ADVANCE PRAISE FOR *IN SEARCH OF PURE LU*

Rarely does a book pop its head above the habit-bound horizon of contemporary North American thought and literature. *In Search of Pure Lust* does. Does, exquisitely. Those anything-is-possible radical feminism decades of the '60s through the early '90s were an astonishing comet that burned and burnt out with equal intensity. In her evocative retelling of her personal and activist experience, Weil spares no one, least of all herself, but her telling increases in insight and tenderness as her Buddhist practice evolves. Her quest as visionary feminist thinker resonates with, and extends, the work of North American writers of those decades like Daly, Rich and Brossard. Weil's inquiry will companion readers seeking to recognize, reinvent or reinvigorate their life beyond the tropes and terrors of the twenty-first century.
—BETSY WARLAND, author of *Breathing the Page: Reading the Act of Writing*

I'm going to cut right to the chase here: I loved this book! *In Search of Pure Lust* is an invigorating ride through the heady days of '70s and '80s feminism, a raw mixture of the personal with the political and the political with the personal. It's also a compelling meditation on lesbian desire. Weil's searing honesty—it's never easy to look in the mirror, never mind reveal to the world what you see—grips you and never lets go. There's tenderness here and pain and compassion also, all the transformative facets of love. If I'd read this book in my twenties, it's quite possible that it would have changed my life.
—EVA TIHANYI, author of *Flying Underwater: Poems New and Selected* and *The Largeness of Rescue*

Intimate, personal, visionary, *In Search of Pure Lust* is the chronicle of a now-vanished golden age of the lesbian feminist movement, a time when we lived the belief that we were reinventing culture and society from root to flower. A page-turner, and a call to remembrance. The reader should expect to stay up all night, and for many nights, reading.
—KIM CHERNIN, author of *In My Mother's House* and *Reinventing Eve*

In Search of Pure Lust explores a wide range of emotions and experiences, from laugh-out-loud moments to love scenes that take

your breath away. *In Search of Pure Lust* is more than a meditation on queer identity. It's an incredible coming-of-age memoir that claims a woman's right to be herself, wherever and whenever she may be.
—*FOREWORD MAGAZINE*

Lise Weil's story weaves among and wisely does not neatly tie together threads of contradictory magnetisms: the longing for maternal acceptance offset and upset by the lure of passion and sexual expression. The search for physical, everyday love balanced by but not assuaged by the communal peace of spirituality. And the lust for individual freedom offset, upset by, and in denial of, the continual need for community activism and social justice. All together this is surprisingly contemporary in its resonance, and compellingly told.
—JUDY GRAHN, author of *A Simple Revolution*

Lise Weil's quest to split the world open and recreate it anew takes her on a physical and spiritual journey that helps shape a movement and ultimately lands her on a Zen cushion where she begins to recognize the gifts as well as the limitations of her own desire. This is the most alive and embodied book I've read in years. I found myself inspired and broken hearted again and again. Weil's story continues to burn in the heart long after the last page is turned.
—DONNA M. JOHNSON, author of *Holy Ghost Girl: A Memoir*

A lyrical odyssey into the shifting politics and alliances of lesbian feminism—alliances that sometimes disrupted a community ethos of love. Weil's memoir is one of the few to portray how women have acted on desire sexually, only to break apart culturally. The women's music references create an authentically remembered background to an era when so many women were coming out as lesbians while discovering their potential in the arts and letters.
—BONNIE J. MORRIS, author of *The Disappearing L*

In Search of Pure Lust provides a window into one vibrant strand of 1980s lesbian feminism. Lise Weil brings to life politics and theories that animated activism as well as heartbreak and conflict. Her personal experiences with debates about sex and sexuality add new insights to these fractious conversations. The history of *Trivia: A Journal of Ideas* is a fascinating one and Weil's commitment to lesbian theory and lesbian writing is inspiring.
—JULIE R. ENSZER, author of *Avowed* and editor of *Sinister Wisdom*

In Search of Pure Lust

Published in Canada by
Inanna Publications and Education Inc.
210 Founders College, York University
4700 Keele Street, Toronto, Ontario M3J 1P3
Telephone: (416) 736-5356 Fax (416) 736-5765
Email: inanna.publications@inanna.ca Website: www.inanna.ca

We gratefully acknowledge the support of the Canada Council for the Arts and the Ontario Arts Council for our publishing program. We also acknowledge the financial support of the Government of Canada through the Canada Book Fund.

Printed and Bound in Canada.

Front cover artwork: Suzanne Langlois, Untitled, 2017, watercolour, pastel and ink, 17.5 x 25 cm.

Library and Archives Canada Cataloguing in Publication

Weil, Lise, author
          In search of pure lust / Lise Weil.

Issued in print and electronic formats.
ISBN 978-1-77133-497-6 (softcover).— ISBN 978-1-77133-499-0 (Kindle).— ISBN 978-1-77133-500-3 (PDF).— ISBN 978-1-77133-498-3 (EPUB)

          1. Weil, Lise. 2. Lesbians--United States--Biography. 3. Lesbians--Identity. 4. Lesbians--United States--Social conditions. 5. Love. 6. Lust. 7. Desire. I. Title.

HQ75.4.W45A3 2018   306.76'63092   C2018-901527-6
                                                                                     C2018-901528-4

In Search of Pure Lust

A MEMOIR

LISE WEIL

INANNA
Memoir Series

For Maurine Stuart, Roshi (1922-1990)
And for Z.

With us it seems to me that everything is accomplished through desire. With us, to desire proves that we are doubly alive. Desire is a grand, irrational invasion which liberates more and more joy. In desire, we know we are united, that through us courses the memory of our grandmothers, the hearts of our mothers. It is nourishing beyond belief, beyond all logic.
—Jovette Marchessault, *Lesbian Triptych*

It is in this way we must train ourselves:
by liberation of the self through love.
We will develop love, we will practice it,
we will make it both a way and a basis,
take our stand upon it, store it up,
and thoroughly set it going.
—The Buddha, *Samyutta Nikaya*

PART I
WINDOW

1.
Woman Loving

...She imagined how in the chambers of the mind and heart of the woman who was, physically, touching her, were stood, like the treasures in the tombs of kings, tablets bearing sacred inscriptions, which if one could spell them out, would teach one everything....
—Virginia Woolf, *To the Lighthouse*

MY WHOLE LIFE I HAVE LOVED WOMEN. Beginning with my first grade teacher Miss Reynolds whom I loved with a fierceness I knew no man could rival, including the one she was planning to marry. For whom the flame still burned so hot seven years later that when my father flew my sisters and me from Chicago to Washington so I could see her again (she had married a Republican congressman), I didn't sleep at all the night before we left. The year was 1963 and songs from the new Beatles album kept repeating in my head: "...*without you I will beyeee in misery....*" To this day those songs have an edge of panic and desperation. If I didn't get to sleep I wouldn't look good for her, and I had to look good for her. It had never been so important that I look good for someone.

On the plane all I could think about was her eyebrows and the exclamatory peak they formed when she got angry or sad. About her plump calves with seams down the back that I used to follow around in the schoolyard, the yard where she'd wait beside me after school on the days my mother was late, one hand resting gently on my head, the other traveling back and forth to her lips with a cigarette. Ever since first grade I had kept her photo under

3

the glass of the night table by my bed (having clipped it out of the yearbook) and glanced at it every night before falling asleep. "Dearly beloved," I would intone silently before turning off the light.

They met us at our hotel, she and her husband.

"There's my little squirt!" she said when I answered the door, though I was twelve years old and tall in a white dress. In an instant all my fears were dispelled; her eyes loved me the same as ever, despite the braces unveiled by my smile. When she hugged me there was the same feel of beloved flesh, of which if anything there seemed to be more now, and the same smell of cigarettes and school.

The year before, when I was in fifth grade, Miss Reynolds had come back to the Latin School to visit. We were in music class and had just struck up a chorus of "Harken Harken Music Sounds Afar" when the piano playing and, with it, our singing, came to a sudden halt. Someone had knocked on the door and was coming in.

It was Miss Reynolds, in a black dress. Married life had changed her. Her hair wasn't wavy anymore and had blond streaks in it. But this foreign woman in the black dress was looking right at me. Then she was walking purposefully up the aisle between the rows of seats, making her way to the rear of the class. Then she was kneeling down beside me. "Hello squirt," she was saying. "How are you?"

She smelled exactly the same. Cigarettes and body warmth. She was looking into my eyes. All eyes in the class had to have been on us, but I saw only Miss Reynolds, her eyebrows gathering in the familiar peak, which this time was a peak of kindness, of concern, of love, for me, her little squirt. I was busy studying every detail about her. There were more lines in her face now. They made her more beautiful than ever.

I think she put her arms around me, maybe kissed me on the cheek, and then she rose and walked back down the aisle and out of the classroom. I suppose she must have addressed the others in the room before walking out but I was too stunned to notice, every cell on overload. The piano playing and the singing resumed, but though I was singing along with the others, I was somewhere else, not there at all, and then I was marching out of the music room with the others and back to homeroom, but I was no longer the same person who'd marched in.

Back home in my bedroom I began to take in the meaning of the event. There had to have been others in those rows from One Blue who'd wanted to see her, whom she'd wanted to see. But she had passed them by. She had come for me. This fact now took its place alongside my other cherished memories of Miss Reynolds and became part of my evening ceremony, intensifying the solemnity and reverence with which every night I gazed at her photo before turning out the light and dropping my head to the pillow.

From Miss Reynolds I learned all the rudiments of love. That it was great, that it was of the soul, that it was pure. That it did not require the presence of the beloved. And that it did not rule out other loves—there would be, most notably, Ricky Spitz's mother in third grade and Mlle. Robert in fifth. In the same way, I now saw—her coming to see me that day in music class confirmed it—Miss Reynolds's marriage had done nothing to diminish her love for me.

"DON'T YOU SEE, L?" A therapist said to me some thirty years later, when I described this phase of my life. "That's how most girls that age feel about their mothers. You must have needed her love very much."

I bridled. I blushed. The shame was reflexive, flooding my veins. Growing up, I knew there was something the other girls had that I didn't, some necessary ballast. Someone to tell you you were pretty all the time, even if you weren't. I felt I'd been caught out. If the love ethos that governed the Miss Reynolds years was one of generosity and abundance, the one that came into play when I began to act on my desires some thirteen years later circled around the something I didn't have—that original lack. The result, once I became a high-profile feminist, was a curious dissonance. Even as I was motivated by, and publicly expressed, only the purest feelings of love and respect for women, my love life was a tangle of lust, privation, and betrayal.

ON THE PLANE ON THE WAY BACK from Washington my father regarded me gravely. "You have a furrow in your brow," he observed, placing his finger in the middle of my forehead. "Do you miss her terribly?"

"I'm fine, Daddy." It was a reflex by now to fend him off. He was always wanting in on my secrets, especially where women were concerned. I missed her, yes, but it wasn't only that. After downing a few drinks with my father, Miss Reynolds and her husband had taken my sisters and me out for spaghetti, and I could tell the husband didn't want to be there. I could tell things weren't working out between them by his silence, her tense frown. How could he not love her the way she deserved to be loved? She of all people?

My whole life I have worshipped women; I have sat at their feet, I have listened with all the force of my being. But sooner or later, from grade school on, the women I loved chose to give their love to men, lavishing on their boyfriends and husbands the same devotion and attentiveness I longed to lavish on them. From what I could see, they didn't get back half of what they gave, and there was little in these men to inspire such devotion in the first place.

Curiously, though, even as I resented the men, I would in time often find myself attracted to them, or at least to some close facsimile. After months of listening to my college roommate rave about her ex-boyfriend, Will, taking in every detail about him—his wiry body, his khaki pants, his cowboy boots—I found myself stalking a man on campus who sported that same country-western look. He called his place "the ranch." Soon I was spending nights at "the ranch" and coming home in the morning to tell my roommate about it. After he and I split up she admitted to me she'd been jealous—not of him but of me. He was exactly the kind of man she wished she could find for herself. I'd been right on the mark.

A few years later a friend introduced me to a wealthy American painter in France. We spent several days with her at her country house on the Seine, drinking and talking about art and literature and sex. She was the most exciting person I'd ever met. There were long pauses in our conversation during which she would stare at me from behind her dark glasses, then casually let fall a penetrating observation. "An emptiness about the heart of life" was one of them. She was quoting the title of my senior thesis—my friend had shown it to her—which I'd taken from Virginia Woolf's *Mrs. Dalloway*. Before that moment it hadn't occurred to me those words had anything to do with me.

One night she and I stayed up late talking, just the two of us. At midnight she announced she was going to her studio to paint. She gave me the choice of going with her or taking off with her chauffeur. "You know he's hot for you," she said.

I chose the chauffeur. Not so much because I was afraid of staying, which I was, but because the last hour of our conversation had been focused on my relationships with men, which admittedly had been pretty tame. She said I was still a virgin, I didn't know what passion was. When she met her lover's plane, she told me, they had to stop the car by the side of the road and go at it in a field.

I was not hot for the chauffeur, who had gold teeth and a greasy ponytail, but I'd been drinking Courvoisier steadily for hours and felt up for that kind of letting go. More importantly, I thought if I went with him it would please her, which—judging from her expression at breakfast the next morning—it did. Of course I didn't tell her about rushing to the toilet right after he fucked me to throw up. Or that as I'd lain in bed that night with my head spinning it was her face that kept breaking through the fog of my consciousness and her voice I couldn't stop hearing. Her deep, beautiful voice.

MY BOYFRIEND WAS WAITING FOR ME at the airport when I got back from Paris. It was 1974, I was enrolled in a graduate program at Brown, and Mitch was a tall, self-effacing photographer from RISD I'd met in the fall. I liked Mitch a lot and we had the same taste in furniture and friends. Also, he was a listener; he stood out from other men that way. In our Hope Street apartment—he talked me into moving in with him soon after that trip to France—we gave large dinner parties featuring vegetables from his organic garden. I was the envy of my sister grad students, even the happily married ones. When Mitch's work took him to

New York in the fall I noticed I didn't miss him all that much. He would come up for the weekends, and not only was I often not happy to see him, sometimes I was genuinely hostile. One time, after a failed attempt to bake bread in his honour, I threw a piece of the unrisen dough at him when he arrived—an incident that prompted me, with his encouragement, to go see a counselor at Brown. She told me this behaviour was not uncommon among Navy wives when their husbands came home from sea and I shouldn't worry, but I wasn't all that reassured.

I was no less doubt-ridden as a student of comparative literature. The professors in our department, all men, enjoyed dazzling us with their learnedness and agility, and my classmates and I spent most of our time in the library trying to bulk up our pitifully meagre minds. I thought if I kept on amassing knowledge maybe the gaps would start to fill in, like freckles fusing to form a tan. But increasingly it felt like an exercise in futility. The spring after Mitch left for New York, I was only too happy to take a leave of absence and move in with him there.

The counselor at Brown had given me the name of a colleague in New York, "in the event you'd like to explore your anxiety further." Mitch was all for the idea; he thought it might help me get in touch with my feelings. We were living in a one-bedroom walk-up on West 87th and it seemed a good omen that Dr. J's basement office was directly across the park. I made an appointment.

Dr. J had a picture of Freud in his office, wore a three-piece suit, smoked a cigar, and sat in a chair taking notes while I lay on his couch and free-associated, or pretended to. My dreams, which I brought in as often as possible (they excused me from free-associating, which felt too risky) tended to lend themselves to meaningful analysis.

The first one I brought in was fairly transparent. I had caught up with Doris Day by the side of the road picking flowers after a Conference of Aging Stars. Though I hadn't attended the conference I began to compliment her on the talk she'd given, assuming from everything I'd heard about her that she'd be pleased. Instead she turned her back on me, snubbed me, as if I were just another groveling fan. On my knees in the dust,

I fumbled desperately in my bag for my cigarettes but when I finally found the pack it was empty. I woke up craving a cigarette.

"Were you breastfed?" was Dr. J's question once he'd finished scrawling in his notebook. When I said yes he scrawled some more.

"And what about cigarettes—what associations do you have with cigarettes?"

"Well, my father's practically a chain smoker."

"Mmm. Anything else?" I racked my brains but came up empty.

Dr. J kept in his office a copy of Andrea Dworkin's *Woman Hating* that was always displayed face-up on his desk during my session. I became convinced it was there for my benefit, to suggest that despite the classical Freudian accoutrements he was a man well-versed in contemporary feminist thought, i.e., a man I could trust. I never walked into his office without flinching at that title, which I instinctively revised to *Woman Loving*. Woman loving, I knew, was the real reason I was showing up to his office three times a week.

When I wasn't in Dr. J's office I was at the Columbia library trying to finish up a paper on James, a loose end from Brown; I was tracing the image of boxes and being boxed in through *The Wings of the Dove*, hoping it would reveal hidden layers of the book. I always emerged from the library slightly demoralized, and the walk down Broadway back to our apartment would finish the job: the scuzzy donut shops and pizza parlors in the West-90s, the same shops same signs every day. It didn't help that I wasn't looking forward to seeing Mitch at the end of this walk, or not as much as I thought I should be.

Whenever I told Dr. J how dead I felt, he'd ask what it would take for me to feel alive. I don't know, I'd say. But the fact is I did. Women. I had a radar for women's things in the city. I'd read *Womannews* and the women's bulletin in City Lights and tune in to the women's programs on WBAI. I'd hole up at Womanbooks on 92nd Street for hours at a time—"Wombbooks," it was to me—and watch women come and go.

Was "woman" a euphemism here? Was I looking for lesbians? It was a question I couldn't have answered at the time. I knew about "women like that"; at Cornell there had been a visible lesbian group on campus and one of the women in the group had approached me multiple times to ask if my roommate and I were an item. I always gave her a disgusted sneer. But secretly I wondered. Abby and I shared a rambling apartment by Cascadilla Gorge. She had a habit of barging into my room to park herself on my bed and talk, or model clothes for me before she went out. On nice days we'd hike down into the gorge and smoke a joint or two on the rocks and usually she'd complain to me about whoever her current crush happened to be. Often late at night we'd sit out on the little fire escape outside her bedroom with its view of Lake Cayuga in the distance, she in her long flannel nightgown, me in my pj's, both of us looking up at the night sky. Sometimes I'd put my arm around her and feel perfectly content.

I loved Abby, I wanted to be with her all the time, but I didn't feel "that way" about her. In fact we'd have long conversations about fucking, our favourite parts. It's true when Abby started seeing Ben I got really jealous. It wasn't the sex, *per se*; it was the fact that she was hardly ever there without him, and after a few days I had to admit that underneath all my reading and writing I'd been waiting for her to barge in.

One afternoon when we hadn't talked to each other for about three days I came home to dishes in the sink and no Abby and I went into her room and wrote "I LIVE HERE TOO" on her mirror with shaving foam, then I left for the rest of the evening and didn't come home till really late. I was hoping when I walked in she'd be waiting up for me all worried. But she was preoccupied because Ben hadn't called that day and didn't say anything. And actually Ben hardly ever showed up again, so if I'd been patient we could have just ridden the whole thing out.

I wasn't dumb. I knew friends don't write on mirrors. I knew I was acting like a lover. What's more, I was aware of an involuntary bulge in my eyeballs whenever I heard the word lesbian. Maybe that activist was right, maybe I did desire Abby. But if I did, how could I possibly allow myself to know it? All through my childhood I had stood out: for my buck teeth, my crooked nose, my lack of fashion sense. (Often on my way out the door I would be arrested by one of my younger sisters and ordered into more suitable attire.) How could I risk standing out now for something deep and red and raw like lesbian lust? Something that, as I saw it, could have only one possible outcome: my being roundly, royally snubbed.

I didn't tell any of the Abby story to Dr. J. I knew exactly where he'd go with it. Especially after that dream that put it all in such a classic analytic context. *Rejected by her own mother, she finds herself creating other rejection scenarios.*

But I had to hand it to that dream. My mother was a wholesome blonde with movie star looks. How clever to feature her as Doris Day! You think someone so wholesome will be kind and accommodating. You come to find out: she's not. You go to her with a compliment and she shoots you down. There she was, unmistakably, my mother.

2.
Womanhattan

Our longing turned into desire. We were alive with desire.
And we knew we could never go back.
—Susan Griffin, Woman and Nature

THE TRUTH IS, LESBIANS EMBARRASSED ME. Like a baboon's behind, they exposed what should stay hidden. And what they did together with their lovers had absolutely nothing to do with what I had felt since the age of five, this enormous welling of the heart for women—not lesbians with butch cuts and husky voices but beautiful women with jewelry and stockings and skirts and round breasts and wavy hair parted just so. It was women I loved, not lesbians, and what I felt for them was a pure thing, a grand thing, there was nothing perverted or queer about it.

And then, I was twenty-five, on the Staten Island Ferry, returning to the city from a conference on women's spirituality. Goddesses were not really my thing but I'd liked the idea of voyaging to an island for a "women's" event. The year was 1976; my own personal bid for freedom was backlit by the anniversary of our nation's independence.

In the summer I had moved out of Mitch's apartment on West 87th Street and into my own tiny place on West 78th. I'd grown increasingly withdrawn and ill-tempered in our New York love nest; the feelings I'd gotten in touch with since moving to the city were not the ones he'd had in mind when he suggested a shrink.

It was a Holly Near concert—advertised on a WBAI program called "The Lesbian Spectacular"—that had pushed me over the edge.

When I entered the hall I saw women spilled out into the aisles and the landings, in couples and in groups, the air between them dense and electric. Near, a California hippie with long golden tresses (she'd made her musical debut in *Hair*) took the stage, radiating peace and love. I sensed instantly that the luminous glow belonged to something bigger than her, bigger even than all the women assembled there, that there was some great light we were all part of. And I knew beyond any shadow of a doubt that I belonged here, in this hall, with these women. When Near belted out a song about factory girls organizing to demand fair wages, I sang along with the chorus with a fervour that surprised me, considering how little thought I'd ever given to factory workers or fair wages. When I came home from the concert I announced to Mitch I'd be moving out as soon as I found myself a place.

The Staten Island conference had seemed so promising when I boarded the ferry that morning along with dozens of other women of all ages and fashion persuasions. There were gowns and turbans, jeans and buzz cuts; I even spotted a sari or two. I felt just right in my khakis and new corduroy jacket. A woman on board was handing out leaflets for a Halloween moonlight cruise "for women and their friends—around Womanhattan." It felt like a pilgrimage.

Once at the conference, though, my hopes ran aground. A group of butch lesbians engaged in hearty backslapping beside the registration table as I studied the program. Workshops on iris diagnosis, on coming out as a witch, on reflexology and womyn's massage ... once you ruled out the how-to sessions and the titles that creatively misspelled "woman," there wasn't much left. The one workshop I decided to attend, "The Politics of Spirituality," came apart over the issue of male children and I walked out before it was over. Afterwards I hung out for a while at the lesbian craft fair in the gym, staring at badges and greeting cards and jewelry, wondering why lesbians in the U.S. had no taste. I finally gave up on the conference and walked back to the ferry.

I was seated on a bench on the rear deck writing out my disappointment when a woman appeared. She had a willowy body and wore a camel-coloured fall coat tailored to her slim figure. *A well-heeled Manhattan professional* was my first thought. Not the kind of woman who attends women's things. She was looking right at me. And she was smoking a cigarette. Just above her hung a large NO SMOKING sign. Suddenly I was craving a cigarette myself. It was uncanny: my Doris Day dream coming to life.

"Were you at the conference too?" she asked when my eyes met hers.

"Yes, how did you guess?"

"The yellow legal pad, the furious scribbling ... is that what you're writing about?"

I nodded.

"Did you think it was as weird as I did?"

"You know, you're not allowed to smoke here." I indicated the sign over her head.

She waved dismissively, then smiled when she saw me reaching for my pack. Unlike in my dream, there were cigarettes in it. I pulled one out and brought it to my lips. She sat down beside me on the bench, offered her lighter. I inhaled, deeply. The ferry had pushed off, there was water streaming by on either side of us. I was happy again about my new outfit and my freshly washed hair, both of which had felt kind of wasted on the conference.

"I never knew 'woman' could be spelled so many different ways," I said, picking up the thread.

She laughed. A willowy laugh. An inviting laugh. I had an urge to read my notes out loud to her, all of them.

"You know, I've never been to a gathering like this where I didn't make any friends."

Who admits they go to these things to make friends? Already I was willing the boat to slow down. "Tell me about it. I went to 'The Politics of Spirituality.' Someone complained because she wasn't allowed to bring her son to the conference and all hell broke loose."

"Clear the room if you don't agree that all men are blood-sucking vampires." She laughed again, exposing a row of beautiful, straight white teeth. Her sunglasses could have come right out of *Vogue*. What the hell was she doing at a women's conference? "You should have seen the lesbian sexuality workshop," she said.

Oh. That involuntary bulge of the eyes. "What happened

there?" I tried to keep my voice as flat as possible. She could have been collecting information; maybe she was a sociologist, or a sex counselor.

"They all wanted to talk about roles. I just don't understand the whole butch thing. I mean if the point is to love women, why would you want to imitate men?"

"Yeah, good point."

"So I brought it up and they were hostile, I could just feel them all staring at my Lord & Taylor pants and thinking who was I to talk." She leaned down, put her cigarette out on the deck, tossed it over the side of the boat.

I wanted to take her side against them, to say, you have as much right as anyone! But on what basis would I say such a thing? And what if she really was a psychologist, doing some academic study? It did occur to me as I stole a glance at those Lord & Taylor pants that maybe they were just admiring her legs.

"It's not that I have anything against men…" She lit up another cigarette, then turned to look me squarely in the eye. "I just don't relate to them sexually."

Oh. Oh … Blood rushed to my head and pounded in my ears. My eyes threatened to pop out of their sockets. Did she come to these conferences to cruise?

The Manhattan skyline was approaching, the old buildings in the banking district looming up on our right; there wasn't much time left. "Lesbians have no sense of history," I said, trying to regain some control. "Did they wear leather jackets on the Isle of Lesbos? I don't think so."

"Have you ever been to the clubs?" she said.

"What clubs?"

"The gay clubs. You know, the Sahara, Bonnie & Clyde's."

"Um, no."

"Well you've been to the Duchess, haven't you?" I shook my head.

"Would you like to go sometime?"

"Yeah. Yeah I would," I said, trying not to sound too enthusiastic.

"Give me your number." She opened her notebook. I handed her my pen.

"Or better," she said, "you know that Unitarian Church on Central Park West? There's a women's dance there next Saturday night."

"I live right around the corner from that church!" I exclaimed, enthusiasm winning out. This was beginning to feel like a dream. "Good. Maybe I'll see you there." The ferry was docking, passengers were being herded off the boat. She scribbled my number down, gave the pen back, and was gone. I had already made my way through the turnstile at the landing when I realized I never got her name.

WHEN I GOT OFF AT MY SUBWAY STOP that afternoon I walked right over to the church on Central Park West and found the notice. "Lesbian Dance," it said, dispensing with the euphemism. "Saturday October 26, 9:00 p.m." These facts became the drawn note of the intervening week: the first thought I had upon waking and the last before I went to sleep. I put myself on a diet, bought myself new jeans, some nights I even danced a bit in front of the mirror. On Saturday I took my time getting dressed, was pleased by the way my black cotton shirt hung over the new pants.

When I arrived at the church a few minutes after nine, the DJ was just setting up in the sacristy. The dancing took place in the nave, but women had spilled out into the several darkened antechambers, talking, laughing, sometimes making out. For the next three hours I wandered through those chambers scanning faces. They all looked rather spectral in the darkness, and to make matters worse I had forgotten exactly what hers looked like. To the very end I held out hope, but she never showed, or at least I never found her. There was something religious about them, though, those hours in the church, seeking, supplicating, praying for her to appear.

Only the next day did I recall she had said "maybe." And that she did have my number and had invited me to the clubs. For days and then weeks afterward I waited for a call. I told myself she might have lost my number—though I had seen her write it in her book. I kicked myself for not having taken hers.

Oddly enough, though, what I felt in those weeks walking the streets of the city was akin to euphoria. Everyone looked different.

Women especially, women in skirts and dresses, mothers walking kids home from school, even women in power outfits. I looked at them now and saw ... her ... and something down there started to open up, or was it my heart opening up, I couldn't be sure, it felt amazing not to be able to tell my heart from down there anymore. Big things were shifting around deep in my hold.

All that fall and winter in New York, I kept one eye peeled for her. I started going out to the clubs by myself, the ones she had named on the ferry. The Sahara on the Upper East Side with its beige walls and upscale aura, where young professionals with hoop earrings sat around bamboo tables looking casually elegant. Bonnie & Clyde's, where serious butches with cigarette packs tucked into their rolled-up shirt sleeves played pool intently while heavily made-up femmes watched from the bar—I didn't stay long there—and its upstairs neighbour, Bonnie's, a cozy restaurant with fireside tables across one of which when I peeked in I saw a couple ardently French kissing. The dark and narrow Duchess on Sheridan Square so right out of a lesbian pulp novel, with its long copper bar where women cruised each other at the counter.

I never got cruised at any of these bars and wasn't ever that tempted to cruise anyone myself. But it didn't really matter. I had a vision now, I knew where I wanted to go. I got Kate Millett's *Flying* out of the library, a big book in a silver cover with shocking pink letters, and kept it by my bed for half a year, so hungry for every little detail it took me that long to finish it. Some pages I read over and over—especially the love scenes in Provincetown with her dear, yellow-haired, aptly named lover Bookie, with whom she would talk about books and make love for hours on end. This was a life such as I longed to live.

Spring semester of 1977 I decided to return to Brown, having found a new feminist focus for my studies, and designed a proposal for a class on "Images of Women" modeled after one I'd sat in on in New York. Back in Providence I was surprised to find myself attracted to a newcomer to the department: a hefty woman with a butch cut who wore leather jackets and was often mistaken for a man. Like Millett, Casey embodied the vast uncharted realm of lesbian desire, a realm that promised untold freedom and joy, and I wanted in. The attraction was mutual; as the weather warmed up Casey and I would hang out together over beers at the Sarah Doyle Centre talking excitedly about lesbian literature and feminist theory.

One night Casey took me to the Italian neighbourhood across the river for spinach calzones and invited herself over to my place after. We sat face-to-face on the rocking chairs in my living room for a while, trading insights about Djuna Barnes and Monique Wittig, until some force drew us both up from our chairs and we lunged at each other, our lips meeting in a great hot flush.

The first time a boy kissed me I had no idea what to do with my arms; I kept casting about for a movie scene that might give me a clue. But now, with Casey, there wasn't a moment of uncertainty. I wasn't thinking about my arms; I wasn't thinking at all. I'd put on a record, *Heart Like a Wheel*, and the McGarrigle sisters were singing about kissing till your mouth gets numb. I imagined Casey, like me, was falling—into the music, into the kiss, I imagined we would just keep falling together as the night wore on, till the day came breaking through. But she pulled away after a minute or so and, looking very sheepish, said she had to leave. She insisted it had been a great evening and it wasn't me and hugged me firmly at the door. Only then did I recall her having mumbled something about a girlfriend the last time we were together. Several nights later she came over to tell me she'd decided two girlfriends was too many and she was choosing the other one.

It was a snub, a real one. I was left to stew in all the red, raw ugliness of my own thwarted desire. My desire for a butch woman, a bona fide dyke. Evidently there was no limit now to the kind of woman I loved. The kind of woman I wanted. If Casey was a pervert then so was I. There was no getting around it now: I was a queer. A dyke. A lesbian.

2.
Apparently

One wanted fifty pairs of eyes to see with, she reflected.
—Virginia Woolf, *To the Lighthouse*

IN MATTERS OF LOVING WOMEN, my father was my mentor, my role model. My primary mediator. I saw the way he looked at them, the women who came to his parties, who sped down the hall, arms outstretched, calling "David!" and then planted firm kisses on his cheeks, who sat across from him in his library with long crossed legs nursing martinis; I saw how his face lit up, how he tried to please them. After the parties he would summon me to the library to "discuss" them with me. "Don't you find Mrs. F. charming? Her husband's dull as dishwater. Can't imagine what she sees in him." "Mrs. G. has such a sweetness about her, don't you think?" (Mrs. G. was a formidable woman with a gravelly voice.) He was captivated by women who had a "certain vulnerability about them," especially if it was a vulnerability only he detected.

Though I rarely contributed to these discussions—his questions were rhetorical, and my nodding was dutiful—not a word he said was lost on me. I was always drawn to the same women as he and wanted every scrap of information I could get about them.

My interest in women was no secret to him—in fact he lost no occasion to rib me about it. About Miss Reynolds he teased me mercilessly. I had a bad habit when seating myself at the dinner table of tucking one leg under me. "What would Miss Reynolds say if she saw you sitting like that?" he would always say. Then he'd shoot knowing glances at her phantom presence in the living room and gesture for her to come in. Rolling my eyes, I'd straighten out my leg.

One day he said it with more conviction than usual and when I looked up there she was at the entrance to our dining room, Miss Reynolds in her powder blue cashmere sweater and pearls.

"Hi Squirt," she said. She came over and gave me a big hug.

I remember little about the hour that followed. A place was set for her across from me and next to my father, who looked unbearably pleased with himself. He poured her a glass of wine and engaged her in conversation throughout the meal. Dinner ended and they resumed their conversation in the library. When I appeared in my pajamas, ready for bed, she was still sitting across from him with a tall drink beside her. She was a frequent visitor to our apartment after that.

I never knew if he was my accomplice or my rival. Only weeks after mentioning my sixth-grade French teacher's fondness for opera, I was sent off with her in a cab to see Beethoven's *Fidelio* with ten dollars tucked in my black patent leather purse. Pinned to the money was a note that read: "This money is to be applied to refreshments however that word may be understood respectively by hostess and guest. *A chacun son gout et ses couleurs*." Mlle. Robert giggled as she read the note out loud at intermission. "What a kind and witty father you have," she said to me, taking my hand and pressing it between her gloved palms. Then she escorted me to the bar, where she allowed me to buy her a glass of white wine. After the opera the two of us reported back to my father's library, where Mlle. Robert accepted the scotch and soda my father tendered to her and politely accompanied him on a tour of his bookshelves.

Later it occurred to me that I might actually have been procuring women for him. Like Miss Reynolds, Mlle. Robert returned regularly to our home after that night to drink at the well of my father's library, with its rich literary offerings and generous bar. Though no longer the pretext for these occasions, I was always invited to make an appearance. My father would beam when I made my entrance and invariably press me to stay—he loved to see me light up in the presence of my teacher.

20

I in turn felt proud to know she was being so royally entertained in my own home. If I was providing a service for him, the pleasure derived from these visits was entirely mutual. When it came to the objects of our fascination, my father and I were in perfect agreement.

And the truth is, no matter how charming and seductive he might be with these women, they were none of them, I knew, serious contenders for my father's affections. In this realm there was no doubt in my mind that I was, and would always be—this was a source less of pride than of anguish—number one.

My mother herself did not seem to be much of a contender. Granted, she was a difficult case. The communications between them—those I was privy to—generally took place between opposite ends of the apartment. "*David,* did you have to leave the bathmat dripping wet?"

"*Aase, please!*" his voice trailing down the hall from the library. "It's already seven thirty, we were supposed to be there a half hour ago." He'd be pacing up and down the front hall with a cigarette and a drink, occasionally stopping to adjust his tie in the mirror. He was a punctual man who hated to be late and she kept him waiting every time they went out. This would have been more forgivable had going out not been their primary shared activity. There were the parties they gave, of course—she had received rigorous training in hostessing from his mother— but they too proved a bitter source of contention. "You're not to lift a finger—let the help do it all. Your duty is to look after your guests," had been my grandmother's first commandment to her. But often as my father made his rounds among the guests he would find his wife, instead of making introductions or oiling the wheels of social discourse, rushing to insert an ashtray under someone's toppling cigarette or kneeling on the floor with a rag and soda water, trying to expunge a red wine stain.

It was at best a mysterious marriage, though my mother's part is not so hard to understand. There was her gratitude to Americans for liberating Norway from the Germans, which eventually drew her to the U.S., in the aftermath of a failed love affair with a Norwegian man. A gratitude that must have spilled over to this Chicago-born American who had served in the war himself, albeit in counterintelligence, and who, though balding and a Jew (something she was repeatedly warned about in Norway before the marriage), was also dashing and debonair and rich, and who promised her culture and luxury—luxury to which she was attracted in part because of the years of German occupation during which she and her family ate only potatoes along with whatever grew in the garden.

My father, on the other hand, a very eligible bachelor of thirty-nine, wealthy, intellectual, a charmer—how to explain his proposal to this Norwegian woman, who though "stunning," as everyone in his family seemed to agree, had no culture (he said it many times at the table) and couldn't care less about ideas? Who showed no sign of that "vulnerability" he claimed to be so taken with in women?

The word most often used to describe my father was "distinguished." It was an effect he cultivated. Mustachioed, rarely spotted in anything but his Brooks Brothers suit and tie, unfiltered State Express cigarette tucked between third and fourth fingers, foreign journals hugged close, he looked the very picture of an English gentleman. As a boy growing up in Chicago he had been taunted for being plump and bookish. He never said "Jewish" but somehow I understood that was at the root of the taunting. It was a fact he did not exactly deny but took great pains to transcend. At Harvard—there were few other Jews there when he attended in the late twenties—he had distinguished himself intellectually, as was attested to by the Phi Beta Kappa key that hung always from his waistcoat and the books that lined the walls of his library and living room. Both rooms were a shrine to European culture, and guests from abroad, of whom there were many, always felt right at home. One of them called our home an "oasis of civilization," evidently assuming that the rest of Chicago was a cultural desert.

My father's living room was appointed in French period style. Two ancient-looking Louis XV chairs with brown leather seats sat on either side of a long sofa against one wall. Against the faux fireplace on the other wall love seats flanked an antique coffee table. At the far end, twin velvet armchairs with matching table lamps sat beside the casement windows that looked out over the lake. French and German literature took up one wall of the living room, English and art the other. It was a room made for entertaining and performing, something my sisters and I were occasionally persuaded to do to the accompaniment of *Gigi* or *My Fair Lady*.

When the waves of Lake Michigan were whipped into whitecaps, my father would turn to his German section, which was right beside the window, bring down a leather-bound book from his Heine collection, and recite one of his *Nordsee* poems. At the dinner table, he would recite Goethe poems by heart. He embraced German music and poetry with a fervour few Jews would admit to and few Germans could any longer afford. He did not believe the fate of the Jews in Germany should rob him of this appreciation, which extended to Wagner's ultra-nationalistic operas. His aversion, he would say if challenged, was not to being Jewish, but to the idea that he should have to identify as a Jew to the exclusion of anything else.

When considering the subject of my father's attraction to my mother, though, it is impossible not to speak of, if not aversion, then at least avoidance. For desire, as I have myself been forced to acknowledge, is often shaped as much by avoidance as attraction. In this case: avoidance of certain biological features, and attraction to their opposite—straight nose, fine blond hair, blue eyes. In other words, avoidance of the stigma that had dogged my father all his life. Not to mention the promise of children who would be spared that stigma, who would not suffer as he had suffered.

But it's possible I am making too much of this stigma. Perhaps when considering their mutual attraction it's enough to point to the time in which they met, the very midpoint of the last century, and to the heavy wave of romance that swept over the nation in that moment, the collective will to move onward and upward out of hardship out of darkness out of history. Perhaps it's enough to point to those evenings of drinking and dancing to the sound of swing bands, to mellow crooners like Bing Crosby and Perry Como or the upbeat lilt of musicals like *Oklahoma* and *Carousel*. My parents' song was from *Pal Joey*—"I Could Write a Book"—a song that as it happens ends on a surprisingly unromantic, and in their case inaccurate, note: *And the world discovers as my book ends, how to make two lovers a friend.*

THERE'S NO QUESTION MY MOTHER was a pleasure to look at. A Nordic beauty with fabulous legs, she attracted attention wherever she and my father went. And her loveliness was uncontested by the women in my father's family, which must have been a matter of pride to my father, who deferred to them in all matters of taste. (During renovation periods I'd come home from school to see his first cousin Francelle standing by the couch with a swatch of fabric, conferring with the decorator.) He liked being seen with her on his arm at parties, especially on formal occasions when she wore long gowns and he sported medals he'd won in the Middle East during his counterintelligence days. He, who beneath all the debonair trappings was still a plump Momma's boy with a hooked nose, must have been proud to have scored this Nordic prize. Yet he never gazed at her the way he did at the women he entertained in his library, or even the women on his side of the family; he did not court her attention as he did theirs. Did marriage put an end to fascination? Did he simply lose interest once the effect of her beauty wore off?

My mother claims that I turned away from her, at a very young age, with something like disdain. Apparently, or so she says, I never needed her. If she's right, is it possible I was following my father's lead in this as well? Or was I reacting, as he possibly was, to something we both experienced early on: the tenuousness of her interest? The capriciousness of her attention? Could she have reversed cause and effect? For what child turns away from its mother as an infant, with disdain?

Apparently, or so she says, I was never hers, was stolen away from her by my father and his mother and given into the hands of professionals almost immediately, all my needs tended to by others. Apparently, she felt like an interloper. Apparently, the women in my father's family lost no time in making her over—as they would later make me over as a teenager, straightening my hair and shaving my legs. (In photos of her from the first years of their marriage, her slim figure is outfitted in elegant designer dresses, black pillbox hats with veils.) Apparently, it took everything she had to hold on to a shred of her own identity.

It is difficult to sort out what my mother claims from what I felt. What I do know is I learned at a very young age to keep a safe distance, and to view her from that distance—as lightweight, if not silly, and hysterical. Above all, as someone not to be taken seriously.

"The moment Aase became a U.S. citizen she voted to cut off foreign aid," my father would say when, as was often the case, she made an ungenerous remark in front of his guests. Or: "You know why Baked Alaska is called *omelette norvégienne* in France? It's hot on the outside and cold on the inside."

Making fun of her was a family sport, and she supplied us with no end of material. At any hour of the night she might storm into our room in a state of panic, saying, "Whosits is this? I found it in the laundry closet." She'd flick the light on and we'd see her standing at the door in waist-high cotton underpants and a pointy bra, brandishing a stray sock. "Why on earth can't you pick up after yourselves," she would fume as she rummaged through the sock drawer for its mate.

She was our running joke, our safeguard against dullness. But the humour was protective, too. "Oh you were all so cute," she would say. Wistfully. Reflexively. She couldn't stop reminding us of our original perfection. I had strayed farther than my younger sisters. Why did my front teeth have to protrude so, they'd been perfect little pearls, how did my hair become so unruly, I'd had silky waves and a natural part. And my posture!

I was only too aware that my teeth stuck out, that my hair was frizzy in summer, that my body had begun to fill out in unflattering ways (my weight overtook my mother's at the age of fourteen). And should I ever forget, she was always there to remind me: the firm hand on my belly ("tuck it in") and on my back ("stand up straight"), the admonitions at the table when I took seconds.

My mother was a beautiful woman, that's what they all said, but to me beauty was dark and mysterious, and there was no mystery about her—she was all surface, all blond prettiness, no secrets, everything must out, immediately! If there was gas it must be passed; any bad air, throw open the windows. She was all for freshness and she had no patience with defects, she thought children with bad ones should be put to sleep, there are too many people on the planet to begin with. She had no comprehension of fat—how people could get fat and stay fat—or wounds, or anything that slowed you down.

My mother was our running joke. Ask me what else she was to me and I draw a blank. If my father was my role model in loving women, my mentor, then this, my initiatory relationship with a woman, was a bust. I had lain inside her belly. I even fed at her breast. But nothing came of it. No bond. No heart connection.

For the Freudians, I know, I'm a classic case. Deprived of mother love, I went looking for it in other women—my attractions, my passions, my aversions all driven by this hole, this primal wound. For a long time I saw it this way myself. At some point, though, it occurred to me that the Freudians might have it all backwards. Not everything I wanted and aspired to could be traced back to my parents. What if I came into the world with a longing for mystery and depth and, not finding it in my own mother, not sated and stopped up by a mother's love as were most of the girls I knew, kept on yearning and searching until I found it?

Somewhere near the centre of Woolf's *To the Lighthouse*, Lily Briscoe, an artist and a spinster, sits with her arms clasped about the knees of the beautiful, serene Mrs. Ramsay. Lily sits as close as she can get, wanting to absorb the knowledge she is certain Mrs. Ramsay has locked up inside her, to "press into those secret chambers," for inside those chambers is everything she feels she most needs to know.

As far as I could tell, the girls I knew who grew up with mother love never wondered about those secret chambers, had no longing to be admitted to them. Like Lily Briscoe, I longed to enter. And over time this longing, obeyed, led me into the presence of the deepest mysteries.

What if my mother—in all that she wasn't—was a window?

My wound a window. In which case I owe her everything.

PART II
BEGINNING WITH O

4.
Beginning with O

like a curviform alphabet
that defies
decoding, appears
to consist of vowels, beginning with O, the O
mega, horseshoe, the cave of sound.
                              —Olga Broumas, "Artemis"

S O I WAS TWENTY-SIX AND BACK IN graduate school and I
was a lesbian. A dyke. All I had to do now was find someone
to love. Because that was the point, after all. All my life I had
been loving women, but now—this was less a conscious thought
than an operative assumption—now I was going to do it for
real. Now I was ready to dance the full-tilt boogie. I just had
to find a partner. My timing was good. It was spring of '77 in
Providence, Rhode Island, and everywhere you looked women
were discovering each other, assembling in places where only
women assembled. Weekends someone was always driving up
to Boston to eat at Bread and Roses, the vegetarian women's
restaurant, to dance at Somewhere, the women's disco, or hang
out at the Saints, the girls' bar in the warehouse district with its
big blond wood booths and giant pool room. Olga Broumas had
just won the Yale Younger Poets Award for *Beginning with O*
and a bunch of us drove down to New Haven for her reading. A
Greek beauty, she closed her dark-lashed eyes, bard-like, when
she read—"oh let me love you / the fathers are off in the distance
nodding their assent"—and we all swooned in our seats and then
gushed in the car the whole way back.

Everyone that year at Brown, it seemed, was nodding their assent. The women's centre hosted one feminist speaker after another, including Jill Johnston, who came to campus to talk about *Lesbian Nation*. When Kate Millett showed up at the Saints late one Friday night with a young girlfriend in tow—a striking brunette whom I took to be Bookie's successor—I felt my life starting to blur with those of my own lesbian heroines. Except for the girlfriend.

My course on "Images of Women in Literature" had been accepted by the Modes of Thought Program and I began teaching it that spring. I wasn't prepared for the number of women who showed up—thirty-three—or the hungry way they gazed at me and hung on every word. How could I live up to such expectation? At the last minute I decided to tack on a lesbian section: Olga Broumas, Judy Grahn, and Rita Mae Brown.

There were two militant lesbians in the class; both sported crew cuts, or "sep cuts," as they were known at the time, and had impressive street smarts. They had already at their young age demonstrated against male violence, marched for lesbian and gay rights, worked in shelters, and organized sit-ins on campus. Who was I to be teaching them about feminism? Or anything, for that matter? Despite staying up most of the night before class preparing, I still couldn't look their way without losing my train of thought. As I was introducing the lesbian section I was sure I saw them passing each other notes and rolling their eyes.

I had to get myself some experience. Soon after the semester ended I read about a women's camp in upstate New York that would be hosting a women's weekend at the end of June. A few weeks later, on a Friday afternoon, I was following a switchback road up the side of a mountain to where a clutch of cabins was set in deep woods beside a field.

It was a hot day with a strong breeze and out in the field a group of women were trying to spread out a huge canvas that flapped intractably in the wind. Cris Williamson's voice issued loudly from a big speaker by the meadow. The movements of the canvas-spreaders seemed to be synchronized to the words of "Tender Lady," which struck me as ironic, since many of the heads were severely shaven and the faces looked pretty fierce. I made my way to the main cabin, where the woman behind the registration table introduced herself as Buckwheat and asked another woman, Sage, to show me to my cabin.

I was relieved when my bunkmate turned out to be a women's studies instructor from Buffalo named Shelly. "How unorganic," I said as she extended her hand, and she laughed. A grad student like me, she was smart and articulate and we shared the same cultural frame of reference. She had just finished *Flying* herself, and admitted to having loved it "in spite of myself." This made me wonder for the fiftieth time why all the academic people I knew professed shame for the books they took to bed with them, especially when they didn't seem that interested in talking about any others.

It was nice to have someone to be alienated with, but before long the conversation began to bore me and when it failed to wind down, even after I'd made several attempts at an exit, I announced I was heading back out to the campgrounds. As I approached the field, a bus pulled up. I watched the women step down one by one: wild hair, lots of it, jewelry, makeup, black leather. Women who squinted as they got out of the bus and felt around in their bags and pockets to make sure they weren't about to run out of cigarettes or Tampax. It had to be the bus from the city.

Soon the New York women were streaming all over the campgrounds and there was rough laughter and irony and cigarette smoke everywhere. I wandered about, watching them settle in and enjoying the general commotion, until I had run out of places to wander and suddenly wasn't sure what to do with myself.

When I was thirteen I went to a girls' camp in Minnesota. I was a social outcast then—a nerd, or queer, in the parlance of that time. As a kid I hadn't really stood out, but come puberty—my mother's clinical assessment was more or less accurate—I had too many things working against me: tight curls, braces, a crooked nose. Plus most of my clothes had been ordered from Bransom's for me by my grandmother. In grade school I'd had best friends I could pal around with, but now I felt clueless in the presence of girls my age. At night in our cabin my campmates would pass pictures of boyfriends from bunkbed to bunkbed, like baseball cards. The photos were never handed to me, as if the other girls knew that I would not appreciate them and that I had none to trade myself.

My bunkmate, Iris Poulette from Kalkaska, Michigan, got up early to go to Mass every Sunday. I'd watch through half-closed eyes as she changed into her church clothes: always the same purple-and-orange-flowered party dress with alternating orange and purple anklets. Iris had kinky blond curls growing out of her armpits and a lumpy body. Like me, she wasn't invited to any of the secret parties, and what I hated most about her was that she never seemed to notice how the cabin emptied out on those nights, except for the two of us and our counselor. She just kept saying how this was the thrill of her life, this summer at Camp Northland, how tickled she was to be there.

I was remembering that summer as I wandered about among the new arrivals, envying them for having been on the bus together, feeling like an outsider. In fact maybe I was having some sort of *déjà vu,* because I soon found myself heading back to my car with the idea of driving down to town to pick up a few things I suddenly decided I needed.

A blue Toyota pulled up next to me as I was opening my door. The woman who got out of it stood up very tall and stretched. She looked a little dazed.

"You looking for the camp?" I said. "This is the place."

She just nodded and looked very shy, which I thought was a strange thing for someone gazing down from such a height.

"You know your way around?"

When she shook her head I jumped out of my car and showed her the way to the main cabin. "Where'd you drive from?" I asked on the way.

"New York."

Had she missed the bus from the city? I asked. No, she said, she liked driving.

"You'll find them all in there," I said, at the door to the main cabin. I was about to say "Buckwheat" or "Sage" but stopped myself. I wasn't sure she'd appreciate the joke.

"Thanks," she said, offering her hand. "I'm Kaye." Her handshake was very warm and deliberate.

DOWN AT THE VILLAGE A&P, in addition to the flashlight I'd forgotten, I bought a six-pack of Rolling Rock and a box of Freihofer's chocolate chip cookies. Then I found myself in the package store buying a bottle of white wine. Winding back up the twisting road I kept seeing Kaye's tall figure in jeans and hiking boots and faded blue tank top. The shy way she stood. I tilted the rear-view mirror down just to check on my hair.

Pulling up beside the blue Toyota I noticed a "Go Navy" sticker on the bumper. Hopefully a borrowed car? By this time, it didn't matter. I knew I had to find her.

She was out in the field where the big tent had been pitched, kneeling by a stake she was pounding into the ground with a mallet. I stood respectfully to the side and watched as over and over again she brought the hammer down onto the round metal head, without pausing or looking up. Her shoulders in the tank top were very strong and brown.

Then finally her head did turn, not because of me but because she had finished. "Oh hi," she said, noticing me at last.

"Good work," I said. "You seem to have settled right in here."

"Just what the doctor ordered," she said. "Very grounding." She got up, moved to another stake, started pounding again.

"Is there another mallet around?" I asked.

"I don't know. Why don't you go ask Sage?" In a matter of minutes, my insider status had slipped away.

Sage was sorry but all the mallets were out. She handed me a scythe and directed me to a hillock by the field where there was tall grass in need of trimming. I found a spot where I could work and keep Kaye in my line of vision. Then all at once when I swung and followed through she wasn't there. I forced myself to keep going a bit longer before returning to the main cabin to surrender my tool to Sage.

On my way back to my cabin I saw a group of women sitting in a circle on the grass out front. Shelly was among them; she motioned for me to join them. When I got up close I saw Kaye sitting in an old rusty chair on the edge of the circle.

"God forbid you should try and bring reality into the classroom," a blond woman with thick glasses was saying. "The worst is when you think you're finally breaking through and then you see this whole block of impatient faces, like, 'When's she gonna get off this personal crap and back to the syllabus?'"

I glanced over at Kaye, worried this shoptalk was boring her. Now that I'd found her again I was afraid she'd take off at any moment. But her eyes were on the blond woman and she had the same look of fierce concentration she'd had by the stakes.

"Of course," Shelly said, "everything in this culture teaches them to individualize. Don't you find it's hard to get any kind of political discussion off the ground?"

"I've been having the opposite problem," I said, surprised to find myself jumping in. I described my militant students, Lorna and Joy, and how they made me wonder where I got off teaching them about feminism. How they made me feel I didn't know anything I hadn't learned from books.

One of the Buffalo women, looking very sympathetic, said, "I think in a situation like that the best strategy is to turn it to your advantage. Why not give those students the floor, so that everyone can benefit from what they know?"

I could just see Joy and Lorna taking over the class, showing everyone how much better equipped they were to teach it than I was.

"I'd give anything to have students like that," Shelly offered.

Then Kaye spoke up. "I bet you have things to teach those kids, though they'd never let on. They sound like know-it-alls to me."

There was a long silence in which all heads seemed to turn her way. *Either she hasn't said a word till now,* I thought, or *they're all as curious about her as I am. Probably both.*

I just nodded and said, "I hope you're right," but I was almost giddy with relief. Kaye's response mattered to me, I realized, in the same way as Joy and Lorna's.

The blond woman asked Kaye if she was a teacher too. "No," she said. "I'm studying to be a nurse. And raising a son." There was a trace of defiance in her voice; in this context, both statements sounded vaguely counter-revolutionary.

The conversation soon ground to a halt and the group broke up shortly afterward. When Kaye started off for the tent I went after her. "Thanks for saying what you did," I called out. "Even if you didn't really mean it."

She wheeled around. "I don't say things I don't mean." She looked me straight in the eye. "Sometimes people get so worked up about what they don't have—they don't see what they have." Her expression was kind; she wasn't trying to put me in my place. But it had that effect.

"Well," I said, casting about for a smooth transition and not finding one, "...would you like a drink before dinner? I have some cold beer in the trunk of my car."

She seemed genuinely pleased at this proposal and followed me to my car. When I opened the trunk she laughed. "Do you always carry a full bar in the back of your car?"

We each grabbed a Rolling Rock and settled down on a little hillock. I was hoping the khakis and green T-shirt I was wearing didn't have "Brown grad student" written all over them. I lit a cigarette and offered her one and she lit up too. For a moment I had an image of my father luring his guests into conversation with Scotch and martinis, trying to charm them with his wit. I saw him standing in front of the hallway mirror before a party, jutting his chin out to make his jowls go away.

"Why did you come here?" she said to me after what seemed like several minutes. There was a distinct challenge in the question, or so it felt.

"Oh, I don't know, I was curious, you know, a camp for all women. I went to a canoeing camp for girls when I was little. I really loved it except for the fact I wasn't very popular.... What about you? What brought you here?"

"I needed a change. Something other than cement under my feet. And then ... the only place I ever meet women in the city is in the bars."

"Oh." This was impressive. Coming to this camp after being in the bars seemed like going backwards. "What's here that you can't find there?"

"Feminism," she said. "All the stuff they were talking about this afternoon." I had to take her word for it, though it was hard to imagine what feminism had to teach her.

I wanted to ask more about the bars but was afraid of betraying my lack of experience. I thought it would be intrusive to ask about her son. So I asked her what made her want to be a nurse She said she'd always wanted to be able to help people, in some immediate way. She said how good it felt to finally be doing what she'd always wanted to do.

The bell rang for dinner. We stood up, brushed ourselves off, her height surprising me again. I matched my stride to hers as we walked to the main cabin, where it was now understood we would sit together. During dinner I stole glances at her profile, the firm set of her lips, her strong nose. She was, I noticed, unusually calm, still. We ate mostly in silence, both of us chewing a lot. The food was a mix of vegetables and somewhat undercooked whole grains. At one point I turned to her and said, "Buckwheat?" When she laughed I was suddenly very happy.

After dinner we sat outside with the wine and Freihofer's box between us, having made another trip back to the car, and I managed to get her to tell me more about her life. At first she kept lapsing into silence, but after I'd jogged her a few times she kept going. She had grown up in the city, she told me, just south of Harlem, had hung out in gangs with mostly Puerto Rican kids. She never finished college and married when she was just twenty. He got drafted and joined the navy and they both went off to Japan. She became pregnant two years into their stay.

I was stuck at Harlem, and the gangs, having grown up in a building with a doorman and an elevator man on Chicago's Lake Shore Drive. Most of my childhood had been played out on a narrow belt between Lake Michigan and the "bad" neighbourhoods to the west. And here, sitting cross-legged on the grass before me with her head down, a corduroy shirt over her strong shoulders, was someone who had not only grown up in such a neighbourhood but apparently knew how to navigate it. And she was confiding in me like an old friend or a kid sister; she was in fact twenty-four, the same age as my younger sister. I longed to sling my arm around her, protectively.

"What about the women?" I asked. "When did that start?"
"Oh, in high school."

36

"Really. Did you actually do it with your friends?"

"I was in love with my best friend. We used to go to her house after school and stay in bed till it was time for her mother to come home from work."

"But ... how could you, you know, how could you get *married* after that?"

"It was an escape, from a lot of things. And ... I was trying to be good. It didn't last very long."

"The marriage?"

"No, being good. It ended in Japan."

"But how did you ... *find* them?"

"It wasn't hard. Women with husbands in the navy have a lot of time on their hands."

When it got cold and we both started to shiver, she took my hand and we went looking for shelter. We needed to be alone, that much was understood.

After maybe ten minutes of poking around the grounds with our flashlights, we stumbled on a tiny cabin near the edge of the property; the door was stuck but gave way when we threw our weight against it. Inside there were no belongings, and—unbelievably—a double bed. It had to be destiny!

We parted to go for our sleeping bags and rushed back. Once inside, we scanned the room with our flashlights. Overcome all at once by shyness, we shot each other a tentative look from either side of the bed. Then, grinning, we put out the flashlights and flung ourselves onto the mattress.

What happened next is a little vague to me now, which is odd considering the momentousness of the occasion. I remember how we found a way to zip the sleeping bags up around us, and how my body found hers in the dark without, it seemed, any conscious volition. I remember being amazed and thankful that the intense liking I felt for her could find its expression so directly in this linking of bodies. I remember our clothes coming off, and the softness of her skin and wanting to graze all over it. I remember never for a moment wondering what to do, how it was done. My hands knew, so did my mouth. I remember the boundarilessness, the ease. And I remember the doubleness of it, the tremendous excitement of knowing what she felt as I moved against her, kissed her, touched her, reached into her. I remember wondering how I could ever settle for singleness again.

But also I remember my confusion when the tough woman I'd been pursuing all afternoon and evening was suddenly gone, completely, and in her place was a girl, vulnerable like the one who sat across from me on the grass with her head down, who seemed to put herself entirely in my hands. Who came almost right away, and then fell asleep in my arms. And who then, as if these competing images were canceling each other out, in the darkness began to fade altogether. Soon she was gone, and nothing I did could bring her back. Beside me lay the body of a stranger.

I BARELY SLEPT THAT NIGHT; there was way too much to take in. As soon as the sun started streaming through the tiny cabin windows I slipped out of bed and off to my cabin to brush my teeth. Moments later I was racing breathlessly back, afraid to find she'd given me the slip for real. But when I forced the heavy door open again there she was, all shy and sweet and sleepy: Kaye. I resisted the temptation to dive right back into bed with her; instead, I hustled her into her clothes and out of our windfall of a love nest.

At breakfast it was hard to get anything down. I could have used some fodder for jokes but the food—waffles and whole-grain toast—wasn't providing any this time. Kaye, on the other hand, ate with the same slow deliberation and silent attention as she had the night before. Sometimes, in between bites, she would look at me in a way that said she was glad. She was happy. I wondered why I wasn't, especially.

After breakfast everyone filed into the main barn to attend a presentation. It began with a brief history of the Athol women's land collective but soon devolved into a series of thinly veiled attacks on Buckwheat, who the others claimed had been usurping authority. Inappropriate laughter began coiling in my belly, threatening to rise up my chest. It crested during the event that followed, an elaborate vagina slide show presented by a tall, energetic woman with a pointer. No one else seemed to think it was funny, which perversely made the laughter want out more urgently. I was getting sick to my stomach trying to keep it in check. Behind that laughter, I think now, was everything I'd ever felt and had to hold back for all the girlfriends I'd loved.

In my cabin, where we retired after collecting her things from the big tent, Kaye and I mused about both events. She was not amused by the bickering at the presentation; we had these women to thank for our having met, she pointed out, and she wished their collective a long life. About the slide show she said she'd had to sit through something similar in nursing school.

"With such a wide array of vaginas?" I asked. "No," she said, smiling.

"With such enthusiastic tapping on monses and labial folds?"

This elicited something like a guffaw and, maybe because of the way we were sitting side by side on my bunkbed for all the world like Northland girls, the laughter I'd been holding in started pushing its way out, and soon I was laughing uproariously and Kaye was laughing with me. At Northland I finally found a friend I could laugh with about Iris Poulette, someone who'd been noticing her too and had been just waiting for an occasion to let it out. This moment was a little like that.

Afterwards Kaye and I sat around and talked like old friends. Except I had never had a friend like this, who took my hand and held it while I talked, who stroked my arm, who liked it when I stopped talking to kiss her on the neck. It was all new, it was exciting, and my heart was pumping furiously. But I told myself not to get carried away. If we kept on talking much longer, we'd both run out of things to say. I'd gotten what I came for, I figured, and that should be that.

When it was time for her to leave, I walked her to her car. *Then and now*, I marveled, spying the "Go Navy" sticker, for which in this moment I felt a surprising fondness. She rolled down the window. We kissed briefly. She said it was hard to leave and I nodded, though I was already looking forward to being alone. Then she was backing out, waving, driving off. I was pretty sure we wouldn't see each other again.

But the first thing I did when I got back to Providence was pick up the phone and dial the number she'd written on my forearm.

5.
Land on Fire

There's wildfire burning in my country, yeah, my land is all on fire
—Cris Williamson, "Dream Child of Desire"

It is the very nature of desire to be driven by a hole....
—Anne Carson, *Eros the Bittersweet*

SHE COMES TO ME IN PROVIDENCE, *I pick her up from the bus— she's left the car and the son with his father. I take her home, she puts herself in my hands, she doesn't say much but keeps looking at me like she trusts me. I put her to bed, she stays there all day, mostly sleeping. When she gets up pulls on her jeans her army boots there's a little frisson of fear no terror. This tall woman with the strong shoulders—has she really been in my bed all day? Does she really want to have sex with me? This tough dyke who, when I was a reject in summer camp, was having sex with her girlfriends.*

The answer comes after dinner, after several glasses of wine, her hand on my thigh, sweetest relief, and back at my place her yes unequivocal we both head for the bed, and this time there is no confusion on my part no disorientation she is all Kaye all the time and I want every last bit of her, skin and hair and flesh, and I decide that black-out at the lesbian camp, that nocturnal lapse in lust, was some freak occurrence triggered by the first time.

When I phoned her that first time there was no answer, no machine to take my message. All night I kept trying, and then all through the next day. Cursing myself all the while. What was I thinking? Messing with someone who used to hang out in gangs, who'd been screwing around with women since she was a teenager, who had probably given me a bad phone number after getting herself off with me in bed.

Finally, that evening, she picked up. Her phone had been out of order ... had I tried calling before? Balm swept through my veins. She was back again, sweet, shy, vulnerable Kaye. Younger than me, this came back to me now.

How all the seeds of a story are contained in its preface.

I come to her in New York. We put her son to bed, sink into her comfortable couch with our gins. Skin scents commingling. Nestle down, burrow in. Not driven, not hurried. Every moment its own thing, not a means to an end. Which is not to say the end, when it does come, is not wild is not blissful.

Evenings when Sam was with his father we'd go out to the bars. The ones I'd gone to by myself the year before. We'd press close in a booth at the Duchess and watch women move on the little dance floor, getting up to slow dance to Billy Joel or disco to Alice Jones. Kaye's hips would grind in a way I knew she'd picked up from her Puerto Rican ex, I imagined the two of them dancing together, Eva shorter, her waist fitting notch and groove into those hips. *I'm not the kind of lover she's used to—too in my head, my body I'm afraid not the kind she loves.*

Nights when Sam was with us Kaye would collapse beside me on the couch after tucking him in. She was asleep in bed not long after, leaving me percolating with questions and lust, too much buzz in the body to sleep or rest. She was exhausted, always, between Sam and nursing school, I knew this, but still I felt spurned, that she could just nod off this way. I'd rise the next morning shaking, jangly, strung out. Later Sam and I would chase each other manically around the park, both of us foils to Kaye's immutable calm.

Mornings I'd find her on the bench in the kitchen listening to 92 FM easy rock—Rita Coolidge singing *"close the window come alive,"* or Crystal Gayle crooning *"don't it make my brown eyes blue."* "Puts me in a good head," she'd say.

In Japan, she told me, while he did his training she sat by the ocean, listened to the ocean, taught herself to breathe with the ocean. *So much she has to teach me*, I thought.

I don't think I saw how hard-won was her calm, just as I was unable to imagine the extent of her exhaustion. I'd never been a mother, never had to wipe anybody else's ass. I'd been living off a trust fund since I turned twenty-five; my idea of hard work was writing a seminar paper. It wasn't only Kaye who suffered from this failure of imagination.

Ever hopeful each time we meet I hustle her into the car and then my apartment.... But first she wants to eat, then she just wants to lie next to me, all quiet. And even if I don't complain—I see her tired eyes—she knows how I feel she says it's written all over my face.

Days at her place revolved around Sam. Shopping, going to the park, cooking, eating. When not hyper from carrying on with him I was often bored. Then and now, I kept telling myself, if she could see you now that hungry girl in the city nose pressed against the glass of bars, clubs, this is what she dreamed of longed for. *But I want I need ... something I'm not getting, what is it?* When she went off to bed I'd be happy to pick up a paper and start grading.

Yale in February. Up in the Tudor tower with my colleagues my peers a graduate convention in comp lit, the talk is of modernism structuralism Marxism. We're subversive we're smart, we give papers with titles like "Luxury Goods for an Elite Clientele." I'm high that night, dancing to "Saturday Night Fever" with my literary friends. Riding the bus down south the next day bound for her little apartment in Washington Heights I feel my world closing in, like a funnel. Of all possible destinations, why this one? She has only one bookcase.

My fidgetiness. Smoking, talking a mile a minute. Her imperturbable calm. Her silence, which has for a while now been a sensitive subject. One night at dinner it explodes out of me: "Why won't you ever talk?" (It did not occur to me that Kaye, who had never finished college, might fear her talk wasn't clever enough for me.)

Her forehead wrinkles just a little. It's cut deep, I can see. A long pause. Then, haltingly, "Are you ever really happy?"

The words hurt her as they come out, I can see this too. And they meet their mark. All evening she's been looking at me with those deep brown eyes so much love in those eyes *why oh why isn't that enough?*

I HAD BEEN BACK IN GRADUATE SCHOOL for almost a year now. The second semester of "Images of Women" was going better than the first. I was more at ease, and this time there were no streetwise dykes in the class undermining my confidence. But as a scholar I was feeling less conviction than ever. Even after making my way through the set books list from Don Quixote to Dr. Faustus the gaps in my knowledge did not seem to be filling in. And as I laboured over papers on de Laclos, Richardson, Defoe—having decided the eighteenth century was a good place to try and gain a purchase even though the writers I loved were all in the twentieth—I sank deeper into a morass of no-meaning.

In late May, almost a year since that first night Kaye and I spent together, I decided we should move in together. The life of the mind was not only stifling my soul, it was coming between Kaye and me, reinforcing the edifice of my resistance. *Oh, come down from your ivory tower and let yourself live for a change. Let yourself love and be loved.* I poured all this out to her in a phone call one night. She was wary at first. Not quite trusting. I managed to bring her around.

She comes to see me, alone. Tanned and beautiful in faded jeans and denim shirt. I can't wait to get her home and into bed. Afterwards we dress up and go out to eat at Rue de l'Espoir to celebrate. I have stories to tell, and though as usual she hasn't much to say, she is listening, and that's all I really want. That and the love in her eyes.

I try and hold on to that feeling in the weeks that follow but little by little it starts to empty out. (*An emptiness about the heart of life.*) She has put herself in my hands. I have brought her around. But now that she wants what I want I'm not sure.

APARTMENT HUNTING TOGETHER, IN BOSTON, in July, with Sam. Hot grey day, calculus of schools, hospitals, neighbourhoods, bedrooms. No place feels right. Sam whines he's tired he's hungry. Am I really ready for this? *Maybe this isn't such a good idea* starts thrumming in me like a mantra. I know I shouldn't say it, it mustn't come from me, she's the one leaving her family, her rent-controlled apartment. In the restaurant it forces its way out with the heat and frustration of the day.

Instantly her face goes white and angry.

I backpedal. Maybe we should just try another day, when it's not so hot. When Sam isn't with us.

Maybe this isn't such a good idea. From the way she is looking at me I see she is taking it all the way.

She closes off. Shuts down. Back in New York she cuts me off. Wants no calls. No letters. Will not be brought around by my begging and pleading. Stops answering her phone now, for real.

Why oh why didn't I see this coming. The tough woman by the stakes with the basketball guard shoulders who doesn't need me. Never did. Waking up now every morning to wanting—to pain I try to kill with cigarettes, and writing in my journal. Writing my way back to the kid sister, the vulnerable girl who trusts me who loves me who always takes me in.

What I couldn't see then, can hardly bear to see now. It was the vulnerable girl—the one who trusted me, who loved me, who'd been ready to risk everything—who cut me off, who had to. She had put her life in my hands. I had trafficked casually with the gift.

It had been over a year since I'd stopped seeing Dr. J, but I knew exactly what his take on our story would be. Your first lover was a mother. And a nurse. How guaranteed to stoke the flames. A mother/nurse with other charges, who wanted you but fell asleep, who loved you but couldn't talk. Dare I say a Doris Day? Opening up that hole, which you're then driven to fill with a cigarette.

Of course it was Dr. J's job to get me to see that hole. Today I see what the hole hid from me. How Kaye's love disappeared into it. How she disappeared into the story of my wound.

6.
From the Stars

Desire: desiderare *to long for, miss, desire, Fr. de-+-siderare*
(Fr. sidersidus—*star, constellation)*
—*Webster's Third New International Dictionary*

BUT I AM NOT ONLY MY PARENTS and my genes, not only my upbringing and my education. I am not only my wounds. Several months after meeting Kaye, I had my chart read at Brown by a semiotics student I'd met through a Marxist prof who'd been making overtures to me. They were having coffee in the Commons Room when I walked in one summer day. "This is Neela," he said, inviting me to join them. "She does charts." "Astrology," she explained.

"Oh," I said, feigning interest. The prof had a reputation for surrounding himself with eccentrics.

"Lise teaches women's studies," he said and they resumed their conversation about Baudrillard and *The Mirror of Production.* As I got up to leave, Neela took my number and not long after she called to invite me to a women's brunch.

Two weeks later I sat in a silk-draped rattan chair in a corner of Neela's living room watching women stream in. None of them looked like semiotics students. One was a Zen Buddhist, another was a midwife. An emaciated hairdresser said she was sticking to her macrobiotic diet even though her strength was ebbing. An acupuncturist wearing what looked like pajamas suggested ways to boost the diet. Minus the dykes, it was the Staten Island women's spirituality conference on repeat. I took mental notes so I could tell Kaye all about it.

Just before I left Neela offered to read my cards. She motioned me into a small room where we sat across from each other at a little round table.

"Oh," she said, looking at the cards she'd drawn. "What?" I asked, alarmed.

"Nothing bad, not at all, it's just so unequivocal. Right now you're at a turning point, especially in terms of sexuality. You're beginning to listen to voices you've been ignoring all your life."

This struck me as oracular. I'd just spent my second weekend with Kaye.

IN LATE FALL, AS WEEKENDS WITH KAYE in Providence or New York were beginning to wear on us both, I returned to Neela for a chart reading. I sat across from her in the little room and listened in quiet amazement as, sentence by eloquent sentence, a curtain was lifted and I stood revealed.

"Sun in Sagittarius, you're a fire sign, you need to burn," she began. "Aquarius moon and rising: all the air in your chart fans the flames. Sagittarius is the missionary sign, the idealist on fire with her vision. She gets an image of where she wants to be, sees it so vividly wants to be there so badly she has no patience for where she is."

Those nights in Kaye's bed, burning up with want....

"Aquarius moon is the sign of the stranger, the outsider. The familiar can become alien in a heartbeat. Aquarius rising, ergo a thinker. You relate to the world through conversation, ideas."

My impatience with her silence....

"With all this air you need lots of space around you, more than you realize."

"And what about Pisces?" Kaye was a Pisces.

"Water sign. Drinker, dreamer, one who feels deeply. It's enough for her just to feel, just to be. In this sense you have everything to learn from her. But watch out: Water, as you know, puts out fire."

It would be years or even decades before I would feel the full impact of this reading. There was only so much I could take in at the time. But in the days and weeks that followed I felt buoyant, as if pumped up with star energy. For the first time in my life,

I was—at least momentarily—released from historical causality. From blame and regret.

Later on, in my grieving over Kaye, I clung to Neela's words. Be thankful, I told myself, you never moved in together. She would have doused your fire and you would have resented her for it. You would have pushed her away and she would have had no home to escape to. Things would have turned ugly really fast.

True or not, all this consoles me. Except that now I am here and she is there and this long year of loving has come to nothing.

7.
Changing

stunned at the suddenly possible shifts of meaning
for which we must find words or burn

—Olga Broumas, "Artemis"

ANOTHER THING THE ASTROLOGER TOLD ME: "You have a writer's chart."

"What kind of a writer?" I wanted to know. After all, I was writing all the time—papers on Richardson, de Laclos, Defoe, Marivaux.

"A *writer writer*," she said.

"Oh," I said. "Ha. Ha." When your models are Woolf, James, Kafka, and Proust, that's pretty much how you feel about the prospect of yourself as a writer.

But in the fall of '78, the fall after Kaye and I broke up, I dropped out of grad school to join a women's writing program in upstate New York. The acceptance letter had arrived around the time Kaye and I began house hunting in Boston. It was surprisingly long and detailed, assessing my strengths as a writer based on the sample I'd sent them. I chose to see it as a test of our love, beside which the prospect of artistic success simply paled, and wrote back to say I'd had a change of plans. Perversely, though, the praise in that letter, and the welcoming tone, would ring in my ears whenever Kaye and I were touring apartments or discussing living arrangements. And, just as perversely, once I was free to say yes to the program, all I yearned for was what I had just thrown away: the chance to live with her, day in and day out. To wake up with her in the morning and go to sleep with her at night.

I wrote back to the director to say I was coming, though without enthusiasm. I saw the program as my consolation. I had lost my chance at true love but, like Proust and Joyce, maybe now I would redeem my losses through writing.

IN AUGUST I DROVE UP TO FIND MYSELF an apartment. When I walked into the country home of the co-director, Janet, she was talking on the phone, swatting flies, and fixing coffee. Books and papers had taken over the kitchen counters.

Between phone calls, Janet regaled me with stories of her previous life as a suburban housewife, her love affairs with a horsewoman and a famous lesbian writer, and a vicious lesbian poet party she'd just attended in New York. À propos of a writing manuscript that spilled across her kitchen table, she explained she was telling her side of the story of her affair with the famous writer, who'd been visiting faculty there the year before and had dumped her shortly thereafter. A kind of redemption, I supposed, but not the sort I'd had in mind.

A student from the previous year came by the next day to show me around the village, which was charming in an upstate New York kind of way, the main street lined with handsome Georgian row houses. We stopped at a little house on a side street. I didn't realize till we were inside and the student said the name "Bella" that I was being introduced to the director, the one who'd written the letter. She was kneeling by an upended armchair in the living room and removing a thick layer of dog hair from its underside, something she continued to do throughout our conversation.

Bella wore old sweatpants and a paint-splattered T-shirt. "Sorry I'm not more presentable," she said in a strong Brooklyn accent, shaking my hand without rising from the floor. It was obvious she wasn't sorry at all. On an end table beside her lay two packs of cigarettes, Carltons and Marlboros. "I alternate," she explained as she caught me glancing at them.

Comfortable, I thought, *what a comfortable person.* The effect she had on me, strangely, was to speed me up. I began firing questions at her: how did this program get started? Whose idea was it? What sorts of people were attracted to it?

Like her efforts to remove the dog hair, Bella's responses to my questions were unhurried and methodical. "We didn't feel women were being served by the creative writing department at the university. Our voices tend to get drowned out.... When people ask 'why split women off from men' I always say 'don't ask me, ask history...'"

I was too busy taking in her face to catch everything she said. Mostly the eyes: the deep creases on either side, the light they gave off, and what I read in them—reserves of both mischief and wisdom. When she looked up from the chair, as she finally did, she seemed to lock my gaze in hers. "I liked your application," she said. It was a tacit acknowledgment that something important had already transpired between us.

"Thank you," I said dumbly.

"You'll be glad you decided to come," she continued. I had the feeling she knew everything: why I'd reneged, why I'd come around, even the fact that coming around hadn't exactly been my decision. When I drove home that evening, having put down a deposit for a room in a boarding house on the main street, I considered for the first time that perhaps Kaye had done me a favour by bailing.

BY THE TIME I RETURNED SIX WEEKS LATER and we were all assembled around the seminar table for our first class, however, I was awash in sadness. Twelve women, none of them Kaye. We go around the table telling our stories. What brought us here. I feel shy as I have never before felt in my life—is it Bella? Some of us are nervously tugging at cigarettes, others chew gum. Penny, a big blond woman from Oklahoma, wears a bandanna, talks tough; her father works on an oil rig. "It's been a long haul," she proclaims in an Oklahoma drawl. Jeanne from Cincinnati, a dyed blonde with a tragic look, says this is a big gamble and she sure hopes it'll pay off. Bibi, a long-haired punk with sleeves cut out of her shirt, hails from Woburn, Massachusetts, "where it smells bad" and says she's just *psyched* to be here, punching the air with her fist. Marla with long blonde hair and a sultry Peggy Lee voice says that after years of standing back from the heat she's finally jumping into the fire. I mumble something about being a refugee from graduate school.

The woman beside me, Jane, whom I've pegged for a suburban housewife, holds up her thumb, which has a Band-Aid on it, and says the power mower just took a slice off it. Everyone waits for her to continue but she doesn't. General laughter ensues. For the first time the tension—the air has been thick with it—eases. Bella has us each pick a tarot card, then write down what it seems to be saying to us. I pick "Temperance," but even after five minutes of listening I hear only the furious scratching of pens on either side. Finally I give up and describe the figure on the card and the pitcher of water he's pouring from. Pass when it's my turn to read. I fare no better in the other exercises she assigns to us. The others, meanwhile, turn out to have formidable talents. Bibi is a whiz at describing an orange through the senses. Marla free-associates in four languages, including Serbo-Croatian. Penny's every sentence is marked by working-class grit and sinew. Jane the suburban housewife is a comic genius.

At the end of the day Bella says she is "energized." She talks of the hopes she has for all of us. What we stand to gain, singly and collectively, in these months of writing together and studying together. There will be courses in women's poetry and fiction as well as writing. Bella wants us to understand that our focus on women writers is not just about righting a historical imbalance, though of course it is that. The writers we'll be looking at are all in some way trying to make connections, to make whole. They reject fragmentation, alienated vision. Writing at the edge of the void. And so does she, she says.

"The abyss seems to be the major preoccupation of most male writers today. Here's what I say we do with the abyss"—she modulates to Jewish mother mode, laying the Brooklyn accent on thick—"fill it with water, chicken bones, some garlic, a little salt. Bring it to a boil, let it simmer for a few hundred years. Then feed it to all the hungry people in the world."

Several of us applaud. I'm cheering inside, where wheels are turning very fast. "Fragmentation" and "alienated vision" would apply to almost all the modern writers we read in grad school. If not to the attitude of my professors. Until this moment it didn't occur to me any other attitude was possible.

We're about to break up when Penny raises her hand. "All this talk about vision, and I can't even see to the other side of the room for all the smoke."

There's a moment of shocked silence. How dare she? The smokers reluctantly put out their butts. In my indignation, I, who've said almost nothing till now, stand up and proclaim loudly that I've spent much of the last ten years of my life in Ivy League classrooms and today is the first day for as long as I can remember that learning is actually making sense to me. Bella nods in my direction then suggests we take a vote on the smoking in the next class.

IN THE FIRST WEEKS THE TENSION in the seminar room steadily mounts. Jane—who, it turns out, lives in nearby Syracuse with her girlfriend—has been blocked; one day she breaks through, has a vision by the lake as wild geese honk overhead, comes home and writes all night long, covering pages and pages. She reads some of it to us in class the next day: it's fresh and funny and alive. Bella looks pleased; she gets us talking about voices—the ones that call to us. How can we heed them? Why don't we listen?

"There are reasons why we don't," Penny says. Her jaw's been clenched, she's chewing gum really hard. "Some of them are damn good ones too."

Colleen, an older woman with hair pulled back in a bandanna who, like me, has been mostly silent, says she regularly burns what she writes because she's afraid of being locked up. Bella nods, knowingly. Marla throws a cup against the wall. Jane ducks under the table. Bibi screams. The smokers—who were outvoted at our second meeting—begin to exit the room, cigarettes already poised between fingers and lips.

"Of course it's scary," Bella shouts. "Who ever said it wasn't scary?"

Each week one of us presents her work. These are the moments of highest stress. Janet the co-director is more merciful with us than I would have expected from the way she spoke of her ex-lovers. She offers precise criticisms and suggestions, e.g., "You don't have enough control of your voice yet; your humour's cutting the wrong way." The rest of us flail about, offering conflicting responses to the work. Heads keep turning towards Bella, looking for a sign. Are we on the mark? Usually she holds out till the very end and when she does weigh in everyone gets very still. It's never just about the work. She tells Bibi she might be able to write something truthful if she could just stop worrying about her image. She tells Penny to lighten up. Even Jane gets worked over: "Have you ever tried writing something that isn't funny? Humour can be a cop-out." Sometimes instead of critiquing the work Bella critiques our responses. Why are they always technical instead of emotional? Why aren't we engaging with our whole selves, why do we leave all the hard work to her?

After class there are griping sessions at Albert's, the family-style restaurant on the main street. Bibi feels she's been dumped on; Jody, a psychologist, feels there needs to be professional back-up if you're going to attack people personally the way Bella does.

"Did you feel personally attacked?" I say to Jane.

"Absolutely not," she says. "I didn't come here to get stroked."

Jody says that's missing the point.

Bella's opening a Pandora's box and it's just not professional.

I ask her has she read what Woolf has to say about the professions in *Three Guineas*. Realizing I probably sound like an academic snob.

Jody ignores this comment. "I'm just afraid some of us are not going to survive this year intact," she says.

Well, I think, *maybe the wheat needs to be separated from the chaff.*

AN ALUMNA OF THE PROGRAM—there are lots of them still around—has a second-floor railroad apartment with high ceilings in an old building on the main street, and one night a week it becomes a speakeasy for all the girls in town. At the end of our first week everyone gathers there for drinks and smokes and dancing on the hardwood floors. Already attractions are forming. Jody, who shares a sweet cottage in the village with her girlfriend, is having a very intense exchange in the corner with Jeanne, the girlfriend nowhere in sight. Bibi and Janet are dancing up a storm; later I see Bibi put her arm around Janet's waist. Brazen, I think, but Janet doesn't pull away.

Bella arrives with a long, lanky blond woman, young, with wire-rimmed glasses. I realize now I've seen the two of them walking in town before, arm-in-arm. They sit down together on a couch and Bella puts her hand on the young woman's thigh and later circles her neck with her arm.

THE NEXT DAY THERE'S A BRIEFING SESSION at Albert's over beer and fried chicken and shrimp baskets; information has been passed on by local alums. Janet's a big flirt but she usually doesn't follow through. Bella's another story. That blond woman is Brooke, they're an item. Brooke was a student here two years ago, that's when it started. The short, dark woman with the camera who was so friendly to everyone and took pictures is Miriam, Bella's life partner. They've been together a long time. Neither of them believes in monogamy.

Penny is staying in the same boarding house as I am. On our walks to and from campus, we have long discussions about Bella and the other students. Despite the way she challenges Bella in class, Penny admires her and, like me, feels privileged to be here. Neither of us has any tolerance for the carping and whining at Albert's.

I begin to be fond of Penny. We spend more and more time in each other's rooms. Talking at first, then, after a week goes by and at her initiative, kissing. I've told Penny about Kaye, she understands I'm not ready for more than this. But it's nice to have someone to be with here.

"PAY ATTENTION TO WHAT THEY TELL YOU to forget," wrote the poet Muriel Rukeyser, who had been visiting faculty at the Centre the previous year and whom Bella often invoked in class. When I think back now to how everything changed for me that year, those words seem to sum it all up. The problem with grad school, I was coming to understand, was not the mind. It was what the mind had been asked to do—and what it had been asked to ignore. Here at the Women's Writers Centre we were reclaiming intuition and magic as vital sources of knowledge. We were waking up to nature. We were tuning into our bodies, our senses. We were learning to put thinking in the service of ourselves, of our own questions. It was all the pieces coming together for the first time. It was coming to see how fragmented my life had been before. It was overthrowing all the male authorities who had ever ruled in my head.

Susan Griffin's *Woman and Nature* and Adrienne Rich's *Dream of a Common Language*, each in its own way a challenge to the male paradigm of knowledge, had been published that year, as had Judy Grahn's *The Work of a Common Woman* and Audre Lorde's "The Uses of the Erotic: The Erotic as Power." All of them were passed feverishly from hand to hand throughout the fall. They kept us company in our subversions. Still today when I read passages from *Woman and Nature* I see the rolling hills of upstate New York and those rushing streams, I hear those honking geese.

IN BELLA'S AMERICAN WOMEN WRITERS SEMINAR, we're reading short stories by nineteenth-century writers. Bella has a way of distilling the essence of a novel or a story into a few sentences or even words that she leaves in the air to resonate until someone, anyone, is moved to respond. Usually I am that person. On this day she's been speaking of Mary Freeman's stories, of the formidable strength of her protagonists.

"Yes," I object, "but the price of that strength is almost always a loveless life." It's a heartfelt objection. As exhilarating as it is to be here, not a day goes by when I'm not painfully aware of what it's cost me.

"Good point," says Bella. "Love for women has always meant self-sacrifice. We've had to choose between love and self, between love and creation. These are false choices. We need to redefine love so we don't get trapped in them." And she quotes poet H.D. "I go where I love and where I am loved ... into the snow. With no thought of duty or pity." Then she tells us she's been writing a poem that begins with the words, "I have been trying to imagine a language in which there is no word for guilt or shame." These words too she allows to resonate in the air for a good long while.

No thought of duty or pity! No guilt or shame! Not since the American painter in France, the one who rocked my world right after college, has anyone made my mind reel this way.

Back at the boarding house, Penny tells me she has a crush on Bella. I would never use such a word to describe how I feel. I don't have words for it, and if I did I wouldn't speak them to anyone. I feel undying loyalty, is all I know.

ONE AFTERNOON COLLEEN INVITES ME to her attic apartment after class. She wants to play a record for me, Kay Gardner's *Mooncircles*. Colleen doesn't speak much but she writes poems that I love, to women and to the stars.

Her apartment is dark when we arrive. She lights candles on a low table and points to a cushion on the floor, where I sit while she slips the album out of its cover, sets it on the turntable. Then she lights incense and settles beside me on another cushion as the music begins. She rolls a joint and we pass it back and forth. It occurs to me I've never been invited to someone's place to sit in darkness and listen to music before, except maybe one time in college with a stoned boyfriend who sat me down to listen to Jesse Colin Young's "Sunlight" and kept getting up to play it over and over again. Which, as it turned out, was all to get me in the mood for sex.

"Changing, changing, changing, changing," sings a rich alto female voice. There are cellos accompanying it and a flute, and I see swirling shapes behind my closed eyes. When I open them, smoke from the incense is traveling up to the ceiling in spirals and Colleen is tendering the joint to me. Colleen, who is ten years older, has only a high school education, and pumps gas at the station next door to pay her rent.

For the first time in my life, I think, nodding to Colleen as I take another toke, *I exist among female forms in all their wild variety.* It's not only to write that we have all come together, I realize now, but to break through the old divisions. To throw over the old rules, the rigid lines drawn by the disciples of the father God, and enter this world of gentle circles and spirals, of infinite, undying change— which, I've been learning, was once regarded as the realm of the Great Mother.

Following the curves of the spiraling smoke, I think: *This is my idea of revolution—not bloody wars but transformation. And I owe it all to Bella.*

APART FROM STUPID LOVE POEMS ABOUT KAYE, I'm still not writing. And tomorrow is my turn in workshop. I linger over dinner at Albert's and have a bad headache when I get home. Around ten p.m. I start writing about why I can't write. It turns into a piece about my father. I write about his library, his sword collection, his Napoleon hat. I write about Miss Reynolds and the time he made her magically appear in our dining room. I keep writing, for hours, on the little wooden secretary in my room at the boarding house.

The next day in class I read it out loud. Nobody jumps on me. Everyone laughs where I imagined they'd laugh. They say they can see my father. At the very end Bella looks at me meaningfully and says, "You've been waiting your whole life to write that piece."

She's right, I have.

THERE'S A HALLOWE'EN PARTY AT THE SPEAKEASY. Louise, the only married woman in the program, comes dressed as a diesel dyke with her hair greased back. Penny is her idol Ida Tarbell, a muckraking journalist from the 1930s. Miriam, Bella's partner, is a wizard with a silver cone on her head; she bounces around the room waving her magic wand, and I notice that somehow she keeps landing at Penny's side. Bella is a gypsy in great colourful robes with a scarf around her head. She stands guard by the door and to everyone who enters she says, "You have traveled far. Rest, drink, later we will talk."

I'm Joan Crawford from *Mommie Dearest* in a low-cut black cocktail dress, heels, and a black pillbox hat with a veil. I speak with mainline lockjaw and only break character once, when Jane appears as herself thirty years from now, with white hair and lined face. "You look amazing!" I exclaim, then instantly resume my cool demeanor. We strut out on the floor and dance a foxtrot together. I feel Bella's eyes on us the whole time.

In a corner on a couch by herself sits Brooke, a prince in brown velvet cape and hat. A sulky prince, judging by her droopy posture and pouting face. I don't dare to presume why.

A week later we all pile into cars and vans and head for Syracuse for a concert featuring Mary Watkins, Gwen Avery, and Linda Tillery. A high school gym, packed with women. No sign of Bella or Janet, but most of this year's students are there, and so are all the women around town we've gotten to know. Linda Tillery gets everyone onto their feet with her drumming and her songs of womanlove, which most of us know by heart. I'm aware of my new friends around me, Jane and Colleen and Bibi. Penny is beside me but not dancing with me because nobody's pairing off, everybody's dancing, alone and together, dancing and singing along with Tillery, "I'd like to get to know you in a special kind of womanly way." I think I couldn't love any of these women more if we were lovers. I can't remember when I have ever been this happy.

BELLA WANTS ME TO TAKE A LOOK at her novel. She says this to me one day at the end of class. I'm floored; why me? Can I come to her house to pick it up, she asks.

She is puttering in the kitchen when I arrive, blending chickpeas for hummus. She wants to know how I like my new place; I've just moved out to a little apartment in the country. I love the hills, I say, and the muted colours of November. I do a little jig around her in the kitchen as the blender whines. "The hills are alive ... with the sound of me!" she quips, once the blender stops. I laugh, we both laugh, but she is exactly right; ever since that father piece I wrote three weeks ago I've been writing nonstop, filling my little efficiency apartment with the sound of myself.

I go on to say how much I love my life here, and how everyone seems to be flowering. "Because of you," I come very close to saying.

We move out to her porch and smoke Carltons, alternating with Marlboros, and watch squirrels darting along the branches overhead. "I always like Sagittarians," she states. (Brooke is a Sag, I've been told.) She admires our energy and speed, she says. But sometimes we rush too much and need to be slowed down. She's a Taurus, she informs me. "We're slow and patient. And we like to indulge."

She tells me a bit about her novel, which is about the making of a revolutionary. It's largely autobiographical, she says. She thinks I'll like the Miss Berg episode—"my Miss Reynolds," as she puts it.

"So you had one too?"

"I think most girls do, don't you?"

At the door she hands me her novel, then gives me a hug. I skip down the street to my car.

ALL THAT WEEK I SLEEP WITH HER NOVEL beside me and every waking minute when I'm not in class I'm reading it. I read about her high school crush on Miss Berg, about her love for Miriam, about their passion for revolution. I'm afraid I'm not reading it the way she wants me to, as a writing apprentice or a literary critic. I'm reading it to find out about her life. When Penny sleeps over we read passages out loud to each other. She asks can she borrow it for just one night, and since I've read it to the end I say okay.

A week later Bella calls me to a conference at Albert's. She says she has something to discuss with me, it sounds important, and so I meet her there after class and it turns out it's her novel. She's upset that I lent it to Penny.

I apologize right away but that doesn't satisfy her at all; she wants me to understand why she's so upset. In class I'm always impressed at the way her words seem to emerge out of silence, how she gives them each their proper weight, letting them come slow and drop heavy and just right. That's the way they come out now.

"What I give to you ... is for you."

There's a long silence afterwards, and it makes me very uncomfortable because from the way they're being said it's obvious the words are meant to convey a particular message and the only thing I can imagine it might be I'm not ready for. Then she says, "You don't seem to realize that most of what I say in class I'm saying to you."

I just say, "Oh," and then grow very silent. It doesn't help that she keeps on staring at me with those mystical greygreenblue eyes that already I feel can see everything. I can't return her gaze. All I know is I have to be alone. So I dash out of Albert's and into my car and all the pieces of the conversation I couldn't take in at the restaurant start flying back at me on my way home, like how we had work to do together, just the two of us, and she didn't want to hold back, and couldn't I see it went both ways, that she was vulnerable to me too. And right away, of course, I start going back over everything she's ever said in class, which is easy since I've written most of it down—I thought it was the mark of a great teacher, to make every student feel she was speaking directly to her—most recently the quote she picked out from *The Story of Avis*, "the intertwined roots of sex and art," and the comment she made about it: that when you work together to bring something into being it's always erotic.

And other things start coming back to me. Like the time at the end of class she said she was about to go do laundry and did someone want to come with her and I could have sworn she was staring at me. And just two nights ago how we were having pie at the diner, she and Miriam and Penny and I, after the auction, and she sat across from me and I could have sworn her leg was pressing into mine. These were things I thought for just a split second and then right away dismissed. But now I think yes she wanted me to go do laundry with her, and her leg that night in the diner, in blue jeans, not only did it press against mine it stayed there, for what could have been minutes. As for that quote from *The Story of Avis*, it wasn't just creative energy she was talking about, how erotic it was—"the intertwined roots of sex and art"—duh, Lise, she was talking about sex.

8.
She Knows

The rules break like a thermometer,
quicksilver spills across the charted systems,
we're out in a country that has no language
no laws, we're chasing the raven and the wren
through gorges unexplored since dawn
whatever we do together is pure invention
the maps were out of date by years....
                    —Adrienne Rich, "Twenty-One Love Poems"

All lovers believe they're inventing love
                    —Anne Carson, *Eros the Bittersweet*

HER BREASTS FLOATING IN THE WATER. *Her wild Jewish hair, pinned up for the bath. Her great, white, freckled chest. She puts a board across the tub for our crackers and wine. She feeds me crackers her fingers smell of garlic. She puts her fingers in my mouth she takes the glass of wine and tips it to my lips then to hers. She likes blending things together, she says I'm too compartmentalized, she takes a doggie bag home from the restaurant and brings it into bed with us, lamb chops and French fries or fried rice and moo shu pork, she likes licking grease off her fingers and mine, she says I think in boxes, why not eat in bed and why not kiss during dinner, she loves to kiss me in the kitchen she loves to get food all messed up in our hair and our fingers. Not since Sappho, she says, have women known the meaning of unrepressed.*

Her little hands, which I forget when I decide I have to get away from her, how like a child's hands they are how like a child she is when she's alone with me, and everything they say, how it's three to one and I need to protect myself, how she has all the power ... it all vanishes. How many looks she has how many women she is, in the bath she's a lady when she's tired sometimes she's an old woman but mostly when she's with me she's a girl. A motherly girl, who likes to buy me gifts, who says Sagittarians don't know how to indulge, who takes me clothes-shopping in the mall, we go in my car because she doesn't drive.

Her father owned an amusement park in the Bronx. I thought she was making it up at first, when she swore it was true I couldn't stop laughing I couldn't stop saying how perfect, you stepped right into his shoes. I didn't even know what I meant then, but more and more now I do. The way she teaches us not to be afraid of pleasure, of fun. She knows the best stores in the mall, she zooms right in on what she wants, she disappears into the changing room and struts out in a new sweater and twirls around in front of the mirror and I ooh and aah. She says she loves to be admired, it's her Leo rising, and I say how perfect since I love to admire you. She makes me try things on and tells me how pretty I look.

Probably it should have stayed the way it was, before that meeting at Albert's. I was so full of her gifts to me then, so full of myself, like the day she sent me off with the mushrooms, she was sending me off on a great adventure, and I let my feet lead the way to the lake and found a tree that felt right against my back and for the longest time I leaned against that tree and just looked, at the piling clouds and the lake turning purple. It felt like I was really looking for the first time in my life, really seeing, and I knew that later I would write about what I'd seen. I was so thankful then, for how she helped me get out of those boxes in my head and come to a place where all I had to do was step out and look and smell and feel.

But after that meeting everything changed. After that meeting everything she said and did was coming back to me pretty much nonstop night and day and finally I had to go over there.

It felt like a week had gone by though it was only maybe three days. She sat cross-legged on the floor. She looked a little afraid to see me, but not surprised. I walked in and lowered myself into her grey armchair. She had on a woolen shirt in grey and blue, the colours of her eyes and hair. She was so completely there in all her beauty. Her mystery. I must have misunderstood, was all I could think. I made myself talk, though I couldn't hear my own words I was shaking too hard, and I had to keep looking straight ahead, not down at her, I said did she think just because my moon was in Aquarius it would have no effect on me, her talking to me that way. What did she think, anyway?

She began to talk. Solemnly. When I looked down her brow was knit, her eyebrows drawn together. She talked about danger, she said it was dangerous, she said she was excessive, she told me everything I stood to risk, she said she was afraid for herself and afraid for me, but after a certain point all of that blurred together and only three words stood out: "falling in love," she said she'd been "falling in love" with me for a long time, she'd been fighting with Brooke she'd had long talks with Miriam, "falling in love" was all I heard, it drew me down from the chair, grabbing her shoes to steady myself, "I don't care, I don't care" I was saying, my mouth heading for hers. Then I was on the floor and she was pulling me to her and my lips were sliding down the length of hers, which tasted faintly of cigarettes and were so full, and so long, like the bow of a cello, I remember thinking, and then I was being held, somehow, against that woolen shirt, she had me in her arms, and it was so impossibly right, the way I fit there, she was so solid in her roundness, *comfortable as the earth itself*, I remember thinking, and on top of everything else that she should feel and taste and smell this way left no doubt in my mind that I had come to the end of a line, there would be nowhere to go after this.

So maybe it's stupid to say it should have stayed the way it was, maybe nothing in the world could have stopped it, maybe it had already started long before, why else would I have hung on every single thing she ever said in class, why else did the words go in so deep? And on the way to the lake that day of the mushrooms when I stopped at the Great American to get a soda at the check-out counter I'd felt waves of something going back and forth between me and the cashier that almost made it hard to breathe.

Refracted light, mistaken for the source—maybe that explained my attraction to Penny too, since we used to lie in bed at the boarding house and talk about her. Okay, so I wasn't writing now, but more and more I saw we were here to learn about living, not just writing, we were creating new forms, not just in art but in life.

Isn't that what I hear in her "yes"? The yes she says from so deep down, what nobody else in the class knows but me, how she is in secret, how she wants, how she wants me to do anything I like to her. Sometimes I don't even remember the part where she does me, not that I don't like it, but mostly I can't wait to get to her there is so much of her so many places to touch and smell and kiss and she puts some kind of rose perfume down there and when I go there she says "yes" she says "yes" and she goes on saying it to the end, like Molly Bloom never existed, "yes," "yes," and the yes is so big it holds all the pleasure and the wholeness women have been denied for millennia ("not since Sappho")....

"Would we love each other any differently?" she said once when I brought up the imbalance—which seemed so obvious to everyone but her—never mind the power factor, her being the teacher, me being her student. And it stumped me, that question, since the truth was nobody had ever loved me like this before, no one had ever asked me so many questions wanted to climb inside my past and look around—*how many floors up was your apartment what did you see when you walked in*—and when I told her stories how she listened, how she remembered every detail. No one had ever stayed up late with me before, like she did, watching TV or laughing in bed, no one had ever been too excited to sleep, eyes wide open just like mine in the middle of the night, ready to talk or make love at a moment's notice.

"You," she says, "you," sometimes over and over, and I feel it completely—it is me and only me she is seeing, and wanting, and wanting to know. Being together is like writing a poem, she said once, you don't know where it's going but you give yourself over to it, all the way. The trick is just not to let myself imagine her giving herself over that way to Brooke, or to Miriam, saying "you you you you" or even worse "yes yes yes" though I know

she must, I know it can't be only me. It's a matter of training, to stay in the moment with her, not to think outside it not to imagine things.

Oh that first week was exciting, sitting in class as she moved around the room in the clothes we bought together, the ones she tried on for me, remembering the deepdown smell of her, the "yes yes yes," and for the first time I didn't take any notes and missed a lot of what she said. One day at the break she whispered "bathroom, second floor" and we each left at a different time and met there and shoved each other inside the stall and I had her shirt unbuttoned and my nose in between her breasts and would have gone on except we thought we heard footsteps and quickly pushed our way out of the stall and smoothed out our hair by the sinks. And I thought of Miss Reynolds after the day I wet my pants in class rushing me to the bathroom and whispering "This will be our secret," and now here I was again having a secret, an even bigger one, with this ultimate teacher, this last one in a long line....

She gets this excited look sometimes. At a dessert on the menu that has Belgian chocolate in it or the shimmer of the lake in the late afternoon light when we come around the bend. She gets it for writing, when writing surprises her, takes her somewhere new. "There's so much," she says sometimes, and I feel that way too, there's so much in life to be excited about, and you never know what vista might be awaiting you around the bend. But sometimes now when I see that look—like last week, when Mia turned up after all that time away—I feel weak and shaky. And I see her as a girl jumping up and down by the Ferris wheel in her father's amusement park, and wonder how it must have been to know she could get on any ride she wanted. For free. Any time.

IN JANUARY OUR RANKS SWELL. Two renowned poets will be joining us this semester for a week each, and we're to read all of their work beforehand. Bella's classroom powers return; like the Bella of early fall, she brings all her vision and energy to these meetings. I see now how much of this energy has been going into me. Days go by without our exchanging a word or even a glance and my doubts flare. But when our day comes I pick her up after class and bring her to my place and we talk and laugh and make love, just like before, and in the morning she doesn't want to get out of bed. How could I have imagined she'd stopped loving me?

But the cold spells seem to be lasting longer. Brooke goes away for a month and when she returns in March I see her and Bella around town, walking arm-in-arm, just like in early fall. Often now when I call, Miriam tells me Bella is over at Brooke's. Each time my stomach seizes.

When the snow begins to melt, I take long, solitary walks in the hills, breathing in the rich, wet smells. Between classes we students sit outside thrusting our faces into the strong sun. Mia, an alum who's returned for this session, has been flirting with me and I find myself attracted and giddy with anticipation. Spring is in the air. The hills and valleys and streams and waterfalls around us are calling out to be explored. I imagine us driving about in her green VW and stopping wherever the spirit moves us to look and smell and listen. And kiss.

Just before spring break Bella comes and spends the night. She's been warming up to me again and this night she's her funniest, most endearing self. She puts on the Nina Simone tape she made for me and takes me in her arms and sings along, "ooh ooh child things are gonna get easier." The way she says, "we'll get it together and we'll get it undone," a little off-key, the words falling over themselves, makes me mad with love for her. I realize I've missed her terribly. We go to bed and get out only to make dinner.

Somewhere in the night she gets me to confess my attraction to Mia. I ask if she minds. She says of course she will be jealous but she only asks that I be honest with her and keep reminding her of "what we have."

I drive her home at two-thirty a.m. and take off for the train station three hours later. All that week, with friends in Boston and Providence, I rave about Bella and my fellow students. We are history in the making, I say.

ON MY RETURN THERE'S A CARD from Bella in my mailbox. She's been sick, confined to her bed. Wishing I were there to minister to her. I call right away. We're watching the news, she says, come over if you like. Thinking "we" must mean Miriam, I get right into my car.

Upstairs I find her in bed in her flannels, propped up on pillows, exactly the way she described herself in her letter. But on either side of the bed there are women. Brooke is there, so is Mia, so are Bibi and Jeanne and Louise and the women who own the health food store in town. Though it's still light outside the room is dark and everyone is staring at the big TV that's been set up at the foot of the bed. My arrival causes barely a ripple.

Bella looks up briefly and cups her hand around my head as I give her a chaste kiss before wedging myself in between the others on the floor. "What happened?" I say.

"The Three Mile Island Nuclear Plant," says Jeanne. "It sprang a leak."

I realize everyone is scared. It occurs to me they're all here not only because few of them have TVs of their own but because— it's obvious from the way heads keep turning her way, just like in class—they're looking to Bella to strike some sort of sense into the event. But Bella herself is nervous and agitated.

I stay long enough to take in the prognosis of several different commentators, which ranges from dire to mild, then get up to leave. In the car I deflate, interested to note I'm less distressed by the nuclear accident than I am by the fact that neither Bella nor Mia offered to take me to the door.

SEVERAL WEEKS LATER THERE'S A BIG PARTY at Bella's to celebrate Miriam's birthday. The damage from Three Mile Island, it now seems, was local and contained; the panic and alarm have dissipated. Alongside Miriam we are celebrating the continuation of life.

Mia, looking especially beautiful in red vest and black Cossack pants, offers me a joint. Ironically, since the groundwork was laid for our affair, she and I have scarcely interacted. Brooke arrives, looking smug in dark glasses, jeans, and leather jacket. She plants herself beside Bella and the two of them lean into each other throughout the evening. When I brush past them at one point I get a whiff of rose perfume. Suddenly I feel weak and want to go home. But my friends are here, Jane and Colleen and Bibi, we take turns dancing together. And then Mia and I are slow dancing to George Benson in a stoned haze, looking into each other's eyes. Before I leave, she kisses me on the lips.

After class the next day I ask Mia what's happening between us. She says she's attracted to me, but she's also afraid. "Don't want to poach on anyone's territory" is how she puts it. I'm disappointed, but I don't argue with her. I'm too relieved to know I'm still seen, by at least someone, as Bella's territory.

SLEEP IS ELUSIVE. I am managing only a few hours a night and making up for it by napping for much of the day. I dream sleep is a sheet carried by the wind that my eyelid is trying, unsuccessfully, to reel in. I dream Bella is a man, older and charming, when I ask her why she's become a man she won't say. I look into her eyes and say, "You have bad news for me, don't you?" She says yes. I say, "After this you don't want to see me anymore." She says correct—"But on those rare occasions when we do see one another I will bring you flowers, treat you special."

She sits at the head of the table in the tweed vest she modeled for me, months ago, the one she said "blended her," and it does, it pulls everything together, her greybrown hair and her pinkbrown pin-striped shirt and her bluegreygreen eyes, she looks smart in that vest, and terribly sexy, but it's for everyone now and not me—and though I've known this all along, have been preparing for it, it is nonetheless like glass breaking along my ribs....

Still it's what I want, to ride with her. Even though I know my turn will be over soon. Even though it's sometimes harder than anything I've done. Even though I'm not writing, or not anything I can show her. It's what I chose, and I'd choose it all again. If only to know ... the letting go ... the floating free ... the waves of joy. Her breasts in the water ... her wildgreybrown Jewish hair. Her visionary smile, which tells me we are part of an experiment, a calculated risk. Her eyes, which say what we're doing here together is part of something so much bigger than I can ever know. But she knows, she knows.

9.
That Hole

Who is the real subject of most love poems? Not the beloved. It is that hole.

—Anne Carson, *Eros the Bittersweet*

"ARE YOU DOING OKAY WITH THIS relationship, when there are so many other people involved?" Louise said to me one afternoon in January when I was visiting the big apartment on South Street where she lived with Bibi and Jeanne. Louise had taken a maternal interest in me from the beginning, and, as the only married woman among us, was the one entitled to ask old-fashioned questions.

I remember going on about "antiquated modes of relating" that we were outgrowing, as women, if not as a species. It was high time, I said to Louise, we started living according to our true capacities for love and friendship, doing away with cumbersome rules that got in the way, especially if what they got in the way of was lesbian erotic energy. Lesbian eros, I declared, was a precious resource and should never be blocked.

It's true I said all this largely for the benefit of Louise and her housemates, who I was pretty sure were eavesdropping. I knew there'd been a lot of whispering about Bella and me; this was a chance to dispel once and for all the myth of my victimhood. But my speechifying was not empty bluster. It was becoming clearer to me all the time that the structures we'd grown up with were designed with men's needs, values, and rhythms in mind and were not only constricting but life-destroying. As lesbians—which most of us in the program were or had become by the time the semester ended—we were here to create and embody new forms.

And in fact, thanks to Bella, I had discovered a form for love that seemed to fit my own needs and rhythms. She had made it clear at the outset that she and Miriam would always be together, live together—they were partners—and Brooke had her own inalienable rights. Common wisdom has it that non-negotiables in relationships obstruct the free flow of love, but in my case, it seemed, they had the opposite effect. With Bella I felt the steadiest flow I had ever known with a lover. There were no dead moments as there had been, with increasing frequency, with Kaye. Evidently my love needed space—and limits—to flourish.

"It will change," she had said. "Not my love, but the way I express it." It was Christmas break then. The other students had gone away for the holidays, and Miriam was visiting friends out West. Bella and I were spending most nights together, and in the evening, if we didn't go out to eat, she would cook extravagant meals for us in her kitchen. I sensed she was warning me this routine was exceptional and I should not get too comfortable. But she was the one who wanted to linger in bed every morning, who shoved her hand in the pocket of my jeans to hold me captive when I got up to leave. "We'll see," I must have thought. "We'll see."

In the spring, her words came back to haunt me. It wasn't the cold spells—I could ride them out just fine. It was Brooke, seeing them together, their leisurely strolling through the village arm-in-arm a replay of the fall. Casting about for some sort of reassurance, I realized how little there was to be found. I was a would-be writer who'd had a stroke of beginner's luck. Brooke was an experienced poet who was now writing a novel. She and Bella had withstood the test of this other love. What were my chances?

Being the chosen one had had definite drawbacks. It had set me apart from the others, made me the object of pervasive resentment, and caused me to forfeit Penny's friendship. At the same time, it had conferred an undeniable status. In fact, during the winter months I had felt myself to be larger than ever before, as if Bella's bigness had expanded me. But now, as it sank in that I was no longer at the centre of Bella's affections, in fact was barely even on her radar, I could feel myself shrinking by the day. The nights she was with Brooke I was unable to forget for an instant that they were together, was unable to prevent myself from imagining to the point of agony the touching the kissing the tenderness, even the laughter. I felt concave and slight enough to topple over at the slightest provocation.

The school year ended, and one by one the students who had entered with me departed. Jane and her partner, Zoey, sold their house in Syracuse and set off to tour the country in their van. I stayed on. Despite the ever-present signs of Brooke's rehabilitation to favoured status, despite the rumours that Bella was making overtures to one of the visiting poets, I waited for her ever-more-infrequent visits, allowed her to reassure me with the scantest of proofs, interpreted her eagerness to explain herself as a sign that she still cared. I was still there in the fall when the next crop of students arrived. By now I had moved back into the village, joining the hangers-on from previous years. At Albert's I would see the new students meeting in pairs and in clusters after class to eat and drink and gossip just the way we used to do. Several times I caught them staring in my direction. I knew word had gotten around.

Just when I was despairing of Bella and preparing to make a definite break she would show up at my door bearing a surprise gift—beige pajamas with white piping, a miniature brass cash register that sharpened pencils. Or she'd call me on Friday and we'd spend all day Saturday going to auctions and barn sales and then carting our loot home with us. She brought tools to my place and taught me how to strip furniture, transforming a dull green chest into a burnished antique. I loved scraping away at the wood with the knife after we'd applied the stripping solution. I loved watching her expression as the green bubbles formed and the grain first began to show through the paint; stripping wood, she said, was just as exciting as writing a poem.

But my lust was a problem. The policy had been strictly hands off since the summer. Anything else, she'd say, was too "precarious." After helping her find an oak table-top one afternoon, then stopping at the diner for chicken-in-a-basket, I took her back to her place and held the table while she drilled holes to fit the pegs. The wanting had been building up all day and my whole body ached with it as I gazed down on the perfect triangle of her face, now given over to the task of aiming the drill. She gave me a sign, I pressed down on the table, and the pegs locked into place. A grunt of satisfaction from her, and then a smile. I had to make do with that smile, then our quick hug at the door.

At home I lay in bed all night in a fever that never broke. And when I got up in the morning and looked at myself in the mirror I could see nothing in that face that would make someone want to kiss it. Before long, it became difficult to look in the mirror at all.

Bella had laid out the terms from the start. She had tried to prepare me. What she could not have prepared either of us for, what she didn't bargain for—in the years since I have played her part often enough to understand this—was what the "change" would unleash in me. Or should I say *who* it would unleash. I had done such an expert job at concealing her—in fact, I had thought her banished forever—yet how decisively she had crept back, that queer girl from camp and junior high, the one with the crooked nose and tight curls who was left out of the other girls' plans and was too clueless to even notice. Who could blame Bella for recoiling? It's not easy to have someone completely at your mercy, especially when that someone is recoiling from herself.

I was on friendly terms with many of the ex-students now and there were plenty of openings to complain, or at least get another perspective. I shunned every one of them. And if anyone ever tried to criticize Bella in my presence I would rush to her defence. Like Iris Poulette insisting she was having the time of her life at Camp Northland, I kept telling myself and everyone else it was all fine. It was good. She had so incredibly much to do, it was amazing she managed to fit me in at all.

Even as I took in the signs of her growing disinterest, Bella began to show up in my dreams as vulnerable, in need of my protection. "You're highly attuned to other peoples' needs," Neela had said during my reading—something to do with

Aquarius rising in the twelfth house. How accurate it was proving now. And convenient. If I stayed tuned to Bella's needs I could remain numbingly oblivious to my own.

WINTER CAME AND WENT AND STILL I held on. My faith in Bella was beginning to waver, but I could not give up on my lust for the world she had inspired me to envision, which meant I could not stop lusting for her. In early April a student from this year's crop told me Bella was getting it on with one of her classmates. A love note had been found; the classmate, when interrogated, had finally confessed. In my friend's presence I shrugged this off, but when she left that night a slow rage began to burn and kept me awake all night. A week later I was putting down a deposit on an apartment in Boston, a cheap fourth-floor railroad flat in Somerville on Union Square that had recently been vacated by a friend. I moved in the next month, buying what I needed in the way of furniture and kitchen things from students who were leaving town. Soon I was writing again, on the metal typing table and handsome old Olivetti I'd just bought for a song. The street below was noisy with trucks and late-night brawlers spilled out from the bars across the way. But the apartment was flooded with light in the afternoon and I had a fine view of the rooftops of Somerville and Cambridge. I spent long afternoons on the daybed in the living room looking out my window. One day I spent hours observing a wounded pigeon waddling on the tar roof next door.

10

The Best Revenge

The becoming who we really are requires existential courage to confront the experience of nothingness.
—Mary Daly, *Beyond God the Father*

I HAD GOOD FRIENDS IN BOSTON, friends from college who like me had been straight then and had since come out. We went to concerts and readings together. We met for ice cream at Steve's on hot summer evenings. There were trips to the ocean and nights out dancing at The Saints and Somewhere. I joined a women's writing group and found it exhilarating to give and receive criticism in a space free of Bella's powerful presence.

My days and nights were full, but it all felt like compensation. It felt as if real life, real deep body-mind-soul-connected life, were going on without me in the hills of upstate New York.

Jane and Zoey were still traveling the country; ever since the previous summer I'd been receiving ecstatic postcards from the road signed "the van dykes." They'd been camping beside mountains and rivers, in the desert, by the ocean. "We are woman and nature!" Jane exclaimed in one of the postcards. In another she wrote she was just beginning to see what it meant to really say "yes" to women, all the way, to say "yes" to ourselves.

Mostly now when they arrived these cards were bitter taunts, reminding me how far back I'd fallen from my exuberant convictions of the year before.

IN NOVEMBER—THE YEAR WAS 1980—Reagan is elected by a landslide, and as darkness closes in I feel myself sinking into a black pit. Three weeks after the election, two thousand women form a circle around the Pentagon to demand an end to militarism. They plant gravestones for victims of the American war machine, everyone from Anna Mae Aquash to the residents of Love Canal. I read all the accounts I can get my hands on and am eaten up with regret. I imagine myself part of that immense female circle bonded by love and rage. Why didn't I hop on a bus and head down there to take part in the action?

At almost thirty I can't help feeling I've done nothing with my life. I who've been given every opportunity. I who only months ago was helping to make history. The writing has now slowed to a trickle and I have no idea where to go from here. I keep trying to say "yes" to myself but the harder I try the more it starts to sound like a stupid New Age mantra. When my parents call on Sundays and ask what I've been up to I can't think of anything to say. My father is worried I've fallen off the degree track. When my mother adds, "and with all the money we've invested in your education," I feel she has a point. Just now I can't remember what it was about grad school that made me want to be anywhere but there.

MY PARENTS ASK ME TO SPEND CHRISTMAS with them in Santa Fe, where most of my father's family now lives. It will be just the three of us, as my sisters both have other plans. We'll stay out in the country with my aunt Francelle, they say, then move into a hotel in town.

I'm just depressed enough to say yes. I've never been to Santa Fe and I imagine if nothing else I'll escape from the greyness and the unrelenting noise of trucks on Somerville Avenue.

Francelle, her sister Nadine, and her daughter Vanna have adobe homes that sit up on a mesa overlooking the Sangre de Cristo mountain range. The views are imposing, as even my father, who prefers urban vistas, has to admit. Inside, Francelle's house is outfitted with impeccable taste, the walls hung with huge abstract oils and colourful tapestries. The only jarring note is struck by a throw pillow with THINK THIN embroidered in jumbo letters.

The last time I saw Francelle was over ten years ago, when they lived in the Hollywood Hills. She had just had her breasts reduced and tried to convince me I should have mine done too. I was not amenable; she had to settle for taking me shopping for a new bra.

Now Francelle is shorter than I remembered but has the same Cleopatra eyes and imperious ways. "You're so thin, darling!" she says approvingly before taking our drink orders. Apparently thin trumps scruffy; I'm wearing worn jeans and a favourite wool sweater.

While my father and Francelle move on to a second round of cocktails, Mother and I go out walking in the arroyo out back. The air is pure and faintly sweet from piñon smoke, the light is ethereal, and there are twinkling farolitos strung above the rooftops. I rave about it all to Francelle afterwards, in her living room with its cathedral ceilings.

"Yes, dear," she says, "it's very beautiful here." But, she goes on to say, they miss LA terribly. John misses sailing and she misses culture.

"'Culture' in LA?" says my father. "That's a contradiction in terms." His low regard for all things Californian is well known in the family.

"Oh David, shush up," Francelle says, and he does. My aunts have always been good at putting him in his place.

Though he clearly adores his cousins, my father is not in his element here. At night he grumbles a lot about men who still have all their hair, and it's not hard to read between the lines. Francelle's husband, Mel, is a tall brawny man who spends most of his time here in chaps and spurs; Vanna's husband, Jim, an economics professor, whom my father had counted on for conversation and whose most striking feature is his full head of dark, wavy hair, seems always to be off riding with Mel. Francelle's avuncular, pipe-smoking husband John, when he's not on the phone cutting business deals, is reminiscing about his sailing adventures. My father is visibly relieved when we move to our hotel in town. And I'm happy to explore the galleries and bookstores of Santa Fe.

On our last night, I'm seated between Jim and Uncle John at The Compound, Santa Fe's toniest restaurant, aware of being underdressed in the cotton turquoise shirt I've just bought on Canyon Road. Jim and John are trying to argue my father out of his aversion to Reagan, to whom he refers alternately as "that hoofer from California" or "that Hollywood cowboy." It's nice to be on the same page with him for once.

"You'll see, David, he'll be good for this country," says Jim, and my mother, who's seated beside him, says she thinks so too. My father just winces.

"Good for business, yes," I blurt out. "But the environment? The poor? The arts?"

The men on either side of me dedicate themselves to setting me straight.

Meanwhile the women across from me are brandishing fingers and comparing rings. Vanna has on one that everyone mistakes for a sapphire. "Woolworth's," she says, triumphantly.

When the main course has been cleared, Uncle John lights his pipe, sits back with a look of consummate satisfaction, turns to me, and says, "When all is said and done, Leeza, living well is the best revenge."

I'm struck dumb. An article with that exact title appeared some weeks back in the *Sunday Times Magazine* about the Oscar de la Rentas. I read through it appalled, looking in vain for a trace of irony or qualification. There is no irony in John's pronouncement either, which goes on reverberating in the air. I'm just bruised enough from my revolutionary ferris wheel ride to wonder fleetingly if he's right. Besides, it would be rude to argue with him—we're his guests tonight—so I just smile and nod.

At the hotel, my parents start angling for information about my life. Daddy wants to know why if writing is what I'm doing I won't show him any of it. "After all I'm cultured, literate," he argues. I'm sorry that he feels left out, but reading any of my writing, I'm fairly sure, would make him feel worse. Mother says I'm being irresponsible by dropping out of school. I say if I'm responsible to anything it's to the future of the planet. "Well become someone," she says, "and then they'll listen to you in Congress." That's exactly what I'm trying to do, I think, but with no conviction at all.

Back on Somerville Avenue, my rundown apartment has never looked so shabby. The view out my living room windows is bleak, especially through the layer of plastic insulation, and some of my plants have died in my absence. Maybe my relatives have a point about living well. At least they're in step with the times.

The Glitter Era is officially ushered in at Reagan's swearing-in ceremony. The faces of Reagan and his VP, Bush Sr., are etched into the Washington sky with fireworks. Frank Sinatra sings a song he's written for Nancy "with the Reagan face" predicting that "the eight years ahead will be fancy, fancy as they come...." Later, I read in the *Times* that thanks to Nancy, high-fashion lovers who've been in hiding all these dark understated years are now stepping out unabashedly in their furs and rubies and Bill Blass satins. I think of my fancy relatives and consider how far I've strayed from my origins.

I just wish I could know who it is I'm becoming.

11.
Making Light

The sparking of ideas and the flaming of physical passion emerge from the same source.

—Mary Daly, *Gyn/Ecology:
A Metaethics of Radical Feminism*

AMONG MY BOSTON FRIENDS all the talk is of the upcoming conference on women and racism. The theme makes me nervous. After reading Alice Walker and Audre Lorde at the Centre, after reading Adrienne Rich's essay "Disloyal to Civilization," I get that white women need to be addressing our racism. But I'm leery of a feminist conference focused on bad behaviour—what's going to happen to female bonding and solidarity? Our "dream of a common language?" I can't bear the thought of feminism being reduced to nothing more than a site of struggle. And maybe, too, being someone who grew up with "help," I'm afraid of being caught out.

Once at the conference though, with the press of women's bodies all around me, there's the familiar buzz of possibility. And in the opening session I'm moved by the testimonies of white directors of women's centres wanting to co-design programs with their black colleagues and activists of all colours who are looking for ways to bridge racial and cultural divides. This is our search for a common language, I realize, feeling ashamed for having been so negative.

In the Jewish Women and Women of Colour workshop, however, things get nasty. When the Jewish women speak out about anti-Semitism, a few black women snarl and say they have white skin privilege; one of them says they could get nose jobs if they wanted. The Jewish women take offense and there is yelling back and forth. At the end, a white-skinned Chicana and an Asian woman complain about feeling invisible; they want to know where they fit in.

No way am I going to open my mouth at this conference.

In the eyes of my Reaganite relatives in Santa Fe I'm a loser, and by the time the conference is over it's hard not to feel the same way here. The only thing I have going for me is the identity I spent the first twenty-five years of my life trying to suppress. But my lesbian credits are undercut by my white skin, my able body, and my privileged background. Having a Jewish father might count for something—but an assimilated, mildly anti-Semitic Jewish father?

REAGAN HAS UPPED MILITARY SPENDING by more than twenty billion, cut funding for food stamps by a third and the NEA in half. It's only minutes away from midnight on the nuclear clock. I have a sense of urgency, if not apocalypse. Thank God for the Women's Pentagon Planning Committee, which I've joined. We're planning a new action, one that calls for surrounding the Bunker. I'm excited; this time I'll be on the front lines! But soon word comes down from the central committee that our plan has been rejected as too dangerous. Our momentum is broken and the meetings fizzle out.

I join a caucus group for Women for Nuclear Disarmament, which is headed by Helen Caldicott. They're planning a Mother's Day March, hoping to attract marchers from all ends of the political spectrum. I'm gung-ho about this idea until our third meeting, when a pale blond woman asks if a poster saying "Dykes Against Nukes" will be welcome and the group leader is not able to entirely reassure her. This makes me rethink my dismissal of the whole identity thing. Soon I stop attending these meetings as well.

IN FEBRUARY, THERE'S BIG NEWS from upstate New York: Jane has begun writing and performing her own comedy shows, with Zoey as her manager. I make a bid to produce her Boston première—a friend has offered her loft at a bargain price—and they accept. We set the date for March 20, the first day of spring; the show is titled "Making Light." An artist friend helps me design posters and flyers.

As spring light floods the city streets, postering becomes my political activism. I show up at every women's concert and poetry reading in town armed with my staple gun and stash of flyers.

In mid-March I'm postering in an atrium outside a hall where Ntozake Shange is about to read when one of my college friends shows up with another woman in tow, short and dark with dancing brown eyes. "Aida," my friend says, introducing us, and the two of them talk me into attending the reading with them.

Shange is electrifying; afterwards, energized, the three of us return to my place. I find out Aida is a working mother raising two children in the suburbs with her partner. And she's a thinker. She's been studying with feminist philosopher Mary Daly and she's now in a study group that's spun off from her classes. Some of the women in the group live in other parts of the country, so they also communicate by letter. She thinks I'd like the letters, especially Grace's letters. "They're amazing," she says, and promises to show them to me.

"MAKING LIGHT" IS A SMASH. Some fifty women are packed into the loft, among them Aida, who is accompanied by a tall woman I assume is her partner. Jane is brilliant and brave and riotously funny. She tells a series of penis jokes ("I grew up with five brothers and my job was to clean the family bathroom; I always knew they couldn't control those things"). She charts her progress as a recovering Catholic, then does an imitation of Pope John issuing a series of papal decrees. She appoints a group of women to get up on stage with her and respond to each decree with a chorus of "you've got to be kidding." At the end she says her whole life she's always gotten into trouble for "making light" and now she wants to reclaim it—as a revolutionary force. She's committed to making light in these dark times, she says, and she's made a commitment to joy in her life. "Let me tell you," she adds, "Joy is not an easy woman to please." When she takes her bow there is, for such a small room, thunderous applause.

Afterwards everyone gathers at my place to celebrate. I uncork wine, we form a huge circle on my living room rug to raise our glasses to Jane, to Zoey, and to spring. Could there be a better way to usher it in? Aida says this is the first time she's felt good since Reagan took office. Her friend, whose face is flushed, says that as someone who grew up Irish Catholic and married an Irish Catholic and is something of an expert in Irish Catholic misogyny, she wants to thank Jane for making it possible for her to claim an identity as a recovering Catholic. She seems to be talking more to herself than anyone else, but I notice that in the course of this long and elegant sentence, everyone around her has fallen silent.

"It never fails," Aida says, turning to me. "When Grace talks, people listen."

So that's who the friend is.

Jane and Zoey want to know all about her: where she lives, what she does. I'm so glad someone else is asking. She's a junior high school teacher, she says. A reading teacher.

"Reading?" everyone exclaims.

"Yes, reading. Which, you may have noticed, nobody does anymore. Sort of a quixotic vocation." Her voice dips down with irony. She could be a Jewish intellectual, I think, between the thick brown hair, the glasses, and the strong nose, but when she smiles I see she has prominent white teeth—Kennedy teeth—which together with the bulky fisherman's sweater say Irish.

As of this month, Grace says, she lives in western Massachusetts. She has just moved from Worcester, where her job is, to a farmhouse in a little village called Leverett. It's a magic place, she says, with trees, birds, a brook, and a great hill across the way. But she isn't totally moved in yet and it's a long commute every day. Plus she's having roommate troubles.

I want to know more—about the roommate, the farmhouse, the village. I want to know why she moved there. What's in Leverett? But now Grace is asking Jane about herself—however did she get the idea of doing lesbian stand-up comedy? I notice Grace's teeth gleaming as Jane responds.

When the party's over and everyone else is gone, Grace is all Jane and Zoey want to talk about. They liked her a lot. They ask—pointedly—how I felt about her. I tell them to back off, but secretly I'm pleased. I know they are looking out for me. They want to see me with someone who's good for me.

THE NEXT WEEK AIDA DROPS A FAT ENVELOPE off at my place. I start with Grace's letters. I had imagined dry intellectual ponderings; instead they are cries from the heart, in the form of philosophical inquiry. I read them once from beginning to end and then I start over again. One is a long meditation on annihilation. Much of her life, Grace writes, has been dominated by the fear of annihilation, whether in the form of the atom bomb, male violence, or, since Three Mile Island, nuclear meltdown. Now she has resolved not to be controlled by such fear. From now on, "like the spider in freefall," she will have the courage to leap from the edge and trust her creative powers to bring her through. After a winter of running from one meeting to another in the hopes of staving off imminent disaster, I feel these words have been written just for me. As I read them, the hopelessness and confusion of this last year begin to dissolve.

Several letters have been prompted by what I guess (she is never specific) was a rift with a friend. Or a lover? As a result of this episode, she says, "large blocks of my memory are now a disaster area." There is a lot of speculation about the nature of romance, which she defines as "being invented according to other people's needs."

I wonder if Grace would mind that I'm reading into these letters for information about her life, especially since "personal" is a concept she says she is coming to question. "I have found myself wondering," she writes, "if 'personal' might be similar to those categories like 'sexual' and 'intellectual' that are losing meaning as we realize our integrity."

I hear Grace's voice as I read these words; I see the woman who sat cross-legged in my living room just a week ago, and very upright, her face flushing as she spoke. I feel enormous space around her words, as I did then around her. And I want to reach into that space; I want to know this woman.

12.
Leverett

The erotic is the nurturer or nursemaid of all our deepest knowledge.

—Audre Lorde, "The Erotic as Power"

I choose to love this time for once with all my intelligence.
—Adrienne Rich, "Splittings"

HEADING WEST ON ROUTE 2 on that Sunday in April there was no question in my mind. I was driving to my destiny. It was cold and raw and rainy. The branches on the maples on either side of the highway were bare, but their tips were red with expectation. Leominster, Lunenberg—even the place names told me I was moving into another dimension. "Exit at Millers Falls. And don't get your hopes up—it's a grimy old mill town and there aren't any falls, at least not that I've ever been able to see." Grace's directions were full of landmarks; the whole way there I was picturing the road winding along the Sawmill River that led to the pumpkin-coloured farmhouse across from the hill.

I'd been trying to picture it all for a week now, ever since the first phone call. From the sound of the ring—muffled, old-fashioned—I'd imagined it was so deep in the country that phone lines barely reached that far. I was on the verge of hanging up when she finally picked up. . "Sorry ... I was out in ... nature."

Her voice ... how was it possible to be so dry and so warm at the same time? She was happy to hear from me. We talked for two hours that first night. Three hours the next. And the whole time I was trying to picture the room she was sitting in and the rooms surrounding that room and the apricot tree she said was growing right in back and the hill across the way.

"It's my qualitative leap," she said about this move to the country, in the peculiar language I was coming to expect from her. Later I would learn it was a phrase from Daly's *Gyn/Ecology*. She had come here to listen to the silence. And to commune with the trees, the birds, the streams. Also because three women from the study group lived in this area and the meetings usually took place here. The house she was renting belonged to Mary Daly, who had plans to move there someday herself.

What else did I learn about Grace during those conversations that swallowed up whole evenings, despite her repeated insistence that the calls were too expensive for me and we should hang up? That she had been a devout Catholic as a young girl and the divorce from God had been traumatic. That the divorce from her husband, after six years of marriage, had been more so. That she'd grown up in Florida, the oldest of four sisters. That she was once a cocktail waitress. This last piece of information impressed me the most. It made me ache that she'd ever had to do anything so beneath her, and fired me up with righteous indignation. She deserved so much more than what she'd been given thus far in life. I would help her get what she deserved.

Leverett. I'd never seen it, I couldn't picture it, but I knew it was going to become part of my history. I was entering the territory of the women whose letters I'd been reading. Anne, who lived nearby in a cabin in the woods, who wrote of the dew crystals on the dried grasses sparkling in the morning sun as she brought up the last of next winter's wood, who was trying to arrive at a satisfactory definition of "wild." Joanne, who lived in Northampton and worked with fibres and wrote about colour and rhythm and light. Nina, who was studying literature and feminist philosophy at UMass. I was driving toward the farmhouse where they'd met so often to discuss philosophy and literature and feminism.

I had Aida to thank for all this. The party at her place. She'd told me Grace would be there, that she'd be spending the night. I didn't really believe it, not until I saw her in a corner of the living room, pouring drinks, wearing that same bulky white sweater. Aida brought me over to greet her. I shook hands with her warmly, but formally, aiming for impersonal.

At supper she sat across from me, but she was talking intently to Aida's partner, who was seated beside her, and I didn't want to interrupt. I kept stealing glances at her profile: the glasses, the gently curving nose, the horsey mouth. I kept trying to catch bits of the sentences issuing from that mouth.

The desire to kiss a woman. Isn't it always to gain entry into the dark cavern from which her words emerge? To know her. Desire. Isn't it always: for knowledge?

I caught something about her not having eaten meat since she read Peter Singer's *Animal Liberation*. "I don't want to take in all that pain," I heard her say.

Later that night, it was just Aida and Grace and me in the living room, working our way through the gallon of Almaden white Grace had brought with her. She explained she wanted to take advantage of her salary while she still had one—she was planning to leave her job in Worcester when the school year ended.

"Oh!" I said. "Like the spider in freefall." A tacit acknowledgment that I'd read the letters.

"Yes," she said, "exactly." And then, "Aida tells me you liked the letters."

So she knew. Maybe she'd been waiting for this moment herself. Aida was beaming and watching my face intently.

"Liked," I said, "is hardly the word for it." And then words tumbled out. About graduate school and how it poisoned thinking for me, but since then I'd realized the problem was what the thinking was in the service of, and now all I wanted to do was take on big questions and think my way through them.

Grace was smiling at me, her teeth glowing in the semi-dark. "Well you should hear us in study group," she said. I didn't dare take it as an invitation, but I couldn't help wondering if it was.

Eventually Aida went up to bed, so it was just Grace and me, and the rest of what I needed to tell her began to rush out: that her letters were on my mind all the time, that I woke up thinking about them. Not all the letters. Hers. How directly they went into the heart of my own questions and showed me new ways to think about … everything.

She liked it, I could see that. I wasn't being too personal. And then, half surprising myself as I'd been so respectful of her space up till then, I moved out of my chair and onto the couch and sort of jumped on her. I kissed her.

A murmur of surprise seemed to bubble up from her centre, but she didn't push me away. She kissed me back. And then we sat back together on the couch with our arms around each other, very shyly grinning at our predicament.

I left soon after, her phone number folded away in my pocket and my heart leaping like an Olympic vaulter.

Later, when we talked on the phone, she asked, "Didn't you think it might have been presumptuous of you?"

"I wasn't thinking about you," I said, and was proud to be saying this, proud to be seen as one who moved from her own desire.

Which is not to say there hadn't been doubts. They had caught up with me on my way home. She hadn't just been startled on the couch when I made my move—there was a guardedness, a self-protective reflex. For which, no doubt, there was good reason in her past. (Up close I'd seen the lines in her face. She was older, she had lived through a lot.) It made me happy to think how little she had to fear from me, and how completely she would come to see this, how all the armour would come down and the lines relax. Still, I sat for a long time in my kitchen with her number on the table and a lit cigarette in hand before I got up the courage to dial.

What would we do when we saw each other? Would we kiss right away? I couldn't imagine it any more than I could imagine the interior of that pumpkin-coloured house. What kind of taste did she have in furniture? The car she had driven to Aida's was bright orange, which might be cause for concern. But maybe it was borrowed. Evidently I was not entirely free of my father's cousins' influence.

I was on Leverett Road now, with the river beside me. On my right was a rundown old shack with a gas pump out in front. A crooked sign on the side read "Chapin's." "If you pass a little general store on your right you've gone too far," she had said.

I did a U-turn and headed back down the road. Coloured Easter eggs hung from the bare branches of a tree in someone's yard. Then there was a long field on my left and, up a little rise on my right, yes, a house that could pass for pumpkin-coloured, and beside it the orange car. As I came up the driveway she appeared on the porch, waving, with a piece of toast in her hand. She had on brown corduroys with a blue hooded sweatshirt that made her look a little goofy.

"My breakfast," she said, apologetically, indicating the toast.

"I don't seem to have been able to get started with anything today."

Once inside, after a brief hug, she said, "Would you like a little tour?" and pulled me right through the kitchen and out the back door. There stood the famous apricot tree, just beginning to bud, and behind it a little cabin, and way out back a big, brown, sagging barn. Just beyond the barn was her little garden, with a larger one beside it.

"The Donnas," she said, explaining that the couple who lived in the other part of the house were both named Donna.

She led me inside the barn and pointed proudly to one wall. Draped across it was a huge white banner painted with the words "WE HAVE DONE WITH YOUR EDUCATION!"

"Wow!" I exclaimed. I'd seen pictures of it in *Off Our Backs*. It was a relic from the great student protest a year ago when Boston College tried to fire Mary Daly. I'd read about the event at the time—there'd been a huge roster of feminist speakers and performers—had even considered driving in to Boston for it. Now, seeing this piece of it here, I felt I was entering the stream of feminist history.

Back in the kitchen I took in the rough-hewn walls, the low ceilings, the giant woodstove, the slate sink with a little red pump beside it. "I love it here," I gushed.

A card table and folding metal chairs sat incongruously in the middle of the room. Grace motioned for me to sit with her while she finished her toast. I shook my head when she offered me a bite. "Your directions were great," I said. "But I still ended up at Chapin's."

"Chapin's. We'll have to pay a real visit there sometime," she said, and went on to say something about a time warp, but I was stuck on that "we," she was saying "we" for the first time, making a plan for "us."

Grace wasn't making much progress on her toast. I pulled my chair up beside hers, she put it down, and we kissed. In between kisses we laughed. Not nervous laughter so much as bemused. After a while she asked would I like to move upstairs. Yes, I would. On our way we passed a small parlor into which were crammed burgundy velour sections of a modular sofa. Again, incongruous. "My plush," she said with that rich, ironic dip of her voice, as if reading my mind. Only one word, but enough to dispel all my aesthetic concerns. On the futon bed in her small room with its pale blue walls and no sound but the rain on the panes and the occasional whoosh of a car on Leverett Road, we made love for the first time.

THE FOLLOWING SATURDAY I DROVE OUT again. I kissed the greening mound of earth when I got out of the car before entering the house to kiss her and this time we moved right up to the bedroom and weren't shy at all. We spent almost all day in bed. There was so much to be learned there. *Desire. Isn't it always: for knowledge? The "oh oh oh" of discovery.* The honey glow of her eyes behind the glasses, their double lashes. Her generous, pillowy upper arms. And our mounting affinities: we both had prominent teeth, wore braces in high school, were made fun of for them. We were both oldest sisters, responsible, protective. And both of us loved to laugh with our sisters, had learned to love laughing from them.

She showed me her secret seal: the labrys tattooed onto her hip, below the panty line, which she said was not only a link to ancient female power but also a bid for continuity. There was so little of it in her life, she said. Right away I thought of the friend she mentioned in her letter, the one who left her. She herself brought up the roommate who had just hauled off the last of her things.It felt too indiscreet to ask why, but it wasn't hard to imagine: she had been too demanding, wanted too much of Grace's attention, as I was coming to see most everyone did.

Both of us were wary of the "dyad" as a basic unit of human relating. Between us we'd seen too many friends disappear into couples that consumed all their time and energy. "The relationship as bottomless pit," is how Grace put it. She told me the Donnas next door set aside a time every week to "bring things up." She put her finger down her throat as she said these words and I cracked up.

"What happened with your last lover?" I asked. I knew she'd been much younger.

"She wanted a mother," was all she would say.

I asked her why it took her so long to be with women—the young woman had been her first.

"I lived in a lesbian household after college. I saw too much pain and destruction there ... and really, I couldn't have loved women any better."

Oh, I thought. *Oh.* I wondered what I had done to deserve someone so pure so good.

Before falling asleep I lie beside her touching her thigh, in my mind I outline her chest, her shoulders, her head, and what I feel is ... such intense recognition of her being ... and I think this is what feminism is all about, what it has to be about, this loving with deep recognition.

IT WAS HARD TO LEAVE THE NEXT DAY. I was in my car, I'd rolled down the window, and we were holding hands. "You light up my life" came on the radio and we both sang along loudly, camping it up: "You give me hope to carry on." Just before I pulled out she said to me, "Do you know how much you 'lighten up my life'?"

I broke out into a very toothy smile. I could make it better. I already had. *She loves me, I can feel it now I love and am loved and my new life is beginning.*

THE STUDY GROUP MET IN LEVERETT the following Saturday and I was invited to join. Aida and Grace both put in a good word for me. I was a little anxious knowing the others all had a background in philosophy but Grace said I'd make up for it with my literary knowledge.

No sooner were the snacks and drinks out on the card table than the women arrived: first Aida, who threw her arms around both of us at once, then Anne, tall and vibrant in a red plaid lumberjacket, who seemed to bring the outdoors inside with her. Nina was short and round and dark and fiery. Joanne, a tall, graceful woman with grey hair, seemed to defer to everyone else. We filled our glasses and plates and then, at Grace's invitation, we all "moved to the plush" and the session began.

Anne was the presenter that evening. She began by talking about reality and the way deconstruction had put us all on the defensive about it; there wasn't supposed to be any such thing as an unmediated, preverbal reality. Anne said the answers to the most profound questions are often found in the humblest places. And she held up a book she had just stumbled across, *The Real World of Fairies,* the title itself a response to the deconstructionists. She went on to read out loud a passage about cloud fairies who sculpted fantastic shapes in the air. So much for my fears the discussion would go over my head.

Anne found this book revelatory. According to its author, fairies were nature spirits. They were "extraordinarily happy—always" because they were in rhythm with all natural things. People on this planet died of boredom all the time—but fairies lived forever because they were in touch with the wonder of life. There were murmurs of pleasure at this point from Nina and Grace.

"What place does talk of fairies have in 'serious' philosophical discussion?" Anne asked. She opened one of the books in the pile beside her and quoted, "'The lovely human beast always seems to lose its good spirits when it thinks well; it becomes 'serious.' Friedrich Nietzsche. *The Gay Science*, number 327."

"Exactly," Nina exclaimed. "The dour seriousness of the academy. It goes hand in hand with the dulling of the senses and the absence of any sense of magic or wonder."

"That's because connection," said Joanne, "is where the magic is." And she went on to talk of how light-filled she felt when she worked with her yarns, which made sense because light is colour and colour is light.

"I'm thinking of Jane now," Grace said, her face turning bright red. "Her idea that making light is a revolutionary act. It's going to be a revelation to her that she's following in Nietzsche's footsteps."

"Very cool," Aida said, and she reminded us of the way Jane ended her show, with a declaration of her commitment to joy. "Wow!" Anne said. "Just listen to this." She turned to another of the pages she'd marked in the Nietzsche book: "'I want to teach them what is understood by so few today, least of all by these preachers of pity: to share not suffering but joy.' Number 338."

"Bingo!" said Grace and everybody cheered. There followed a chorus of voices pleading for me to get Jane to come visit and join us for study group.

THE NEXT DAY WAS WARM and Grace and I spent most of the morning working out in the garden and going back over the previous day's conversation. Everyone had assured me what a valuable addition I was to the group, and Grace wanted to be sure I'd taken it in. "So ... do you think you might finally be persuaded to start reading Daly?" she asked.

Considering how tuned into their thinking I was, it was a matter of curiosity to everyone in the group that I had yet to open one of Mary's books. Jane had been trying to get me to read her for over a year now but I kept resisting. I liked my feminist illuminations to come by way of poetry, if not experience; I didn't want them all spelled out for me in heady prose. But now, having met these remarkable women whose common denominator was Mary and her classes, I decided the time had come. Yes, I told Grace. I would begin reading *Gyn/Ecology*.

Our lovemaking that afternoon was long and languorous and seemed to draw into itself all the meetings and weavings of the previous day. Afterwards I sat on the front porch gazing out. It had rained all week and the earth was really waking up now. The pasture across the road was pale green, the trees on the hill were bursting into bud. The week before, a friend in Boston had handed me a mushroom—a potent one, she warned me—saying, "You'll know when to take it," and I knew this was the moment. Before long I found myself being drawn out back to the meadow up behind the house. There was a big maple right by the garden that Grace had referred to as a "particularly benevolent tree." I leaned against that tree, feeling Grace's presence in it, feeling her behind me, supporting me.

As I stood there, looking out at the field, the earth began to move. It broke up into plates that heaved and swelled like waves. I began to rock with it, until my whole body was rocking with the rhythm of the earth. It was the same rhythm as our lovemaking, and in fact it was our lovemaking, for the earth I now saw was also Grace, opening, welcoming, and now I was opening, I was caressing the rolling field, I was making love to the earth, her perpetually shifting plates, her unknowable centre.... *There is absolutely no difference,* I thought, *between loving her body and loving the earth*. Making my way back to the house I was filled with new knowledge: there had been another way of life. We were at the centre of it. Not on top, but at the source. Everything flowed from us.

The power of Grace's empathy was such that it often felt to me as if she were able to lift out of her own skin and enter mine. "Yes," she said, knowingly, when I told her, or tried to tell her, what I'd just seen and felt. And soon her face began to flush and she said, "Let's go for a drive." We grabbed sweaters and went straight for her orange car.

She drove very fast up Leverett Road, then took a sharp right onto a dirt road that led us to a small stream. "Rattlesnake Gutter Road," she said. "Word has it there've been fairy sightings here." She parked and we began walking up a spiraling path through the woods. Beside us was a deep gulch with huge boulders; we were flanked by tall trees. Their needled branches were delicate fingers scratching patterns into the darkening sky.

All at once, we both became conscious of the moonlight. Everything was bathed in it. We climbed higher until—there it was!—the moon between the branches, huge and bright. When I looked at Grace I saw her teeth were shining just like the moon.

"Your teeth!" I said. "They're glowing."

"Well what do you think yours are doing?"

Our teeth, which had brought us so much grief in high school, now little moons!

"You know," she continued. "I used to love the song 'Moonlight Becomes You' until I found out what it really meant."

"What *does* it really mean?"

"You know, you look good in moonlight."

"NOOO!" I cried. I had never heard it that way either. We fell silent then. "*Peep peep peep!*" rose up from the bogs, growing louder and shriller and more voluminous as we listened, as if to tell us ours was only one of infinite conversations being carried on all around us in thousands of other languages, that we were one with this massive swell of burgeoning spring life, all of us becoming moonlight and moonlight becoming us. And I thought of the postcard from Jane and Zoey when they were camping out West saying "we are woman and nature" and in this moment understood exactly what they meant.

"I haven't seen any fairies yet," I said to Grace. "But I kind of think we are fairies. Don't you?"

"Without a doubt," she said.

"IT'S PURE ROUSSEAUISM!" MY FATHER SAID, the one time I tried to explain it all to him: these new friends, this farmhouse in the country where I was spending more and more time. I think I had mentioned that in my new circle of friends, all of whom were very smart and literate, we had decided Descartes was the root of modern evil. What kind of brain comes up with a statement like "I think, therefore I am"? What about: "I feel, I hear, I see"?

"Well," my father said, "I suppose you all believe in going back to nature, embracing the earth." He made it sound insufferably stupid. "Go back and read Rousseau if you think you invented these ideas. Or better yet, the German Romantics."

As a matter of fact, I had been thinking a lot about the German Romantics lately. I had felt such an affinity with them, back when I was still trying to translate male experience into my own. Like us, they believed in the power of the imagination, in kinship with nature, in striving for integrity of life, work, and thought. But the parallels only went so far. It was inconceivable to me that males had ever cared this passionately about the world. Besides, the Romantics were reacting to the movement that had preceded theirs, another band of men who had in turn displaced the band preceding them. Periodic fluctuations of the male psyche.

Whereas we ... we were the first in recorded history to see as we saw. Never before in this span of time had the perceptions of women entered the realm of representation; never before had women in large numbers attempted to reclaim not only our own bodies but the body of knowledge that had been stolen from us. No one in recorded history had lived or loved this way before. And the way we lived and loved—I was, we were, certain of this—was of significance for all living beings.

LIFE IN LEVERETT BEGAN TO TAKE ON a rhythm. Friday afternoons I would arrive laden with fruit from the truck on Somerville Avenue I passed on my way out of town: strawberries, peaches, bananas. Grace and I would rouse each other every morning with murmurings about cereal and fruit and maple syrup. After breakfast we would sit out on the front porch and gaze at the hill across the way; there were tiny white blossoms now, and more shades of green than I ever knew existed, and purples and mauves and pinks, and the air was impossibly sweet. Saturday we would run errands in Amherst. One time I insisted we stop at an antique store and there we found a drop-leaf pine table to replace the card table in the kitchen.

Study group met every other week, and each time more connections were made, more threads spun, and when it was over I was both achingly full and hungry for more. The women in the group became more beautiful and amazing to me every time we met. Finally, we—women—were rising to the level of my very highest intuitions about us. I was pleased with myself for having had such intuitions for so long, for having loved women my whole life. The thought that any kind of stigma could be attached to this love was now simply laughable.

Often we were joined in study group by Eleanor, an ex-nun from an activist order who'd spent a lot of time in prison. She was there the day it was Grace's turn to present, and her presence somehow reinforced everything Grace was saying.

Grace started by apologizing for not having prepared a talk for us. But she had some questions to put on the table about love. Is love a function of the will—i.e., can we choose whom to love? According to the language of patriarchal romance, not at all. "We 'fall' in love, we're 'helpless as a kitten up a tree,'" she said. "But if we don't exercise choice in this arena of our lives, where does that leave us?"

"'I choose to love this time / for once / with all my intelligence,'" I quoted. "Adrienne Rich: 'Splittings.'" Bella had given me that poem to read my first fall at the Centre, well before we became lovers. It had seemed momentous and meaningful to me at the time. Now it was feeling even more so.

"Yes, exactly," said Grace.

Anne, nodding furiously, said she was coming to think that no real political change for women could happen without deep friendship—and cultivating and sustaining friendship was a matter of conscious, deliberate choice. Ergo, what Grace was saying was of the essence for our entire movement.

The outcome of this session was that we all decided to overturn the patriarchal verdict and proclaim love the supreme function of the will. In addition to being in vehement agreement with this edict, I couldn't help feeling proud because implied in what Grace was saying was that she had chosen to love me.

THE WEEKEND OF THE LESBIAN POETRY READING in Boston, Grace came to stay with me in the city. It was a much-heralded event, featuring some of the great lesbian poets of our time, among them Adrienne Rich, Audre Lorde, and Judy Grahn. At the Centre I'd come to know women's poetry readings as great celebratory events. There was rarely a reading there that did not create communion among its listeners, that did not leave us all vibrating with the words we had heard, solemn and expansive. For weeks I had been looking forward to partaking of such communion with Grace by my side.

When we arrived at the Arlington Street Church that Saturday night in June, there were the usual rowdiness and high spirits that attend lesbians convening in large numbers, and as Grace and I took our seats up in the balcony, we saw the church was full to the rafters. As one poet after another took the stage and read, though, the voltage began to plummet. The celebration I was waiting for never happened. Racism was the pervasive subtext; several of the black writers read angry poems that seemed to be directed at the audience, and most of the white writers seemed to be weighed down with something I later decided was guilt. Towards the end, Adrienne Rich read a poem about a cripple and a skier that ended with the words "the skier / and the cripple must decide / to recognize each other." As she read I saw Grace's hands go to her stomach and when I looked up I saw there were tears in her eyes.

The next day we attended a reading by Audre Lorde at my friend's loft, the same place where Jane had performed three months before. Lorde read a story called "Tar Beach," about sunning with her lover up on a city rooftop which, in the course of an afternoon of feasting and making love, becomes a piece of paradise. It just so happened Grace and I had spent part of that afternoon on a blanket up on my roof in Somerville taking in the spring sun and the panoramic view of city rooftops now veiled in green. We listened with complete abandon, our chairs pulled close together and our hands on each other's legs, bathing in the sensuous detail of Lorde's prose. Here was transport, and sisterhood. Almost enough to make up for the day before.

And it is happening now this is the big one the one I've been building toward my whole life. Great. Pure. Of the soul. Bella not the end of the line after all. When Grace tells me the title of the book Mary Daly is writing—Pure Lust—I know exactly what it means and everything it connotes. This movement toward her this desire to know her, knowing and loving not being separable. Embracing the object of my lust and my lust itself with the most absolute, unconditional "yes"—yes this was meant to be and yes all the fairies are backing us up yes this is what I was put on earth to do. What Dante imagined in his Paradiso: *"Will and desire become one."*

ONE SUNDAY EVENING IN MID-JUNE I sat down at our new old pine table and said, "Grace, let's have a talk." In my mind was an Adrienne Rich poem she had read at the Arlington Street Church, a poem in which her life with her lover was braided into the lives of the feminists who'd come before them, which ended with words written to Susan B. Anthony by Elizabeth Cady Stanton: *"Yes, our work is one, / we are one in aim and sympathy / and we should be together..."*

Grace had to go pee first and while she was gone I took a look around me. It was almost too much to take in: the flowers on the table, fruit in the wooden bowl, supper cooking on the stove: mushrooms, eggplant, summer squash. The red door open to the spring rain. What more could I want?

"Well it's Sunday and we haven't had our session yet," she said when she came back in. "Is there something you'd like to bring up?"

I laughed, but was not to be deterred. "Grace, I've been thinking so much about it and now I just have to tell you."

She nodded, smiling, and sat down across from me.

"How do you think it would be if I moved in here with you?"

"I thought you'd never ask," she said. She confessed she'd been waiting for me to say something.

"Really?" I asked. "For how long?"

"Well let's just say it was reaching critical mass."

The house was too big for her to manage all by herself. She needed my help. Those were her words. But beneath them were layers of unspoken longing, and unspoken love. We both knew it. "Come live with me. Our work is one," she might as well have said. She didn't say it, but I knew.

13.
Dwellers in Possibility/
Companions of the Flame

...Now we are ready
and each of us knows it I have never loved
like this I have never seen
my own forces so taken up and shared
and given back
    —Adrienne Rich, "Phantasia for Elvira Shatayev"

THERE WAS A CONSTANT HUM that spring and summer of 1981; it filled all the rooms of the farmhouse on that country road in western Massachusetts. The house was the hub of a great wheel. The women in the study group came from all directions and the walls absorbed all of our sounds: the laughing, the cries of epiphany and delight, the occasional roars of indignation. Even the sounds of our listening—for we listened to each other with an intensity that seemed palpable.

Jane wrote an essay at the time that began with women sitting at a round dinner table and talking and laughing so hard the table lifted up off the earth and became a flying saucer spinning out into space. That's how it was in study group sometimes; as we sat in our circle the energy would start to build until we were all careening on the edge, like those tilt-a-whirl cars you can get to spin madly by turning the wheel in the centre, and you keep turning harder even though you're giddy and dizzy with laughter.

It was what we thought conversations were for: those moments of lifting off, weightlessness, being propelled through time and space by the sheer voltage of our connections, words traveling the channels that we'd opened. For it was always more than a matter of feeling connected to each other, and to ourselves—that recurring "yes, yes, that's just how I've always felt too!" or "yes, I think I've always felt that way, but till now I didn't know it." It was also the opening of a vast space—for many of these were yeses that had never existed before, and there was no telling where they would lead. Our territory was the unexplored realm of possibility, H.D's "unwritten volume of the new."

In *Gyn/Ecology*, I found a whole chapter devoted to this phenomenon—Daly called it "Spinning." Like the spider, we were in freefall through space, "whirling and twirling the threads of life on the axis of our own being." When a conversation brought us to the point where we felt suspended, weightless, lightheaded, and somehow not ourselves—then we knew we were on to something. What was coursing through us was nothing less than sheer evolutionary energy.

All of which is not to say we were a bunch of starry-eyed idealists. We saw the sickening of the planet—the spreading poisons, the dying out of species, the numbing of psyches. We saw that the disease was pervasive and possibly terminal. And we saw that it was being visited upon the planet primarily by the male of the species and his need for ownership and control.

I had now finished *Gyn/Ecology*, which spelled out the ravages of two thousand years of patriarchal pollution. (My instinctive preference for women, my instinctive urge to protect them from men, to protect myself, had an objective status to it, I saw now. History backed me up on it.) How could I have resisted this book for so long? In its critical analysis of patriarchal myth and ritual and its celebration of female bonding, it was the theory to our practice. Maybe I had needed to wait until I was fully engaged in that practice so that as I read, every word of it became flesh in my mind's eye.

As unblinkered as its vision was, *Gyn/Ecology* was not a bleak book. Like Virginia Woolf in *Three Guineas*, Daly saw that women, this culture's perpetual outsiders, were free "from unreal loyalties," and thus in a position to bring about fundamental change. How much more so was this true for those of us who centred our lives around women. We thought of ourselves as the last hope on earth. To the destruction we saw all around us, there was only one answer—creation—and when we began to spin together, we felt we were following the lines of the double helix itself, the very spiral of life, the most fundamental unit of creation in the universe.

Grace had grown up in Florida, and when it came to hospitality, she said, she was a Southerner at heart. Among the study group women her pet name was "gracious," and the more time I spent with her, the more I saw why. Anyone who came through our door was always welcomed, not only with offers of food and drink but also with that exquisite attention she knew how to pay, and that I was beginning to notice many women couldn't get enough of. Perhaps that's why it seemed Grace and I were never alone in those days. Someone was always dropping by— to retrieve a forgotten bag or borrow a book or just to share a thought that couldn't be sat on one day longer.

But it wasn't only people. There was almost always some accompaniment in the form of lines from philosophy or poetry. The poems in Rich's *The Dream of a Common Language,* which all of us had read many times over, were constantly present, especially the "Twenty-One Love Poems" which it often seemed to me we were all living out: "this we were, this is how we tried to love, / and these are the forces they had ranged against us, / and these are the forces we had ranged within us...." Maybe it was this other layer of language that made the air so thick always. Maybe that was the hum.

The house itself seemed thick with history, and the tiniest acts— waxing the wideplank pine floors or pumping water at the slate sink—had a way of taking on an almost sacred significance, as if hallowed by the travails of the farmwomen who had lived there before us. This was even more the case after Aida introduced us to a play she had discovered, set in a nineteenth-century prairie farmhouse, called *Trifles.* She recounted the plot to us during study group one June night. A farmer is murdered; the sheriff and his henchmen are called in but find no clues. When the neighbouring wives appear they are able to solve the crime by attending to the disarray in the kitchen—the very details the men dismissed as "trifles."

We all loved the way women took justice into their own hands in this play. We were so taken with it we actually performed it one night in the kitchen of this nineteenth-century farmhouse. Aida played the first of the wives to discover something was awry, rifling through the things on the kitchen counter with a studious eye. I played the sheriff. Eleanor played my wife, and it was eerie how completely she managed to embody the fury and compassion of Mrs. Hale as she pieced together the story of the farmer's wife: "No, Wright wouldn't like the bird—a thing that sang. She used to sing. He killed that too." The sounds of Susan Glaspell's play too were absorbed by the walls of this house, becoming yet another living presence here.

In study group we talked a lot about something we called "the third thing." Patriarchal thought presented us with an endless series of false alternatives: we could be either powerful or loving, either subject or object, either body or spirit. When confronted with such dualistic thinking, we always looked for a "third thing"— something greater than either of those alternatives and in light of which they could be resolved. Joanne liked to remind us of the history of philosophy, with its eternal tug-of-war between perception and cognition. As if the two functioned independently of each other! As if the eye did not take in everything—texture, colour, shape, and meaning. To prove it, she brought in one of her graceful fibre creations, which testified to this fact more eloquently than any words could do. The third thing, we agreed, was also the dimension we entered as we sat on the plush and spun together, that made of us something greater than the sum of our parts.

One day when we were walking the long loop that led up into the hills in back of the house and wound back down along the stream, Grace said to me, "I just had a flash!" She often had epiphanies on our long walks, and I loved to be the first to be privy to them. "Maybe it's the third thing that can save the number two," she said.

I asked her to please back up and fill in.

"You know, the dyad, the couple. What prevents you and me from lapsing into the dreariness of conventional coupledom?" We often talked of the dangers of "Donnadom," the insularity and self-reflexivity of couples. We used to wonder if there was something inherently dysfunctional in the configuration of two. In study group we tried to avoid referring to ourselves as "we," or indeed to give any indication by word, gesture, or intonation that our relationship differed in any qualitative way from that between any other two women in the group.

"Isn't it this whole we're both a part of?" Grace continued. "This web of women we feel held by, these thoughts that travel back and forth between us? Isn't that our third thing?"

Yes, I said, I could see that was so.

In the month of July, however, when I was still living in Boston and spending long weekends in Leverett with Grace, the third thing became objectified in a very literal way when Maxine, the Berkeley outpost of the letter-writing group, wrote to say she planned to move in with Grace for a month, "while there's still room for me there."

Grace thought the news would please me. Maxine was doing graduate studies in German literature and I'd enjoyed her group letters, which were peppered with references to some of my favourite writers. *"Zum Erstaunen bin ich da!"* ("I am here to marvel!") she once quoted from Goethe, reminding me of how I had resonated with that line in college.

A weekend with Maxine would be great, I said, but didn't Grace think a month was a bit long? She insisted everyone in the study group was thrilled—Maxine lived for ideas—and she had a feeling the two of us would talk each other under the table. She assured me it would work out somehow.

MAXINE WAS JUST AS I'D IMAGINED HER: short, impish, bespectacled, and quick-witted. She arrived on the red-eye on a Saturday morning, and Grace and I had decided to bring her to Crane Beach for the day. It would be our first time at the ocean together and a good way to ease Maxine into the Northeast.

The conversation as we headed north with me at the wheel was mostly a running dialogue between Maxine in the passenger seat and Grace in the back. Maxine was fulminating about the anti-racism fever currently sweeping the East Bay women's community. Its latest target was *Gyn/Ecology*. We had all read

Audre Lorde's open letter to Daly calling her out for not including African goddesses in her account of gynocratic cultures—a critique that struck us as both important and respectful. But in Berkeley criticism was ratcheting up to censorship. Maxine told Grace that women—presumably, white women—had entered the feminist bookstore A Woman's Place armed with little DayGlo stickers, which they then applied to every copy of Daly's book on the shelves. The stickers said "don't read this it's racist."

Grace was appalled. She told Maxine about the orgy of white guilt at the Lesbian Poetry Reading. At the beach it was grey and windy and the ocean was very alive. I longed to be running down the length of it. When we came up close, I thought I saw Grace do a little, irrepressible hop. I felt sure if the two of us had been alone together we would have gone skipping down that beach. Instead we fell into line with Maxine between us and walked sedately along the shore, she and Grace attempting to make sense of this latest instance of implosion in the women's community.

I liked watching the two of them riff off each other, but at the same time I so wanted to be silent with Grace, to be looking out together at the water, the dunes, the hawks overhead. When Maxine moved on to the subject of her dissertation, which had something to do with imagining a subjectivity free of domination, I began to get a headache. It was a relief to get in the car and drive back to Boston.

"DON'T YOU SEE SHE HAS A CRUSH ON YOU?" I said to Grace on the phone that night. On the beach I couldn't help noticing the way Maxine kept staring up at her through her thick glasses. And in the car, though she and I had shared a few animated exchanges about the inanity of academic thought, her attention had always seemed to veer resolutely back to Grace. They were both back in Leverett now, and it was late enough that I assumed Maxine had retired.

"An intellectual crush, yes. Nothing to worry about," Grace whispered, then said she had to get off the phone. Maxine was waiting.

When I arrived in Leverett later that week Grace was fixing supper. Maxine had books and papers spread all over the pine table and I was interrupting what appeared to be an in-depth conversation. I had the sense Grace welcomed the interruption but was making every effort not to show it. She made no move in my direction and something told me it would not be right to go over to her. Instead I went upstairs with my things and then called down for her, as if I'd just discovered something that needed her attention on the second floor. It was juvenile, I knew.

I grabbed her when she came upstairs. "Aren't we even allowed to kiss hello?" I asked.

"Of course we are, silly. I'm just trying to be ... sensitive." She was happy to see me, even more so than usual, holding on to me, hard, and kissing me back. I pointed out that she'd been up early and had worked all day—she was teaching summer classes— so why was she waiting on Maxine this way? And why was Maxine allowing it? Grace said they only saw each other once a year so she wanted things to be special for her. She insisted it wouldn't go on like this. But that night Maxine went on talking as before, and Grace went on listening.

It was true Maxine lived for ideas. She didn't seem to live anywhere else. And she made you feel petty for caring about anything else. She would work all day at the kitchen table and always look a little put out when it came time to clear the table for a meal. Then she'd be impatient for us to be done eating so she could put her books and papers back on the table. She said it inspired her so much to be in this house that she hardly needed to eat or sleep anymore. And sure enough, when I got up in the middle of the night once to use the bathroom, there she was at the kitchen table, scribbling away.

To me it was obvious why Maxine wasn't interested in food or sleep but I didn't want to insist on it. I only knew that when Grace came to bed at night I could feel the release coursing through her limbs. And one night she did say, in a low whisper, that she wanted to spend a long time alone with me, just the two of us.

"Just the two of us?" I said, "You mean, without the third thing?" We both laughed really hard.

As taxing as Maxine could be, she also brought us incomparable gifts. Foremost of those was the writing of Christa Wolf, who was the focus of her dissertation. Wolf was an East German novelist and essayist whose name I had never heard in all my years of studying German literature in college and grad school. Maxine was hard at work translating a speech Wolf had just given on the occasion of receiving the Georg Büchner Prize for literature. When Grace left for work and we were alone together she read passages from it out loud, first in German then in English. It was about the fate of literature in the nuclear age, at a time when words ring hollow. The language was stark, poetic, and unforgettable; it seemed impossible the original could have been more powerful. Maxine read more of her translation to Grace and me that night, her voice conveying such rich, deep feeling that all of my irritation dissolved.

A WEEK INTO MAXINE'S VISIT, on a Saturday afternoon, Jane and Zoey arrived in Leverett, fulfilling a longtime dream. Study group was meeting at the house that day and they would be part of it. When they pulled up in their famous van right after lunch there was great jubilation. The last time Grace and I had seen them had been after Jane's show, and they were thrilled to see her again, even more so to see the two of us together. When the study group women began filing in there was even more excitement. Most of them knew Maxine from before and she was welcomed with great fanfare. Aida, Grace, and I had given everyone an earful about Jane's show and I had circulated her essay about the spinning table, along with photos Zoey had taken on their trip. So the two of them were instantly surrounded, mostly by women they hadn't met before wanting to talk about making light and lifting off and women and nature.

It took an hour or so before we were ready to settle down on the plush and get to work. Maxine was the designated presenter. Sunk in the crimson cushions she looked more diminutive than ever, but once she began to speak she commanded the room. She began by saying she wanted to pay tribute to the spirit of place by quoting from Emily Dickinson, who was born and died only fifteen minutes from where we sat, a fact that had never been far from her mind since she first arrived. Dickinson, we might be surprised to learn, was a poet who knew a few things about women's power. And then she read:

We never know how high we are
Till we are called to rise
And then if we are true to plan,
Our statures touch the skies
The heroism we recite
Would be a daily thing
Did not ourselves the cubits warp
For fear to be a king.

Seeing the puzzled look on some of the faces in the circle, Maxine explained what the poem said to her: that women—she was certain this "we" was female—are natural giants, but, afraid of the greatness that's in us, we diminish ourselves. And she read the poem again, after which Jane issued a wolf whistle and deferential Joanne uttered something like a groan of delight. This was a far cry from the dainty, unassuming "Belle of Amherst" image of Dickinson that had such a hold on the popular imagination.

Next Maxine delivered a report on what was happening inside the women's community in Berkeley. She repeated the account she'd given to Grace in the car about the guerrilla anti-racism actions in the Berkeley bookstore targeting *Gyn/Ecology*. Why, she wanted to know, did some women go to such lengths to bring down powerful women and powerful thoughts? Why were women's communities dedicated so exclusively to validation and support? "If we put even half the energy that goes into witnessing each other's suffering and salving each other's wounds into praising our strengths..." she said.

Aida, her dark eyes flashing, talked of the ascendancy of the disability movement in Boston. Yes, accessibility and signing at concerts were positive steps, but it was now getting completely out of hand. Healthy, able-bodied women were being asked to consider their condition provisional, if not to apologize for it. To take health and strength in any way for granted was now unacceptably "ableist."

Nina chimed in with a firsthand report from the five colleges, which she said had been infected by a "ramp first" mentality; before you could even start planning a women's event you had to make sure it would be accessible. She knew of a ramp that was constructed so early in the planning stages the concert it was built for never took place. She wondered if the love affair with oppression in the women's community wasn't itself a form of romance.

"The romance of disability," Grace added, her face flushing. And she brought up the Lesbian Poetry Reading and Rich's having chosen to read her poem about the skier needing to acknowledge the cripple. "I guess she's right in step with the times," she said sardonically.

Jane, her jaw working very hard, said she had sent her essay on feminist humour—it was titled "Making Light"—out to a lesbian publication and had gotten a letter back saying they liked her ideas but were concerned about the light imagery. Had she not considered the racist overtones?

"NO!" we all screamed.

"I'm not sure why they stopped there," Jane went on. "Didn't it occur to them it was fat-offensive too?"

Everyone cracked up, and Grace said if it went on like this it wouldn't be long before we saw a ban on dancing and singing in solidarity with women who were sick, disabled, or just dispirited. That prompted an invitation from Jane to join her on the road for a lesbian comedy tour.

When Maxine finally managed to get the reins back, she said she had resigned herself to the fact that we could no longer limit our search for strong women to self-identified feminists and lesbians. And these days she herself was deriving inspiration from women of the past, like Emily Dickinson, and women of the present like Christa Wolf. At which point we understood this had all been a prelude to her presentation of the Büchner Prize speech, which she had finished translating the day before.

In Büchner, Maxine explained, rising up as high as the plush allowed, Wolf found a soul mate, a man who stood at the dawn of the Industrial Age, a gap between eras, a fractured time, who saw that—and here she began to read from those pages that had been multiplying on our kitchen table for weeks now—"the pleasure people took in the new age was rooted partly in a desire for destruction," and who foresaw a "civilization which treasures money and flawless technology above all else...." From

Büchner Wolf took the word *verkehrt*—meaning "upside down," or "reversed"—and used it to describe the present state of the world. "The condition of the world is ... 'reversed,' we say, tentatively, and notice ... it is so," Maxine said. "We can stand by this sentence. It isn't beautiful, only accurate. And so is a balm to our ears.... Could this phrase become the first in a new, accurate language which we could hear with our ears but not yet speak with our tongues?"

I was again mesmerized by Maxine's words, which seemed to be channeling Wolf herself. Looking around at the others, I could see they were enthralled as I was. Grace's face was luminous—mainly, I imagined, from the effect of that last passage. Nina was glowing. How confirming it was, she said, to know that this writer from a socialist country without the benefit of feminist theory saw exactly what we saw. And had we noticed the astonishing resonance with Daly's notion of "reversal" (her word for the tendency of male thought to turn things on their ear—e.g., Eve as born from Adam's rib)? Yes—we were all nodding—we had.

Aida stayed over that night and slept on the plush. Jane, saying she wanted to lighten things up a bit before we all went to bed, told some new penis jokes based on an article she'd just come across about "fractured penis syndrome." Sunday morning Grace and I were awakened by moaning outside the bedroom door; we looked up to see Jane's finger sticking through the crack, bent at the joint. We got out of bed laughing.

MONDAY, THE LAST DAY OF JANE and Zoey's stay, was sparkling and warm and we wanted to make the best of it. Grace called in sick to work, Aida called her partner to say she'd be late, Anne came back, and we all piled into Jane and Zoey's iconic van and drove to the end of Leverett Road to a sacred hill Anne knew about called Temenos. She led us through the woods to a series of cave dwellings, deep in the ground. One was big enough for us all to fit in; we arranged ourselves around the perimeter in a circle. It was dark and cool and damp.

Maxine began to chant—she knew some Indian ragas—and we let the sounds reverberate around and inside us. Afterwards, mainly just to try out the acoustics, I started singing a camp song, one we used to sing around the fire as camp was ending. "Little did we know when we met you, we could learn to care for you so, now we know we'll ne'er forget you, little did we know ..." It had been my favourite song at camp, even though there was only one person there I actually cared about. But now, in this dark chamber, with all my new and old friends around me, it really fit. Everyone else seemed to think so too; they made me sing it all the way to the end.

The night before we'd been talking about Virginia Woolf and her idea of "moments of being." "Why settle for moments?" Maxine had asked, "why not heaven now and forever?" And she quoted H.D.: "we are voyagers, discoverers/ of the not-known, / ... possibly we will reach haven, / heaven."

It seemed to me in that moment we were all very close to heaven.

14.
Third Things

A space must be maintained or desire ends.
—Anne Carson, *Eros the Bittersweet*

AFTER JANE AND ZOEY LEFT I noticed Grace was tired. Like me, she'd been too excited to sleep well and between work and Maxine was unable to catch up. I'd been ordering her to take naps in the afternoon over the weekend. Though Maxine seemed to dote less on her after our visitors left (having had her dose of attention), Grace continued to cook for her. We were both doing a lot of chauffeuring her around as well. Some days it was all I could do not to explode. Toward the end of her stay, I had a dream in which Grace and I were taking a baby out for a walk in a stroller. Suddenly the baby burst out of the stroller and did a perfect cartwheel on the grass, then hopped back in and let us wheel her home.

I had been keeping my feelings about Maxine to myself, but I did tell Grace this dream before leaving for the city one Sunday. She agreed it was apt. I mentioned how drawn she was looking and reminded her of the idea she'd had of us spending time alone together. She had the following week off. Could we maybe go to the ocean together? Just the two of us? To my great surprise, she said yes.

Aida agreed to put Maxine up for the week—we would drop her off on the way. Serendipitously, Mary Daly was planning to be in Maine around the same time, staying at an old guesthouse she knew at Old Orchard Beach. She would reserve a room for us there—it was cheap and right on the beach.

IN AN EERIE ECHO OF MY DREAM, Maxine was testy and petulant on the way to Aida's. Once we'd deposited her there we were both almost giddy with relief. We confessed we had each been wondering if bearers of vision always took this sort of toll on the people surrounding them. But once we landed at the guesthouse—a funky old lodge sitting right on a wide, sandy beach that seemed to go on forever—my mind was emptied of all other thoughts. We were at the ocean together at last, just the two of us.

Or would be soon. We had breakfast with Mary the next morning. I had met her once before, when Grace took me to see her at her home in Boston. She was a tall, sturdy woman who—I was surprised to discover—took herself far more lightly than one would expect from someone with five PhDs. The wood-shingled diner sat right on the beach and Mary was waiting for us at a table by the window. She seemed delighted to be by the ocean and announced she was very glad for our company—though she was looking at Grace as she said this. It had been evident to me at our last meeting that she enjoyed unburdening herself in Grace's presence—and how could I blame her? No one listened like Grace.

We'd barely gotten in our orders when Mary started in on the attacks in the Berkeley bookstores. What did we think was really behind all this anti-racist hysteria, she wanted to know? Before we could say anything, she pulled out a pink plastic pin and laid it down on the table. She'd felt something sticking out of her mattress that night, she said, and this is what her search had uncovered this morning. She seemed quite undone by the discovery. Later Grace explained to me that, for better and for worse, Mary saw connections everywhere.

After breakfast I took off on my own down the long beach, wanting Mary and Grace to have some time alone together. Now that we were free of Maxine I was feeling generous about Grace's time. On the way back I noticed the white sand was dotted with children and parents speaking French with a Quebec accent. At lunch, Mary explained Old Orchard Beach was a watering hole for French Canadians. In fact, she said, she had plans that afternoon to meet up with two friends from Quebec. She invited us to join her.

A few hours later we were driving down the coast in her old Ford Pinto. Just after Ogunquit, she turned into a hotel parking lot and we made our way down a winding path to a little cove protected by large rocks. There they were, the two friends, sunning on a big beach towel under a colourful umbrella and waving at us. One of them was darkly tanned and in a bikini; the other one wore a one-piece suit and had boyish good looks. I guessed them to be in their early forties. When we got up close I saw on the towel between them a big book I had heard about but hadn't seen before: Luce Irigaray's *Speculum de l'autre femme*.

The boyish one jumped up and kissed Mary on both cheeks. "Nicole Brossard—someone you both need to read," Mary announced to us when the kissing was over. She introduced Grace to them as one of her most promising students and me as Grace's "literary friend."

Nicole introduced us to her partner, Marisa. They motioned for us to sit down with them. "How do you like her?" Mary asked, pointing to the book, and so began a fiery three-way discussion about Irigaray that touched on Freud, Plato, and Lacan.

Mary told Grace and me more about Nicole's radical work with language and the movement of Quebec writers she was part of over lobster dinner that night. This was not the Maine vacation with Grace I'd imagined, but Mary was leaving in the morning and I wouldn't have missed this day for anything. It seemed the study group net had now been cast even wider, and whenever I thought of Quebec I would see these two warm and stylish women on the beach, reading French theory and spinning words into revolutionary forms.

GRACE AND I HAD JUST WALKED IN From the beach for lunch the next day when the manager called her to the phone. Mary's car had broken down on the road—an overheated engine. I heard Grace offering to pick her up and drive her home. It was Sunday and the garages were all closed, she explained when I protested. In that moment it seemed I'd been waiting to be alone with her for weeks. "We'll still have four days," she said, reminding me we had just had a morning on the beach, just the two of us.

So Sunday was spent driving back down the coast to Boston, stopping to pick up Mary on the way—there was lots more talk in the car of ominous signs from the universe—and then making our way back up the coast just exactly as we had two days before. We arrived back at the guesthouse late Sunday night.

In fact, since we had to drive back to the city again on Thursday to pick up Maxine, there were only three full days left. But we made the most of them. We drove up to Camden and checked into a motel there, exploring the coast and the used bookstores in town. In one of them we found an old copy of *Mrs. Dalloway* and read passages out loud to each other at night. We'd both read it before but it had new meaning now. Our last day found us picking blueberries on a mountain that towered over the sea. We had entered a state of timelessness and seemed to be light years away from our other lives. Later we would refer to these as our three days of grace.

THAT SUNDAY NIGHT GRACE CALLED from Leverett, her voice sounding grave. "I have some upsetting news. Aida seems not to be the woman we thought she was."

By now I was getting used to her ellipticism; I asked her please to elaborate. She said Maxine had been privy to a lot of nasty talk while staying at Aida's, and much of it was about me. The gist of it was that Aida seemed to harbour some deep resentment of me and the study group could no longer go on as before. It was a painful conclusion to come to and she had resisted it as long as possible. But now, having pulled the whole story out of Maxine, it was no longer avoidable. She would spare me the details, she said, until she saw me.

I was busy packing that week—moving day was less than two weeks away—so I had plenty of time to try and digest this information. Not that it was really digestible. Waves of disbelief kept washing over me. Aida was my friend. It was she who had opened the door into this world of Grace and Leverett and the other women in the study group in the first place. It just didn't make any sense.

Thursday night when I arrived, Grace embraced me solemnly, then sat me down at the kitchen table. She held a lit cigarette and the ashtray before her was full. She told me she had just sent off a letter to Aida, explaining she was no longer welcome in her home.

"Can I have the details now?" I asked.

Grace nodded at Maxine, as if prompting her. Maxine began by saying she didn't like being in this position. She liked Aida, and she probably didn't really mean half the things she said. But on the other hand, as she'd said to Grace, we did need to know what sorts of things were being said about us.

"What exactly is being said about us?" My patience was running out.

Finally, Maxine came out with it. It seemed Aida and her partner, Cheryl, were both concerned by certain changes they'd seen in Grace since we'd been together. They thought I treated her like a princess and encouraged her fragility—by constantly urging her to take naps, for example. They were afraid I was creating an unhealthy dependency. And—Maxine screwed up her face to show how absurd she thought this was—they even speculated that I was using her to get to Mary Daly.

On the heels of our emergency rescue of Mary on I-95 that Sunday, this was actually comical. It also occurred to me round about now that the position Maxine was in was not all that unpleasant for her; she had had star billing for several days running.

"That's very perceptive," I said sarcastically. "Anything else?"

But Grace wasn't amused. She said under the circumstances she could not imagine being in the study group with Aida, never mind having her stay over at the house. I had to admit I couldn't imagine either of those things myself.

Maxine left the next day to see family in New Jersey. That afternoon Aida called. Grace took the call up in her room. She stayed up there several hours, and when she came down her face was deathly pale. I had already cooked up a stir-fry for both of us and eaten my portion. I offered her some but she didn't want any. Instead she sat down with a cigarette and started shaking her head.

"What is it, Grace?"

After several moments, she began to talk. Aida had not

denied saying most of the things Maxine claimed she'd said. She apologized profusely for all of it. But she wanted Grace to understand that it was all said in the heat of the moment.

"What heat, what moment?" I asked.

"Well that's just it, it appears our dear Maxine was not exactly an innocent bystander." From the moment she arrived at Aida's, Grace said, Maxine had wanted to talk about nothing but Grace and me. She felt abandoned by us, felt Grace was no longer the woman she had known before. She and Aida and Cheryl had sat around the dinner table one night with a bottle of wine, coming up with theories—you know how good Maxine is at that, Aida said—and at a certain point the speculation just seemed to run away with all of them. Aida realized soon after that most of it had been over the top, and she regretted it sorely. She wasn't even really sure anymore who had said what. She just hoped Grace would be able to forgive her.

We spent what was left of the weekend trying to fathom what to Grace was unfathomable. Not Aida now but Maxine, her dear friend for whom she had been putting herself out for a month, not only talking behind her back but carrying tales, driving a wedge between friends. It was just this sort of discrepancy between words and actions, she said, that made her want to despair.

I suggested that maybe it wasn't as grave as all that and reminded her of what I'd said about Maxine that very first night. Didn't she think a lot of this boiled down to simple jealousy?

In her own way, Grace was an innocent in the realm of lesbian desire. She didn't seem to have any idea of her own attractiveness to other women, or of how powerfully women could be driven by such attractions. Probably unrequited feelings had played a part in the whole roommate debacle as well, and in the rift with her friend that so obsessed her in the letters. I thought getting her to see Maxine's behaviour in this light—as frustrated desire—would diminish her outrage. It didn't.

"If I'd wanted to be lusted after I'd have stayed with men," was all she said. Her tone was bitter. When I left early Sunday afternoon—I had to go back to Boston and pack—she was still distraught.

WEDNESDAY NIGHT GRACE CALLED to tell me she had confronted Maxine that afternoon when she returned from New Jersey. Maxine had taken it all very badly. She said how hypocritical Grace, with all her talk of friendship, was to run off with her lover and leave her behind when she'd come all the way across the country to spend time with her. Then she called the airlines and booked herself onto the next available flight out West. She would be leaving the next day.

"This is not surprising, Grace," I said. "She's hurt. That's how people act when they're hurt. They fling accusations around. That's all."

Grace said she wished she could take it as lightly as I did. There was reproach in her voice, as if I didn't understand, hadn't fully grasped the horror. It was the first time I'd felt distance between us.

15.
Haven, Heaven

we are voyagers, discoverers of the not-known,

the unrecorded;
we have no map;

possibly we will reach haven,
heaven.

—H.D., "The Walls Do Not Fall"

MORE THAN ANYTHING, Grace and I used to say to each other, what we looked forward to about my moving in was going to sleep together every night and waking up together every morning. The small taste of this we'd gotten during our days of grace in Maine had made us long for more. But when at last we had it—an unbroken line of nights spent side by side—it went mostly unnoticed. The first week after my move Grace's every free moment, it seemed, was spent going back over her interactions with Maxine or having long phone conversations with Aida, trying to convince her she was hardly a fragile victim of my charms. I, meanwhile, was busy unpacking, installing my dishes and glasses in the old pantry, setting up my books in the little room in back that was to be my study.

If the joyful mornings I'd anticipated of waking to each other's presence didn't materialize, at least there were moments of mutual pleasure at the way my furniture seemed to fit right in. A set of antique cane chairs I'd bought in upstate New York replaced the folding chairs around the pine table, and there was just enough space in the parlour alcove for my cherry desk. The wine-coloured plush section it displaced was eventually passed on to Anne. On the bathroom wall, facing the old tub where we both liked to linger, I hung a friend's frankly erotic painting of a conch shell.

STUDY GROUP MET IN LEVERETT AGAIN the following Saturday. Joanne had brought a blueberry pie, Grace made coffee to go with it, and we celebrated my move by eating pie on the cane chairs, which were widely admired. Nobody said a word about Maxine's absence. To Grace's relief, Aida had offered to sit this one out, and Grace made up a plausible excuse for her.

The book under discussion tonight was *Mrs. Dalloway*— the others had been reading it along with us for the past two weeks—and it was Grace's turn to present. Once we were all seated on the plush, Grace said she wanted to come back to her perennial theme, love, and friendship, and the enemy of them both: romance. "What is it about romance that's so destructive?" she began. "It's the way it falsely constructs the other, deprives her of her real existence, her Selfhood. Clarissa Dalloway herself understood, deeply, the negative power of constructs. 'Clarissa would not say of anyone in the world now that they were this or that.'" This was why she was so horrified by Drs. Holmes and Bradshaw, with their tyrannical ideas about health and sanity. It was why she was repelled by Doris Kilman, with her creeds and prayers and bullying. It's why she chose over the passionate, possessive Peter Walsh a sober man who always kept a respectful distance. "And there is a dignity in people, a solitude," Grace quoted, "even between husband and wife a gulf, and that one must respect...."

Grace ended by stating that a woman who is surrounded with people who are re-creating her according to their own needs is in the greatest conceivable danger— that of losing her own rhythms, of losing herSelf. Even—she added meaningfully—if those people happen to be lesbians. And then she announced her decision to quit the study group.

There were immediate stammers of protest and disbelief. I was stammering along with the others—I hadn't seen this coming.

Prompted for some sort of explanation, Grace said that recent events had made her come to doubt the reciprocity of words and actions, and the possible efficacy of words. When Nina asked her to be more specific, she began, in a grave voice, to recount the events of what between the two of us was now known as "the week of horrors." She repeated the things that had been said about me, and about her, by two women whom she said she had come to think of as dear friends, as companions. The others listened attentively, but when Grace got to the theory that I was using her to get to Mary Daly, Anne, her large frame convulsing, emitted a series of snorting laughs. And when she'd finished the story of Maxine storming out when accused, ranting about betrayal and friendship, Joanne's shoulders were shaking. It took me a moment to realize she, too, was laughing.

Nina went even further. "So much for the new ethic!" she roared, mocking Maxine's parting words.

I looked over at Grace, afraid she would feel slighted. To my surprise, I saw something like relief on her face; it had lost its hard set. Only now that it was breaking up did I see the heavy, dark cloud that had hung over us ever since Maxine's departure. I wanted to throw my arms around all the women in the study group; I'd never loved them so much.

As it turned out, the others had all been biting their tongues for some time. They'd seen the toll Maxine was taking on Grace and were worried about her. Maxine had brought them inestimable literary gifts, they said, and they would always be grateful for that. But if it took this kind of drama to shake her loose from Grace, they seemed to think, so be it. As for Aida, it was her fiery impulsiveness we all loved about her, and she seemed to have learned her lesson, so if I could forgive her, they could too. Anne pleaded with Grace not to let one episode of runaway emotions interrupt what we had here, which was sacred. "Yes!" Nina and Joanne exclaimed in unison. And without even waiting for an answer, we began to pick up the threads of Grace's presentation and do what we'd always done so well together: spin.

On Maxine's recommendation, I'd been reading Christa Wolf's novel *The Quest for Christa T.* Excitedly, now, I began to outline it. The narrator's task, it seemed to me, was precisely about the task of seeing another human being clearly—in this case, not making up her main character according to her own needs and projections. I shot a look at Grace to see if she was still resisting the flow that was undeniably moving us along.

A trace of a smile flickered across her face. "Do you think it's possible Maxine didn't actually *read* the book?" she said.

I was so relieved. She was with us again.

STUDY GROUP CONTINUED—Aida rejoined us at the next meeting— and so did our life together on Leverett Road, which, perhaps because it had begun to feel precarious, now seemed terribly precious. I repeated the news to all the friends I could think of: I was living in a wonderful house in the country with the woman I loved. Never before had I had the occasion to say those words: "The woman I love." Grace made me want to say them over and over. I reveled in waking up every morning to bird-song and the sight of the great green hill across the road, in driving into Greenfield or Amherst for groceries and supplies.

As Maxine's visit receded into the past, Grace's generous, expansive self returned. I basked in her Southern warmth and slow tempo. Some mornings she would set up a lounge chair on the porch and just laze out in the sun for hours. Other days we worked in the garden. The Donnas had taken up most of the garden space with their rows of vegetables and flowers, but there was a corner with just enough room for us to put in several rows of tomato plants. We hauled a load of horseshit from a nearby farm and worked it into the soil before planting.

We were careful to garden only during the day, when the Donnas were both at their jobs. They had never been very neighbourly to begin with and now had taken to complaining about noise levels at study group meetings. We were counting the days till October, when Mary Daly would be taking over their apartment. She was hard at work on the last draft of *Pure Lust* and was planning to use the loft behind the house as her studio.

Afternoons, if it wasn't too hot, we would walk one of the several loops that spun off the house. Our neighbour had a sugar house, and one afternoon in mid-August we decided to stop over there for maple syrup.

Mr. Ripley, who lived alone, was busy baking a cake when we arrived. "A friendship cake," he explained; he would be taking it over to a friend's house that evening. In addition to the syrup we bought from him he tried to send us home with zucchini, corn, and tomatoes from his garden. We explained that we were on our way around the loop and he said to come back for them any time.

We mused about Mr. Ripley as we set off up Chestnut Hill. What sort of man baked a cake for a friend? We had both of us resonated to the chilling line from Christa Wolf's Büchner Prize speech, "The men of this age cannot love, or they love only death." But Mr. Ripley seemed to love his life, and he wasn't sucking off any woman's energy. "I didn't know men like him existed," I said. Grace guessed he was part of a dying breed, a vestige of pre-industrial society. Before long we were back inside her perennial questions, which had begun to be mine too: What is friendship? What is love? And are women any better suited to either of them than men?

We were now rounding the bend at the top of the hill where the homes and the woods gave way briefly to meadow. Not that either of us was paying attention. In Wolf's *The Quest for Christa T.*, Grace was saying—she was now deep inside my copy—the narrator's struggle to see Christa T. set for her a new standard for love, and friendship. This seeing was active; it required relentless self-questioning on the part of the seer. In her mind, there was no better definition of love than this unstinting effort to truly see another person—as she was, not as one wanted her to be.

Thanks to Grace, thanks to Wolf, I thought I was now beginning to understand something about love myself. It required a kind of discipline. Not acting on impulse but waiting, watching, attending. I tried to do all these things with Grace. "I consider it far more flattering to be 'an object of thought' than 'an object of desire,'" she had once said to me, borrowing from Hannah Arendt, and I'd taken it as a mild reproach. I thought of how I had jumped on her that first night at Aida's; I thought back to the first week of Maxine's visit, when it seemed if I had to wait one more day to be alone with her I would die. Tumescent was the word that came to mind. Swollen with impatience. A fire in my blood. Granted, I was a fire sign, with lots of air in my chart to fan the flames. But that was no excuse.

Grace never showed any signs of impatience or urgency where I was concerned. For her I had always been first and foremost an object of thought. And wasn't this what I had come to depend on? That whatever I was experiencing at any given moment, she would always give it her deepest consideration, would try to think how I might feel? I wanted to grant the same kind of thoughtfulness to her. To see *her*—not as I wanted her to be but as she was.

IN AUGUST I LEFT FOR NORTHERN MICHIGAN to spend three weeks with my family in the summer home they rented there, one of a row of houses that sat along the bluffs overlooking the lake. Most of them were owned or rented by people I had known since childhood. They congregated at the tennis courts in the morning and on their porches over gin and tonics in late afternoon. In the past, I'd been amused by the Chekhovian nature of our family interactions: my mother's scoldings about sandy floors and wet towels interrupting my father's Mr. Ramsay-like fugues of thought about Marcuse or Foucault, the steady stream of jokes generated by my sisters and me to show we weren't paying attention to either one of them. Now it all felt like tragedy of the absurd.

In study group we were fond of quoting a line from Peter Berger's book *The Sacred Canopy*: "Sometimes reality hangs on the thin thread of conversation." Only now did I see how much my world depended on those conversations in study group, and with Grace. Without them, I felt lost and adrift.

I broke up the drive back by spending the night in Syracuse at Jane and Zoey's. Their best friends Bonnie and Deirdre joined us for dinner bearing three bottles of wine, two of which they uncorked right away, and we all went to work in the kitchen to the sound of the Eurythmics. Deirdre was naughtily irreverent, as ready with stinging one-liners of her own as she was to collapse in hilarity at Jane's jokes; Bonnie was more serious, almost formidably so. I liked watching them work side by side in the kitchen, Deirdre's blonde ponytail beside Bonnie's jetblack one. Their love for each other was palpable—and they were both so warm and kind. As the night wore down we started to joke about the latest trends in lesbian sexuality, which led to an impromptu performance of lesbian S/M acts by Jane and Deirdre to the tune of Cole Porter's "You're the Top." I was so sorry Grace wasn't there with us; they made me promise to come back soon and bring her with me.

THE HILL ACROSS THE WAY HAD GROWN sparser when I returned to Leverett, and a shivering in the trees heralded colder times. But as I walked into our kitchen, the sight of our beloved pine table, the old slate sink, and then Grace herself coming down the stairs, grinning from ear to ear, were as warm a welcome as I could imagine. We walked each other back up the stairs, into her room and onto her futon, where we lay for the rest of the day, mostly talking about missing contexts. Maybe, we speculated, once having found the place where you finally fit, it got harder to feel at home anywhere else.

"I guess I'm just going to have to stick around here for a good long time," I said, and she reckoned that would be just fine with her.

I'd forgotten about the bounty of late summer in New England. Even as the trees and bushes thinned, the farmers' markets began to bloom with teeming stands of local fruits and vegetables. Our tomatoes were thriving, as were all the vegetables and flowers in the Donnas' garden.

As fall arrived, I was feeling exceptionally buoyant and vigorous—Grace, too, as far as I could tell. She was about to begin a job at Leverett Elementary School, and in February she would be entering the doctoral program in philosophy at UMass. I had plans to sit in on courses at UMass myself, and to get started on a thesis proposal. Thanks to the discussions in our study group, I now felt I actually had something to say.

Everyone told me I looked blissfully happy. "How could I not be?" I would say. I had friends such as I had never had before, who inspired me to think and create; Mary Daly herself would soon be our next-door neighbour. And I felt more solidity beneath Grace and me than ever, as if we'd been just drifting about before but now had dropped anchor.

The only niggling concern I had was that my tumescence seemed to have become a thing of the past. When I first noted this in early September, it was mostly a relief. But as weeks and months went by, I began to worry. Far from being impatient for time alone with Grace, more and more now I felt I could wait indefinitely to feel her lips on mine, to feel her skin beneath my fingers. It was not that I loved Grace any less, or thought of her any less—in fact, I wondered sometimes if maybe I'd worked too hard on making her an object of thought and not desire. We still made love, but there was no urgency about it, so it tended to happen less and less often. Was this what happened when you lived with someone? Was it a secret carefully guarded by the other women I knew in couples? Or was it me? Was it true what I'd discovered with Bella, that I needed space—and limitation—for lust to flourish?

As ashamed as I'd been before of my tumescence, this lack of urgency seemed even more troubling. What if I never felt it again? I couldn't help wondering if Grace noticed and missed it in spite of herself. I would continue to wonder about this in the months that followed.

CONSIDERING HOW EVERY DETAIL of that spring and summer of 1981 stands out in lapidary relief, it's odd to me now how little I recall of the fall and winter. Perhaps because, after all the euphoria and epiphanies of those earlier months, we were finally settling down to the reality of day-to-day life in this old farmhouse—which, as Grace would point out to me later, was as inconvenient as it was charming. Nestled in a valley as it was, already in September the house was shrouded in darkness by mid-afternoon. The first three cords of wood delivered to us were caked with mud, and as neither of us had ordered firewood before, we didn't know to refuse them. The logs did more hissing than burning, and we were often cold. Once it warmed up, the kitchen was cozy and quaint, but, as Grace began pointing out with increasing frequency, it had no counter space to speak of. And it was a chore, she made it plain, to have to drive all the way into town to do laundry.

What I recall of study group that fall and winter is that it often seemed to hover on the brink of disintegration. Nina was overwhelmed with schoolwork and preoccupied by an unrequited love. Anne was juggling three demanding jobs. Aida's daughter was going through a difficult phase. And Grace and I had our own troubles. But we all kept on showing up. I remember the word Grace used to describe us one bitterly cold Saturday when we all dragged ourselves out of our warm homes to drive the snowy roads to Anne's place in Shutesbury: valiant. It felt apt.

Anne's presentation that day, on creation myths, was a just reward. All male creation myths, she began, reflected men's fear and dread of chaos and wild nature. And most of them featured some form of rape, beginning with the Babylonian story of Tiamat, in which Marduk the great sea monster repeatedly assaults his consort Tiamat. She reminded us of Jane Caputi's brilliant article in the lesbian journal *Sinister Wisdom*, which analyzed the movie *Jaws* as a modern variation on the Tiamat myth. As dramatic counterpoint, she then read to us from *Daughters of Copper Woman*, a book of stories based on Northwest Indian myths that had just come out. In one of them, the first male on earth was conceived out of a woman's loneliness, in the mucus of her tears, and was, accordingly, named "Snot Boy." In another, girl children were born of the love and happiness of mother and daughter.

By way of conclusion, Anne moved to one of her pet subjects: parthenogenesis, or virgin birth. She cited documented instances of women giving birth without male intervention, along with scientific research that supported this claim. Then she spoke of the symbolic implications of parthenogenesis—virgin birth as a way to name a woman's creative power, her power to create her own wild self.

Driving home along the snowy roads, Grace and I talked of wild selves and how hard it could be to stay in touch with them. "But imagine if we'd had Snot Boy instead of Adam and Eve," Grace mused, and I grinned, though my mind was already jumping ahead to the mud-caked firewood.

My own wild self was getting plenty of nourishment that winter. I was sitting in on a feminist studies course at UMass taught by Jan Raymond, a philosopher friend of Mary's. The theme of the course was feminist vision and how to see beyond the almost universal rule of men and the male imagination.

Jan drew on the work of visionaries like Matilda Joslyn Gage, Elizabeth Gould Davis, Monique Wittig, and Mary herself. Between study group, *Gyn/Ecology,* and Jan's class, I was getting a pretty good grasp of the philosophical underpinnings of patriarchy and the kind of vision that was possible when one managed to free oneself of its assumptions. More and more I was amazed at what I'd graduated from two Ivy League universities without knowing: for starters, that women were the originators of just about everything that mattered on this earth. In the thesis that was now taking shape in my mind, I planned to make up for that.

IN EARLY OCTOBER, THE DONNAS PACKED UP and left. Their garden had had a bumper crop and they left us several baskets full of newly harvested vegetables, which made us feel terrible for having wanted them gone so badly, not to mention for having made them the butt of so many jokes.

The following Saturday afternoon, Mary pulled up the driveway in her Ford Pinto, trailed by a moving van with her things. Mary had never lived in the country full-time before; she was nervous and cranky when she arrived. Grace and I gave her a warm welcome and pitched in as best we could, helping to set up her furniture in the small apartment next door.

The last items in the van were a washer and dryer. When it became clear there was no place for them in her apartment, Grace offered our bathroom.

The bathroom had come to symbolize luxury and abundance—to both of us, I thought. It was large and light-filled and we had spent many hours in the big tub lolling and soaking and rubbing each other down with a loofah. It was hard to watch the room fill up with appliances. I thought I could live with the washer, once it was in. But when the movers tilted the dryer off the dolly and onto the floor it stuck out over the doorframe by a good three inches.

I looked to both Grace and Mary for some indication they saw this for the violation it was. There was none.

"Look," I said to both of them, "it's sticking out beyond the doorframe." No one responded. "Grace?" I prodded.

"Well the door still closes," she said, "and a little extra metal isn't going to kill us."

We had spoken of this room as our sanctuary, our witching well. Mary pointed out that the workers were being paid by the hour; there was no time for discussion. I reminded them both that we did have a clothesline. When this failed to make an impression, I said simply no, no I didn't want it here. The movers set the dryer back on the dolly, pulled it up the ramp and back onto the truck. Mary turned on her heel and walked out.

It was not an auspicious beginning. Grace disappeared into Mary's apartment shortly afterwards and didn't emerge for what seemed like several hours. I knew she must be trying to calm her down.

I could understand Mary's point of view. This was, after all, her house we were living in, and she'd been giving us a break on the rent. Moreover, Grace must have felt, accommodating a dryer was a small favour in return for the priceless gift of Mary's work. It wasn't until later on I remembered Grace's complaints about going to the Laundromat and realized she probably wanted the dryer for herself.

When she finally returned that night her pale, tight face said I was right. Whatever reproach she'd prepared for me I pre-empted with my own *mea culpa*. I should have given in, I said, it all just happened way too fast. She said she understood and it was all right now, but she kept her distance in bed that night so I knew it wasn't really.

Mary herself, to my great relief, did not seem all that put out. She was curt with me, but then she was curt with everyone. She had come here to write her book and she did not suffer interruptions or impediments gladly. True, one afternoon she knocked on our door to show us the lint sticking to her newly-washed corduroys. But in the months that followed, the three of us often went out together to dinner or the movies and when we did there was always an electric charge in the air, a feeling of high adventure. I remember one Saturday night driving down to the Hampshire Mall to see *Looker,* a very creepy film about ad agencies that replace real women with holograms. The whole way back to Leverett we took turns ranting about this civilization run to plastic and neon. It was not at all hard to believe Mary when she said the film was prophetic, and she could foresee a time not too far into the future when the depth dimension would have become a thing of the past.

It was a blessing, I thought, that as I began to really take in the sickness and ugliness of our culture I had such friends as these to critique it with, and a place to retreat to that was free of the toxins that seemed to have seeped in everywhere. Spying the porchlight as we rounded the bend on Leverett Road, we knew we were coming home to our haven, our home in the hollow with its old wooden pantry and slate sink, with its fields out back and hill across the way. As we stepped out of the car and looked up, we were rewarded by a magnificently star-studded sky. I felt that if Grace and I could just hold on to this life we were living right here, with all that we were coming to know and the work that arose from this knowing, all would be well.

Sometimes, though, despite all the classes and discussions and readings, the knowing was hard to summon. I felt far from the epiphanies of the spring and summer, those moments of fullness that succeeded one another like beads on a string, the convictions that arose from them. Though our lives were still steeped in friends and meetings and ideas, Grace and I had fallen out of the habit of holding events and experiences up to the light, watching them take on new meanings as we considered them from multiple angles. When we talked now it seemed it was always about wood or storm windows or how badly Nina was behaving in study group. And though I persisted diligently in my efforts to really see her, there was no denying she was proving ever more difficult to read.

More and more, too, I was having to admit, Grace was not always good at reading me. One night in early December she came downstairs briefly from her nap, then turned on her heel, went back upstairs, and stayed up in her room the rest of the night. The next day she told me it was because I had made fun of the way she looked coming downstairs, all groggy and disheveled. This was shocking to hear. Yes, I had smiled, but not *at* her. It had been—how could she think otherwise?—a smile of sympathy and affection.

16.
The World as It Is

the world

> *as it is   not as we wish it*
> *as it is   not as we work for it*
> *to be*

—Adrienne Rich, "The Spirit of Place"

B Y DECEMBER IT SEEMED TO ME Grace and I had both fallen into a rut. She was chronically sleep-deprived due to her new routine as elementary school teacher, and her "gracious" summer persona was not often glimpsed. The new schedule was not conducive to evening socializing, so we were mostly alone. This should have brought us closer, but Grace seemed to be pulling back into herself. Sometimes I thought we'd gone too far with our wariness about coupledom, our allergy to the dyad. When I mentioned one day that we hardly ever did anything together anymore, Grace said only that her schedule was onerous and she found it hard to keep up with me. Did I have something specific in mind?

As a matter of fact, yes, I said. I was thinking of going to the MLA conference in New York this year. Would she consider coming with me? We could stay with my sister. And it would be a break from our difficult life on Leverett Road. After an hour of deliberating, she agreed.

I hadn't attended a Modern Languages Association conference in years. For the most part, they were stuffy post-Christmas affairs where academics delivered boring papers with snappy titles in hotel ballrooms. But since the late '70s the conference had also been host to a sidebar of feminist and lesbian panels featuring some of the great women writers of our time. At various times I had heard Monique Wittig, Susan Griffin, Judy Grahn, and Mary Daly at MLA. This year Audre Lorde would be there, as part of a panel devoted to her work. Since Grace did not want to attend the whole conference, we decided I would take a bus down ahead of her and she would drive down in time for the Lorde panel.

UNLIKE MY PLACES OF RESIDENCE, my sister's apartment bore more than a passing resemblance to the one we grew up in. Her taste in clothes was similarly upscale. "You're not going to the conference in that, are you?" she said when I showed up at the breakfast table the first morning in jeans and a pullover. I dutifully changed into corduroys and she lent me a suit jacket to put over the sweater.

This turned out to be a blessing. The scene in the Hilton lobby was a whirl of heels, cashmere coats, Hermès scarves—it could have been a corporate convention. As I made a beeline across the lobby for the escalator that would take me downstairs to the panel on Irigaray, someone called my name. It was Casey, my grad-school crush. At first I didn't recognize her: she had traded in the leather jacket and butch cut for a long camel coat and jaw-length hair. We gave each other a firm, friendly, water-under-the-bridge hug. Under the coat, I saw as we drew apart, she wore a tweed suit. Possibly by way of explanation, she told me she had just delivered a paper at a panel on "Intertextuality." Not daring to ask her what that meant, and unable to think of a reply, I explained I was late for a panel and tore off down the escalator.

Grace arrived the next afternoon, worn out from having driven through a snowstorm. She was a sight for sore eyes after a day of lacklustre panels and half-baked exchanges with colleagues from Brown. I gave her a big hug when she walked in the door. But once she'd settled in to our room, I let her know the purple turtleneck she was wearing didn't go with her brown sweater. My tone was light and teasing, but the moment it was out I knew it had been a big mistake. Grace blanched and left the room. I came after her, apologizing profusely. My sister had been rubbing off on me, I explained, only realizing how true this was once I'd said it. Then there was the fashion show of a conference. I described to her the scene in the lobby.

Why had I dragged her to the city for a conference like this, she wanted to know. She was gathering her things. I pleaded with her to stop. I'd had no idea it would be like this, I said. And I told her the story of bumping into Casey, reliving the shock of it as I did. "She used to be fearsome," I said. "Unassimilable. Or so I thought." The story reeled her in; I could even feel a hint of her empathetic attention returning. We wondered together about the academy's powers of assimilation, and eventually recovered enough to have dinner that night with my sister and her boyfriend, though from time to time Grace would glare at me in a way that frightened me.

THE FOLLOWING MORNING WE ATTENDED a panel on Marxist feminism. We had studied the program the night before, looking for a shelter from the corporate crowd, and this looked like the best bet. The panel was well attended but tediously academic, and we were both nodding off when we heard Mary Daly's name. The last speaker, a professor from UMass, was accusing her of something, it wasn't clear exactly what. Then she was critiquing her "overblown" style. I thought she could just as well have been describing her own, but there was plenty of snickering in the audience, so clearly not everyone shared this perception. I was disgusted; Grace just shook her head, as if this were a grim confirmation of something she already knew.

What sort of women used public space to hold other women's passionate thoughts up for ridicule? And what sort of women go along with them, laugh at the in-jokes, at the feminist writer's expense? There was so much self-hatred among women, even self-avowed feminists. These were some of our musings as we walked uptown to find some lunch. The kind of musings that would have brought us together in the past and made us feel close. Now I was just grateful we were talking at all.

We had pinned all our hopes on the Audre Lorde panel. Apart from Lorde, the panelists, we saw when we entered the

Regency Ballroom that afternoon, were all white. Lorde, seated at the far end, looked on inscrutably as, one after another, the presenters delivered impassioned speeches about how her writing had changed their lives. Lorde's own talk at the end was angry and accusatory: white women had yet to deal with our racism, and she was losing patience. She did not cite specifics, though the constitution of the panel was an obvious case in point. As worshipful words continued to flow during the question period, Lorde looked merely annoyed. When she rejected one woman's question as "intellectual and unfelt," the questioner bowed her head like a penitent. It was a painful spectacle. Our heads, too, were bowed as we hightailed it out of the hotel.

The ride back to Leverett was full of heated discussion. At least the conference had gotten us talking again, even if it was mostly Grace talking. "'Every woman wants a boot,'" she began. She was quoting Sylvia Plath, but she spoke the words with such dark intensity I thought at first they were hers. She had thought feminism was about refusing the boot, she said. But maybe Plath was right, maybe none of us could resist it if it came from someone we saw as powerful, all the more so if she was a feminist icon, and black on top of that. Maybe this was the logical conclusion of white feminist guilt. Maybe all white feminists were ultimately masochists. This kind of speculation continued all the way home and persisted at the dinner table for days if not weeks afterward.

When we were first together I was in awe of the way Grace could take the tiniest incident and worry it, elaborate, build on it, pulling in relevant quotes and anecdotes, until it had grown huge with implications and symbolic power. "Are you bored yet?" she might interject halfway through, with that ironic dip in her voice I so loved. "Are you kidding?" I'd say. She was the spider in freefall, weaving everything around her into coherence, how could I tire of that? But now when she began spinning one of these webs I'd often feel panic rising, and as she persisted I'd be seized by the same violent impatience I used to feel as a child at the dinner table when my father willed me to stay while he lingered over the last drops of his coffee. *May I please be excused?* I wanted to say.

Sometimes my restlessness showed. "Don't let me keep you," she said one time in that bitter tone I'd come to dread. And then I protested, made an excuse: there was something that needed doing and couldn't wait.

It was puzzling to me, this impatience of mine, since for the most part I agreed with Grace's perceptions and admired her argumentation. And not so long ago it had seemed I couldn't get enough of her intensity. Why and when had I begun to feel, once she got started on one of these harangues, that I wanted to be anywhere but here?

IN JANUARY, A HEAVY SNOWFALL transformed the landscape and lifted both our spirits, especially when school was called off for two days. The first day we walked the long loop around Chestnut Hill and for a few hours it was just the two of us amidst the white sculpted shapes, mostly speechless with wonder. We came home smiling, built a fire, cooked up a big pot of soup. Happy as we hadn't been in so long.

Then the snow iced over and the barn roof caved in under the weight of the frozen snow. There went everything we'd stored in that barn, including the famous banner. Grace's car spun around twice on Leverett Road as she was driving back from school one day and no mechanic could figure out why. The stress was compounded once she began driving to classes at UMass. Then Mary announced to us that the results of the well inspection had just come in the mail—"as I was sipping my morning coffee"— and traces of E. coli bacteria had been found in the sample. This explained the occasional stomachaches Grace had complained of ever since moving there. From now on, heaving big jugs of bottled water was added to our list of daily chores, which also included stacking and carrying wood and scraping ice and snow off our cars.

Study group was our weekly solace. It had been a hard winter for just about everyone, but once we sat in a circle telling our troubles—whether on the plush on Leverett Road, in Joanne's living room, or around Anne's dining room table—the listening seemed to suck them right up.

Once we'd all been heard, it was time to roll up our sleeves and get to work. In February, that meant putting together a collection of our writings for publication. There had been talk of this for a while, but now I especially was urging action. Grace's annihilation paper was not far from finished and Jane's essay on feminist humour was all set to go. Anne was working on a piece about parthenogenesis and Joanne had the beginnings of an article on Picasso called "The Masterpiece and the Mistress in Pieces."

At one of our group meetings that month, "collection" morphed into "regular publication." A journal would help to create a body of knowledge. It would foster more work of its kind. It would help us to go on thinking together, and extend that thinking out into the world. A journal it would be, then!

A title came to us soon after. In *Gyn/Ecology* we had learned that one of the names of the Triple Goddess had been "Trivia"— She Whose Face Points in Three Directions. The reversal of the word's meaning over patriarchal time reflected the progressive devaluation of female thought and action (a devaluation which Glaspell's play *Trifles* had brilliantly subverted). We would reclaim the word by making it the title of a journal of serious thought by and for women—thought that issued from our ordinary, "trivial" lives.

On a cool day in March, Grace and I set off for a walk up Chestnut Hill. Smoke was billowing from the roof of the sugar house. As we climbed, I began to talk excitedly of *Trivia*. The first issue was already beginning to gel. In addition to the material in progress, Jan Raymond had committed an article, as had her partner Pat, an ecologist. How amazing it was going to be, to get our visions out into the world, to publish the thoughts of other like-minded women!

Grace was not offering any encouraging sounds as I spoke. She wasn't saying anything at all. Finally I asked—what was she thinking?

She said I had no idea what was involved in starting a magazine and neither did any of the others and we needed to come down to earth. And she said not to count on her, as she was barely keeping her head above water trying to juggle work and school.

Now it was I who fell silent. I told myself she was just trying to look out for me. But I felt like a horse being reined in.

ON A DAY IN EARLY APRIL, when the brook in the meadow across the way was so high you could see it foaming from the house, in the course of a study group meeting that lasted eight hours, we composed a mission statement for *Trivia*; it stood, we explained, for the "gatherings of wise women where our ideas originate and continue to live." Joanne designed a logo to accompany the statement and presto, we had ourselves a flyer.

That accomplished, we went out for a walk in the windy evening. Peepers were screaming, trees creaking and groaning. Exquisite fungi were growing on stumps in the meadow along the brook. I felt a lot like that brook, which was coursing and bounding with no end in sight. *So much for Grace's dire predictions,* I thought. I half expected she would take them back that night when we were alone. She didn't, but I was sure she had felt the high of creation with the rest of us.

IN LATE MAY, JANE WAS TO PERFORM her first college gig in Syracuse. I knew Grace needed cheering up, and if anything could do it, I thought this would. The show was on a Friday night and Grace had a term paper due that day, but she was determined to finish it in the morning so we could get an early start. In fact she didn't finish till mid-afternoon, so we had to race all the way down the interstate.

The show had already started when we arrived. Jane was performing in a real auditorium this time, and it was jam-packed. Bonnie and Deirdre were saving seats for us in the front row; Bella and her latest girlfriend, Bonnie informed me later, had tried to nab them just ten minutes before we arrived. Apparently they were now sitting in the aisle just behind us, as I kept hearing Bella's expansive laugh coming from that direction. Occasionally a delicate foot would appear beside me on the floor and I guessed it belonged to the girlfriend, though I never looked back to see. Jane's act was brilliant and polished and funnier than ever, and it was so good to be laughing with Grace again, to be together among so many other women laughing. She actually gripped my knee for several minutes toward the end of the performance.

As Jane and Zoey were full up, we were billeted with Bonnie and Deirdre. Their little house sat on the edge of a golf course with a large screened-in porch, and Grace and I felt instantly at home there. In fact it seemed to me we were enveloped in the same kind of attentive, receptive welcome Grace used to extend to our guests on Leverett Road. It wasn't long before Grace was delivering a full-blown account of the Audre Lorde spectacle at MLA. Deirdre reciprocated with MLA stories of her own—which she had in spades, as she and Bonnie were both finishing up doctorates in English literature. Just as I'd expected, Grace was delighted by Deirdre's irreverence.

Saturday was filled with long, leisurely conversations about H.D. and Woolf over drinks in wicker chairs on their porch. When Bonnie talked of the poets she loved she seemed to hold them between her long, tapered fingers and her brown eyes blazed with intensity. Grace listened with a kind of rapt attention I hadn't seen in so long, and her face reddened the way it used to when she got excited in study group. I didn't know if our new friends sensed how battered we both were—I hadn't said a word to either of them about our difficulties—but their exquisite consideration was wonderfully restorative. I could feel us slowly coming back to what Grace would call "ourSelves."

Bonnie and Deirdre wanted us to stay another night, but Grace worried we were imposing and we thought we should get back for the garden, so we left the next morning. For the longest time I would regret this decision bitterly. Just one more day with them might have done it, I thought, might have turned us around—one more day under that canopy of calm and gracious living they seemed to spread over us.

We left after lunch and came home to rain. In the car I made the mistake of asking why we never had fun anymore and Grace curled up into herself the way she did when I'd been insensitive. Granted, it was a tactless thing to say, I knew it even as the words were coming out. But I felt someone had to say something. Why wasn't there between us the kind of joy and lightness I always felt around Bonnie and Deirdre, or Jane and Zoey? Things had been grim for so long.

And there were times it felt to me Grace wanted it that way. On a balmy green evening some two weeks after our trip, we set out on an after-dinner walk along the dirt path that led past the farm and over the brook to the cow pasture. The mayflies were out and Grace was making twitching movements with her hands and head to flick them off. She was not enjoying this walk and I knew it, but was willing her to keep quiet about it. Spring had come at last. We'd been waiting for what seemed like forever, and now here it was. There were daisies and buttercups and blue vetch on either side of the path, the trees had grown huge in their greenness, and the warmth recalled happier times, *how in love we were at this time last year how we would walk these footpaths and count our blessings.* Why did she have to focus on these little gnats? Why did she always let things get to her? No wonder we never had any fun.

After only ten minutes, Grace turned back. She said she was getting eaten alive. In that moment, I think I hated her.

NOT LONG AFTER, GRACE GOT SICK. She had big red welts on her neck that she kept wanting me to feel. It was the bugs from that walk, she said. She complained of pains in her stomach and said she was getting weaker and weaker. I knew in her mind I was to blame. If I'd taken the bugs more seriously maybe I wouldn't have insisted on her taking that walk with me. "Your problem is you don't have any problems," she had said to me not long before. "So I have to have them for both of us." But hadn't she once said she wanted to be lighter? Hadn't she once said I lightened up her life?

One afternoon, she took to her bed and locked the door. I begged her to say something to me, to tell me what was wrong. No response. Every few hours I would approach the door and plead again. "Grace, please talk to me." Nothing.

I stayed nearby in my study, on alert for the sound of her door being unbolted. The sound never came. I left the house a few times so she could go the bathroom and get herself something to eat. On the evening of the second day, when I returned from one of those outings, I found a piece of yellow scrap paper on the kitchen table. "At the risk of my physical and emotional well-being," the note read, "I have tried to become the woman you want me to be." For the sake of her well-being, it said, she was going to have to move out.

Oddly, this news did not crush me. The feeling that swept over me as I read the note was mainly relief. This was Grace's handwriting, which meant she must be alive. I hadn't been all that sure she was.

17.
Not to Have

Nothing is so difficult as turning one's attention to things as they really are, to events as they really occur, after one has spent a long time not doing so and has mistaken their reflection in wishes, beliefs, and judgements for the things and events themselves.
—Christa Wolf, *The Quest for Christa T.*

And then to want and not to have—to want and want—how that wrung the heart, and wrung it again and again!
—Virginia Woolf, *To the Lighthouse*

I.

THERE WAS A SUDDEN, SHARP DESCENT from holding the dream entire to trying to salvage pieces of it. Adjusting down, discovering how little I could really make do with. There was a woman I knew and loved—the Grace of last spring and summer, she of the letters, brilliant and visionary, she of the loofah in the bath, gracious and indulgent—whom I was in peril of losing. In my desperation to keep her alive at all costs, and to keep alive the Grace who knew and loved me, I had missed all the cues. "At the risk of my emotional and physical well-being...." This was surely not only about bug bites. What kind of pressure had I unknowingly been putting on her? Who exactly was this "woman I wanted her to be"? Someone like me, without the problem of having to work for a living? These were questions I didn't ask.

Grace found an apartment in a housing development north of Greenfield. It had all the modern conveniences, and a laundry room just forty feet away. She would move there in September.

Once this was settled it seemed some pressure had been lifted from us. A friendly exchange on the stairs led to our having supper together one night, and thereafter things eased back to a semblance of what they'd been before. I could see she was trying to be better to me.

But every few days I would say or do something to trigger a withdrawal. Again she would go cold, shut herself in her room, ignore my pleadings. In those rare moments when we were getting along we would plan a meal out. Usually by the time we made it to the restaurant something would have robbed one or both of us of appetite.

In mid-July, Grace left for Florida to see her family. She sat in her car in the driveway with a lunch I'd packed for her on the seat beside her and then didn't leave. I opened the car door, lowered myself to her lap, and draped my arms around her, and we both broke down and wept.

That night there was a full lunar eclipse; I set the alarm so I could see it and never got back to sleep. The next day she called from Charleston, missing me. We talked of the eclipse; she, too, had been up half the night taking it in. I thought: *We are still women looking out on the world together. When something wondrous happens—or something horrific—we will always witness it together, no matter what.*

Jan Raymond and I had become tennis partners; on our way back from a vigorous game the week after Grace's departure Jan said she'd been reading about Vera Brittain's friendship with Winifred Holtby and musing about friendship as a "thoughtful passion." "Thoughtful," as she understood it, meant both "considerate" and "full of thought." I enthused about this idea. Those were exactly the qualities that drew me to Grace, I said. By the end of the conversation I had confessed to her that Grace was moving out and Jan had mentioned an apartment she and Pat owned in Montague that would be available in August. I said I'd go over for a look.

Montague was just down the road—a classic New England village with a steeple, a town green, a library, and a feminist imprimatur. Jan and Pat had built themselves a house just outside of town. Adrienne Rich and her partner, Michelle Cliff, who had recently taken over editorship of *Sinister Wisdom*, lived right on the main street. The apartment for rent was shabby on the outside but spacious and handsome indoors, with shiny, wide plank pine floors and a solar sun porch designed by Pat. There was a large room in back that could serve as the *Trivia* office. And just across the street was the post office, which would come in handy once the journal was up and running. I signed a lease that week.

BACK FROM FLORIDA, GRACE WAS BROWN and relaxed and guardedly friendly. A letter from UMass was in her mail; after opening it, she took to her room and stayed there for several hours. On emerging she announced she'd failed the semester and would have to repeat it. That had to be a mistake, I said.

It was no mistake, she assured me. She'd barely been able to keep up all semester; her work had been shoddy. That was all she would say about it.

When study group met the following Saturday, she announced that she would be withdrawing her essay on annihilation from *Trivia*. She was no longer the woman who wrote that piece, she insisted; the vision expressed in it was no longer hers. Though all of us tried, there was no talking her out of it.

Moving out of the house on Leverett Road was a bigger job than either of us had foreseen. We spent several days packing boxes and loading our cars. A friend with a truck came by one day to move the big pieces. It was not easy to pack up my study, where I had passed so many intense hours pulling my thoughts together. Dismantling the parlour, where the air had been thick with our spinning conversations, felt like a desecration. It did not help that Grace seemed almost cheerful as we worked, handling objects that seemed sacred to me—the pine table in the kitchen, the chairs—in a spirit of "good riddance."

Grace's place wasn't ready yet, so we moved everything into the Montague apartment. The plan was for her to stay there and set herself up while I joined my family in Michigan.

MY FATHER WAS PACING UP AND DOWN the driveway and smoking a cigarette when I pulled up beside the old frame house on Michigan Avenue; my sisters ran out to greet me when they heard the car. Dinner was being held up for me, they reported, and Mother was happily prolonging her stay at the beach. As they escorted me into the house with my bags, the sun was just setting over the lake. It was surprisingly good to be here.

Word had gotten around town that I was helping to start a magazine, and Mrs. Gilbert, the local doyenne of entertainment, dropped by the next day to welcome me to the world of publishing. She handed me a copy of her latest book: a practical guide to parties, full of whimsical tips (example: April Fool's Day party—wear clothes backward). My sisters and I took turns reading parts of it out loud to each other on the beach that afternoon. I'd forgotten how good mindless laughter could feel.

After several days of sitting in the sun, playing desultory games of tennis, and cracking jokes over meals with my sisters, an old but almost forgotten self was beginning to revive. Someone who slept at night and had an unusually healthy appetite. Someone jocular and contented. I understood why I let myself get drawn back every summer. Life among the wealthy Jews on Michigan Avenue was serenely untroubled. A jovial hum seemed to accompany all activity here. Even my parents and their annoying habits were somehow part of the fun. I allowed myself to sit back and relax into it and was not particularly pleased when it was time to leave.

THE JUMBLE OF FURNITURE AND BOXES awaiting me in Montague—and my jumbled feelings for Grace—did not impinge on my consciousness again until I was heading back East. I was tempted to stop in and see my friends in upstate New York but instead left at dawn and drove straight through, feeling compelled to get back to the mess I'd left behind. When I arrived in the evening, however, I found that all boxes and bags had been emptied, their contents stowed in appropriate cabinets, closets, and bookcases. The closet shelves were lined with paper, linens, and towels neatly folded with used soap bars inserted between them. The fridge was stocked with milk, juice, and eggs. There was no sign of Grace herself and no note on the table.

I unloaded the car and drove straight to Greenfield, picking up a six-pack along the way. There was no car at 9 Orchid Lane so I waited. She pulled up not long after and seemed glad to see me. She invited me inside, explaining she'd been to the Franklin County Fair. With her carpets down, the apartment wasn't as bad as I'd feared. "Thanks for moving me in," I said. "I hardly expected…"

"It's my way of thanking you for allowing me to stay there."

"*Allowing?*" Her formality was unnerving. I poured us each a beer, we sat down at her kitchen counter, and I began discharging some of what I'd stored up to tell her over the past weeks. She listened with her usual attentiveness, but something was off. I couldn't put my finger on it, but when I hugged her good-bye I noticed she smelled different.

"It must be the sausage and onion sandwich I ate at the fair," she said when I remarked on it.

"*Sausage and onion?*" I was no purist myself when it came to food, but ever since I'd known her Grace had been citing brutal statistics from *Animal Liberation* to explain why she didn't eat meat.

"I'm experimenting. I want to know what it's like to act with less consciousness." This was not reassuring.

We ate out twice at the Minuteman that week. Both times I fired off a series of questions aimed at stoking her back to life, but she seemed mostly intent on finishing everything on her plate. One night that meant steak and homefries.

TWO WEEKS PASSED DURING WHICH WE barely spoke. I called her one evening—low-grade fear was ramping up to full-blown panic—to ask when we could see each other. She said it just wasn't good for her to see me, it set her back too much.

"Why?"

"You still have the faith."

"Faith?"

"You still call yourself a lesbian, don't you?"

"I love you and I'm attracted to you."

"Then you still believe in love."

"So you don't love me anymore?"

"I don't know what love means. And I want out of this conversation."

"Please," I said. But she'd already hung up. I got in my car and drove straight to Orchid Lane. When there was no response to my ring, I began knocking, pleading. Finally she cracked the door open and peered at me very sternly. I must have pushed my way in, since I remember her trying to blockade herself inside the bedroom. When I managed to push my way through that door too, she dove into the bedcovers. I drew up right beside her, in jacket and sneakers, held my arms tight around her. I was dimly aware that I was forcing myself on her, but it seemed I had no choice. I had to bring her around to what was true about me, about us. If I could just make her feel it, the force of my love would bring her around, would bring her back.

But it wasn't working. She remained curled up tight as a fist. After many long minutes of listening with my whole body, straining to sense the faintest stirring in hers and sensing nothing, I finally let go. I stood up and walked out the door, leaving her there on the bed in a fetal heap. It felt like I was leaving the scene of a crime. What the crime was I wasn't sure, but I knew I would pay a big price for it.

II.

TRIVIA WAS A WELCOME DISTRACTION. I had been crowned editor-inchief at our last study group meeting. It wasn't exactly an honour. The editorial pool had narrowed to Anne and me at the previous meeting and Anne, who had a full-time teaching job, had been relieved when I offered to take the reins. Her title would be associate editor.

Before I left for Michigan, we had opened a post office box in North Amherst and put ads in several women's papers, and, amazingly, manuscripts were already starting to trickle in, along with letters of interest. By happy coincidence, Harriet Ellenberger and Catherine Nicholson, founders and original editors of *Sinister Wisdom*, had just moved to nearby Shelburne Falls. They invited Anne and me over for a coaching session one Sunday afternoon. In their sunlit kitchen, over slices of Catherine's deep-dish apple pie, they lavished us with advice and encouragement. Harriet offered to serve as production advisor for the first issue. They still had most of their old paste-up equipment and would gladly put it at our disposal. When Anne and I drove away we felt we were being borne along on the wings of feminist sisterhood.

That the job was going to involve much more than reading and editing manuscripts somehow hadn't really occurred to either of us before that afternoon. Neither had the fact that we were starting a business. Harriet and Catherine had given us the name of an accountant and a week later, in her upscale Northampton office, both of us had a rude awakening. We were going into business as a non-profit corporation, the accountant explained to us; she was entering figures into a computer as she spoke. We would have to open bookstore and subscriber accounts, keep several ledgers, write out invoices. There would be bulk mailings. We would have to type mailing lists onto address labels. Make arrangements at the post office. Apply for tax-exempt status.

Anne and I exited her office in a daze. We'd managed to get this far without even thinking about money. How were we going to pay for the first issue? That night we put our heads together and came up with the idea of a feminist lecture series as a fundraiser for *Trivia*. Within a few days Smith College, Anne's alma mater, had agreed to host and sponsor the series.

Trivia was gradually taking over the spare room of my new apartment. Anne came often to go over submissions and to work on her parthenogenesis paper, which I was helping her to shape into an essay. Editing was a great outlet for my ardour for women's ideas, and I realized I had a knack for it, an instinct for how to bring forth the essence of a piece and prune away what distracted.

The apartment itself was slowly growing on me. In back there was a big garden framed by raspberry bushes and orange poppies. Off the bedroom in front there was a tiny study that looked out over the post office parking lot. It was here I kept materials for the thesis that was continuing to form in my mind. I liked to look up from my reading to watch people departing with their mail or striking up conversations in the lot. Hours would go by sometimes without my giving a thought to Grace, and some days I could feel happiness starting to steal up on me again. But every time I drove up Route 63 from Amherst and had to turn left instead of right my heart sank.

THE FEMINIST LECTURE SERIES WAS OFFICIALLY launched in November with a talk by Anne on parthenogenesis. The room was packed, with friends old and new. But when Grace arrived, in familiar brown corduroys and white jacket, she was all I saw. Anne spoke eloquently of parthenogenesis as a metaphor for the as yet unrealized possibilities of female being. A deep hush fell over the audience the moment she began and held on till the end. When she finished there was explosive applause. Grace rushed through a hug with Anne afterward, apparently aware of my eyes upon her, and then dashed off. I went out with Anne and a group of friends to celebrate, but the whole time I was thinking of Grace, how I'd robbed her of her slow, gracious, well-timed self. Of her friends. Why wasn't she here with us, celebrating?

In December a large van deposited five pallets at my doorstep and Anne and I lugged the cartons up the stairs and into my living room. Inside, we ripped open one of the boxes. Slim volumes, with black titles on glossy white background, spare and elegant. Anne's parthenogenesis essay was among them, as was an excerpt from Jan's book on female friendship and an article by Kathleen Barry denouncing lesbian sadomasochism.

Anne and I went into gear, packaging single copies for subscribers, multiple copies for bookstores. I invited friends over to stuff and stamp envelopes. Soon responses were coming in—fan letters, submissions for the next issue. In two weeks, bookstores started calling, wanting more copies; the issue was selling fast, and we had to order another printing. This was exhilarating, and far more than we'd dared to hope for. But there was a place in me it failed to touch. Nothing would ever feel really right as long as Grace and I were estranged.

Study group attendance had been falling off ever since the end of the summer, when Grace dropped out. I had hoped we would all come together to celebrate the birth of our parthenogenetic love child, but this never happened. Though I missed our meetings, my life was rich in friends. Sometimes, just when I was sinking, Jan would call me up and propose dinner. Soon she was collecting me in her jeep and in a matter of moments our minds were clicking into gear. One evening it was the Hannah Arendt biography that had just come out, another her book on female friendship, which was now nearing completion.

Often I stopped in to see Joanne at her house in Northampton: an oasis of calm and creativity. She would walk me around her garden, show me her new tapestries, or play a few bars of music as she reminded me of the principles of creation. In Northampton there was also Lena, a young writer and student of Jan's I'd been getting to know, an intense, jumpy chain-smoker with hair like lamb's wool. We'd meet for dinner and talk about poetry— we shared a fondness for Gerard Manley Hopkins—and love. Lena was trying to separate from a woman who drank and was overdependent on her. She realized she was dependent, too, in her own way. Listening to her made me realize how I longed for this kind of honest talk, how taboo it had been between Grace and me. Sometimes as Lena talked I'd feel like rubbing her woolly head.

And always there was Anne, our editorial conferences, our long winter walks. On one of those walks, Anne talked of her meeting with Grace and Eleanor the night before. Eleanor, she told me, had been badly hurt by a woman she loved, so hurt she said she didn't think she'd be able to be close to a woman again. So hurt she said she felt last year she was dying.

"I bet Grace latched right onto that," I said. Anne nodded, yes she did.

IN LATE MARCH, ON A DAY OF WARMTH and sunshine, I was biking the country roads that looped around Montague and breathing in the rich sweet smells of spring, which also conveyed to me spring on Leverett Road and everything I missed about Grace.

I'd written her several letters apologizing for having barged in that night and proclaiming my determination to really see her, if she'd only give me a chance. All had gone unanswered. But for a few days now I'd been immersed in *The Color Purple*, steeped in the element of Celie's letters to Nettie—which was also the element of our love—and here on my bike I was composing a love letter to her. I imagined writing it down and, if I could muster the nerve, sending it.

At the post office later that day two envelopes were waiting for me in my box; her handwriting was on one of them. It was ominously thin but at home I ripped it open eagerly. What, specifically, did I remember about the dryer incident? And: how does communication end, if it even existed in the first place? The wind was knocked violently out of me.

The other letter was from Deirdre. Life was agreeing with her so well lately, she wrote, and with Bonnie too. She said she thought the secret was very simple: kindness. Active kindness. Which Bonnie exemplified, unfailingly, with her. Case in point: This past weekend Bonnie had gone out and found an antique desk chair for her, to replace the one she had, which was falling apart. The letter felt like a missive from another world, genteel and gracious, a world Grace and I once inhabited but had now slipped out of, possibly forever.

III.

IN SEPTEMBER I DROVE TO THE HOUSE on Leverett Road to pick up the galleys for *Pure Lust*. Anne and I were assembling material for *Trivia*'s third issue, and Mary had agreed to let us publish an excerpt. Turning into the driveway, I saw a "For Sale" sign planted in the front yard. Shaken, disbelieving, I walked around to the loft in back. Mary emerged when I knocked, galleys in hand.

"What's this about?" I said, pointing toward the yard. We were standing by the apricot tree between the loft and what used to be Grace's and my home. This tree I had already begun to imagine before I ever moved out here. This house where we had, at first, been one in our work in our vision in our aspirations.

"I finally had it inspected," Mary said. I knew Grace had been urging her to do this for months. There'd been complaints on and off from tenants and guests about swollen faces and runny eyes. "The report came back two weeks ago. Ureaformaldehyde foam—the attic's full of it." She didn't have to say more; the dangers of ureaformaldehyde had been all over the papers.

"You didn't think of having it removed?"

"Of course I thought of that," Mary snapped. "But it's expensive and then you have to reinsulate. I don't have that kind of money.

And…" She cast her gaze about the property. "Maybe it's just as well. Given the history here, all the creepiness. You know what I mean?"

"I'm … not sure."

"People just leaving … walking out of your life … without saying a word."

I knew by "people" she meant Grace. I gathered she hadn't spoken to Mary since moving out. For the first time I saw how this must feel to Mary. How hurt she was, and confused.

"Well," I said, "I guess people do what they have to do." Sidestepping the opportunity to meet Mary on common ground. Out of loyalty to Grace? Or did I want to believe that my case was different from Mary's? Not as definitive?

"At least it's been a good place to write," Mary said as she handed me the manuscript.

"It certainly looks that way," I said. It was a very thick bundle. I let her know how honoured I was, and how excited, to have it in my hands.

OUR HAVEN, OUR HEAVEN, insulated with toxic foam. On my way home I tried to take this in. Imagining how Grace would have brooded over it for days, going round and round at the dinner table, teasing out all the implications. "Your unknowing is powerful," she'd said to me during one of our fights. How vindicated she would feel now.

Over the next few days I made my way hungrily through the galleys of *Pure Lust*. It was a passionate, gripping book. Like *Gyn/Ecology*, it juxtaposed the destructive forces of patriarchy with the regenerative power of women and nature. Like that book, it balanced on the razor's edge of rage and faith. But nowhere in it did I find even a trace of what I had imagined all this time, what I thought the book was about:

that sacred motion from me to her   this desire to know her knowing and loving not being separable desire   pure, unmediated, unconditional   holy yes from the entire universe

Could it be this version of pure lust was entirely my own?

PART III
HOMEWARD

18.
Homeward

Homesick for myself, for her—as, after the heatwave
breaks, the clear tones of the world
manifest: cloud, bough, wall, insect, the very soul of light:
...

—Adrienne Rich, "Transcendental Étude"

DURING THE TWO YEARS I lived in the apartment on Main Street, I was almost always tired. The Montague church bells tolled every hour on the hour, and mostly, it seemed, I was awake to hear them. In desperation I would lie in bed in the deep hours of the night, listening to the hours of my life being ticked off one by one.

Some of my sleeplessness during this time was due to *Trivia*, which more and more I was editing alone, and which had fallen way behind schedule. But most of it, during the first year, could be traced back to Grace—her long withdrawals, my panicked fears, then the spiraling dénouement. In the end, it seemed I was falling into her own hole, and there was nothing I could do to break the fall.

Our final encounter took place on the UMass campus, where I was postering for another event in the lecture series. At first I didn't think it was Grace; she looked so much like everyone else, in jeans and a denim shirt tied at the waist. Then I saw it was. After a few dazed seconds, I ran to her. The look that came over her face when she saw me was cold, steely. The words that finally came out were: "I'm going to yell if you don't leave."

For weeks after, those words, that look were either waiting for me at the edge of sleep or holding me back from it. I could not imagine a time when I would not be haunted by them. Yet   than a month or so after that encounter I noticed myself beginning to lose sleep over Lena.

Lena and I were friends, that was our bottom line. We met often to discuss *Trivia* submissions; I trusted her judgments, even if they sometimes seemed a bit harsh. And I loved attending cultural events with her. We brought out the literary snob in each other, especially at lesbian poetry readings. Lena and I were committed to remaining friends, and had determined neither of us was truly ready for a new relationship—and therefore, when our wits grew sharp from sparring and the air between us was filled with our ribbing and jabbing, we both smelled danger and knew to withdraw. Or at least she did. I would wake up when it was still pitch black outside simmering with rage, or lust. I'd stir myself a vodka and grapefruit juice, sit myself down at the kitchen table and wait for sleep to take hold of me again, which it rarely did before the sky was full of light.

It was the winter of '84, and Lena was living in a house on Graves Avenue in Northampton with three housemates, all of them women in their forties. Women who, for the most part, did whatever they pleased all day long. Lena referred to them in awestruck tones as witches. There were huge stacks of books by their beds, where they seemed to spend most of their time. The titles—I stole glances at them whenever I could—ranged from medieval history to quantum physics to Gnostic mysticism. The shades of the house were always drawn, so whenever I visited, no matter what time of day, I felt enveloped in darkness. A rich, creative darkness. On one door a sign would go up regularly that read "Remembering. Do Not Disturb." All three women were fans of *Trivia,* and I used to stop in sometimes with bulk mailing materials, hoping to get them to fold and stuff with me. But I never could count on getting them all to pitch in at once. The cardinal rule on Graves Avenue was you didn't do anything you didn't want to do.

I decided I wanted to live in a house again—a house full of women. As it happened, a friend of mine needed renters for an old colonial house she'd just bought at the edge of town. It would be perfect for me, but I'd have to find a housemate. I began postering and putting ads in bookstores, laundromats, *The Valley Women's Voice.*

It was stressful trying to imagine intimacy with a series of strangers, each with her own history and agenda. Usually I knew right off when it wasn't going to work, though I got less picky as the September deadline approached. Twice I thought I'd found the housemate of my dreams but both women backed out. At night—when I wasn't in torment over Lena—the faces of the women I'd interviewed, their histories, their hairdos, their handbags and satchels, would swirl around in my head. It was beginning to feel like my love history all over again.

IN THE MIDDLE OF AUGUST, I broke off from my search and from stripping in corrections to the fifth issue of *Trivia* to sit a Zen sesshin at a retreat centre just down the road. Apart from a brief flirtation with transcendental meditation in New York, I had never had much truck with Eastern religions. But this retreat was to be led by a woman roshi, one of the only ones in the world, and Anne, who had studied Buddhism in Japan, insisted it was an opportunity not to be missed. Which is how I ended up at the Temenos Lodge at 6:45 a.m. on a Saturday after only a few hours of sleep, having been up late the night before bent over the light table.

To me a country retreat meant outdoor activities. The roshi's name, "Maurine Freedgood," seemed a nod in this direction. I wore shorts and a T-shirt.

The roshi made her grand entrance at seven sharp, sporting several layers of long, flowing robes in shades of black and white. Her voluminous grey hair was done up Japanese-style in a bun and she carried herself like a queen. My first thought was: I've worn the wrong clothes.

We seated ourselves on two long rows of black cushions on the floor. My bare legs, the only ones in the room, were painfully conspicuous. Maurine—she asked us to call her by her first name—took her seat at the head of the rows and said a few words about posture: the importance of keeping the spine straight, the gaze steady. Then she rang the bell beside her three times. After a half hour of silence, the sound of the bell came again, at which point everyone rose and bowed to their cushion. Maurine gave a sharp strike with a pair of wooden clappers, announced "kinhin," wheeled to her left, and led us all single file in brisk circles around our cushions. After ten minutes the clappers sounded again and we all took our places, bowed again, first to each other, then to our cushions, before seating ourselves. The whole morning passed that way, with alternating periods of sitting and walking around the room, broken only by chanting and a tea service.

The silence at the beginning of each sitting period, once the bell stopped resonating, was deep and seductive. I wanted to abandon myself to it, as all the others seemed to be doing, but my body, which was still racing against the clock, seemed to be tugging me in the other direction. The issue I'd torn myself away from was to have gone off to the printer two weeks ago. I wanted to be back home, finishing it up. As if to underscore that wish, fiery blades of pain began shooting through my shoulders and neck. Rubbing them or changing position would have helped but you weren't allowed to move, let alone get up and go out for a stretch. During the rare moments when the pain let up or even disappeared I was unable to feel anything but dread of its imminent return. The latter half of each sitting period my ears would strain to hear the sound of Maurine's robes rustling as her hand reached for the bell. I knew almost nothing about Buddhism except that it had to do with learning to stay in the present moment, and by that measure I was failing miserably. Whatever had possessed me to sign myself up for this hell? Especially when my work was waiting for me back home, together with my comfortable couch.

The walking-around-in-circles struck me as particularly absurd. I could not chase away images of Madeleine and her little French schoolmates following their strict teacher, Miss Clavel, down the Paris sidewalks, imitating her very purposeful walk. The difference being our bodies were upright and this walking had no purpose at all. The others seemed to take it in stride, but then quite a few of them, I noticed as we circled around, were clad in black robes. When we began chanting in Japanese before tea, most of them seemed to know the words. There was no Anne to confer with, as she'd been called away by a family emergency at the last minute; I wondered if she had any idea what she'd gotten me into.

Then, at the end of the first sitting of the afternoon, Maurine touched me. She'd been circling around us as we sat, the whoosh of her robes faintly audible behind us; I guessed she was checking on our posture. She pressed her knuckles against my back and ran her hands over my shoulders. Almost instantly something released in there, and I dropped down and found myself HERE, in my body, breathing. Breathing as it seemed I'd never breathed before, from deep down in my centre. After maybe ten minutes of this I was just as suddenly hit by what felt like a huge wave and then, just as hard, by the need to weep. As soon as the bell rang I escaped outside, into the woods, where I knelt down in the bushes and delivered my load of tears.

When I returned to my cushion afterwards it was as if a switch had been flipped. I was now perfectly comfortable in the sitting posture. In fact, there was at this moment nowhere else on earth I wanted to be. It was as if I had intersected with time and space in some deeply fated way. This cushion right here on this wooden floor in these woods was now home.

Only the next day, when Maurine gave her talk, was I able to begin to put words to what I felt, sitting there, enjoying my breath. "You will have heard that we sit to get rid of our ego," she said. "In one sense, this is true. However it is also true that when you choose to sit in this way, to stay firmly on your cushion hour after hour after hour, you are granting to yourself the greatest possible importance. You are saying, 'I matter.'"

That was it. That was the reason for my tears. For as long as I could remember I had felt myself to be someone whose thoughts mattered, whose ideas mattered. But in some other, deeper, more fundamental way I had not ever mattered. Not to myself. Until now.

That afternoon I felt the energy of the trees surrounding us and reveled in the deliciousness of the breezes through the windows. I began to appreciate the pale grey wood of the lodge, the old maple tree trunks that thrust up through the floorboards, and the purple flowers in the window box I spied every time I rounded the south bend. I stole glances at Maurine during *kinhin*—how she walked at the head of the line, bearing absolutely upright, face tilted slightly forward. Fierce concentration was written on that face, but just beneath it I was sure I could read something like thrill. As if each time the firm padded foot met the ground was the first time. I was beginning to think that for all its rigours and demands, what this practice was really about was pleasure, or at least something akin to it, something bigger than pleasure towards which that word merely gestured. This was confirmed on Sunday when Maurine ended the lesson—she called it a "dharma talk"— by reading to us from *The Color Purple*: the scene where Shug tries to get Celie to see that God is not the punitive old white man she's been praying to all these years, but a lover of pleasure and fun. "Oh, she say," Maurine read, taking on Celie's dialect, "God love all them feelings. That some of the best stuff God did. And when you know God loves 'em you enjoys 'em a lot more."

Maurine was not especially convincing as a poor Southern black woman and she may have had no idea these lines referred to lesbian sex. But Shug was obviously talking about something erotic, and they were still some of the most subversive lines I knew. Maurine too, I now understood, was a lover of "all them feelings."

I emerged from the lodge at the end of the retreat that Sunday into the humid August afternoon feeling deeply rested and happy. My drive down the steep dirt road to the bottom of the hill seemed to take forever and I liked it that way. The grey sky brought out the tropical green of the leaves, splashes of ruby red and orange in the woods. How longingly I had thought during the retreat of my couch, my books, phoning my friends. I was now in no rush to get home.

I BEGAN SITTING EVERY MORNING, in the *Trivia* room, facing the big maple tree in back. At first it was to keep the feeling of those two days, the way you try and keep a summer tan through the fall. As time went on it required more and more discipline but I kept doing it. It made me happier, and calmer. Had I come upon Kaye's secret, I wondered; was this what the ocean had taught her in Japan?

The more I sat, the more my life seemed to organize itself. I started getting rid of junk that had been sitting around for a long time. Problems and entanglements that had been weighing me down had a way of working themselves out. And when, not a week after the retreat, a "For Sale" sign appeared on a little house right down a street off the main road, it seemed to have materialized out of my morning meditations.

It was a house I'd barely noticed before, modest with white asbestos tiles, green trim and a porch facing the street. A wooden garage and a small yard abutted the bus garage next door. I made an appointment to see it.

The man who met me in the yard the next day was a farmer from Vermont; the house had belonged to his sister. When I walked in though the side door my heart opened. A big country kitchen lined with cabinets, a little pantry out back, and a mudroom to the side. Upstairs a hush and a sweet, starchy smell that reminded me of Charlevoix attics. Wide plank wood floors and little rooms lined with old wallpaper. Sloping ceilings. From the smallest room, a view of the poplar meadow in back.

Beside the kitchen porch, a little path led down a steep grade bordered by lilac bushes and then veered to the right to meet the lower level of the garage, which, it appeared, had once served as a barn. Its windows were mostly broken and inside were some pieces of rotting furniture and the remains of an old chicken coop.

He'd grown up here with his sister, Lillian, the farmer told me. Back then it had been a farmhouse.

It wasn't my dream house, it was not Leverett Road. The house had no bathtub, only a shower stall. There would be fumes from the buses next door, and there was enough of a slope in the kitchen floor to send you slightly off balance. But I was charmed. The house had character. And great possibilities. I could store cartons in the garage, and lots of women could stay here and help out with *Trivia*. Even the address—11 Union Street—seemed auspicious.

I TOOK POSSESSION THE LAST WEEK in October and spent several days transporting boxes and furniture from apartment to house. Anne came to help one day, Lena another. One day, my new neighbour came by with a cheque for two hundred dollars: the annual fee for grazing rights for his donkey, Poncho.

After my friends had gone, I spent a few days just getting to know the place. Compared to the apartment, which had been right on the main street, this house was quiet, the silence broken only by the occasional sound of buses pulling in and out and sometimes gunning their engines. The church bells were muffled here, especially in the small room upstairs. Instead, several times a day and sometimes at night too, I would hear the sound of Poncho braying—a prolonged, pitiful moan into which he threw his whole being.

That week I dreamt intensely of both Kaye and Grace. They were presences that followed me around those rooms. Especially Grace, because so many of her things had been unearthed during the move. Her old turtlenecks were now my rags. The contact paper she'd used to line the closet shelves of the apartment I was now applying to the shelves in the pantry. In the months since that encounter on the UMass campus, I had found myself melting with forgiveness toward her. From Anne I'd found out that her husband used to beat her. Grace had written to complain about an article we'd published advocating violence, and Anne had offered this piece of information by way of explanation. She was shocked to find out I didn't know. At the very least I should have guessed it from the annihilation paper—it was right there between the lines—but I hadn't.

"Your unknowing is powerful." How right Grace had been about that. But it wasn't only me; I was beginning to see this. Each of us wanted to go on being seen by the other as she was in our first weeks together: I light-filled and happy, infectiously so, she wise, gracious, and strong. We were there to help each other rise, to lighten each other's lives, to bring brightness and expansion— not to drag each other down by "bringing things up."

In my morning meditations these past months I thought I had begun to understand the way Grace had reacted at the Lesbian Poetry Reading when Adrienne Rich got up and read the poem about the cripple: her tears, the way she gripped her stomach. Her hands had gone to her stomach in the same way when I told her Audre Lorde was in the hospital again, the cancer having

160

returned. At the time I attributed these responses to her bottomless capacity for empathy. But now I saw them from another angle. What if feminism, beginning with Mary Daly, had been her ticket out of pain and victimhood? What if she was counting on the women around her, and on the feminist writers and thinkers she admired, to sustain her belief that another way of life was possible? If all this was true, then being with me, in the end, must have called up her worst fears, thrown her back into that weak state she thought she'd left behind forever, upended her faith all over again.

At the same time I'd been having to look at some troubling things about myself. I recalled our last months together on Leverett Road, those interminable meals, thinking I couldn't take another moment of her obsessions, her defeatism, her spirals of doom. Had I fallen out of interest, grown impatient? Distracted? Bored? Indeed I had.

Yet wasn't it her knowing I had fallen in love with? The woman who wrote about annihilation, having been haunted by it her whole life, in one form then another. Wasn't it just this I'd loved about her? That she felt everything so immediately so intensely, was not able to disconnect from what she knew, in fact could not get free of it, would stay with it until some sort of meaning could be wrung from it?

ON HALLOWE'EN I HAD A HOUSEWARMING party. Lena and Harriet came early and helped me set up. The house was full of women for the first time—most of them in costume. Anne was an earth priestess. Harriet was Tinkerbell. Lena was George Eliot. There were several guests I didn't recognize at all. Once everyone had arrived, Anne lit a bowl of sage and then led a procession through the house, up the stairs, in and out of all the rooms, smudging every corner. Later in the evening, I requested everyone's attention and announced we were going to perform a commitment ceremony. "This is as close as I'll ever get to a wedding day," I said, and, with Anne officiating in her priestess robes, I proclaimed my intention to love and cherish this house "till death do us part." Everyone applauded and struck up the chords of the wedding march. It seemed propitious that this ceremony was taking place on the eve of the Witches' New Year. Already my dreams for this house were coming true.

A WEEK LATER, IN NOVEMBER 1984, Reagan was re-elected by a landslide. I went over to a neighbour's to watch the returns on her colour TV. Other friends and neighbours had gathered to watch with us. We moaned and groaned together as Republicans swept the country, domino-style, and we all departed early in a funk. I expected to continue feeling bad about it in the days and weeks that followed, but after two days I noticed it wasn't even on my radar. Was it just that it hadn't sunk in? I thought about it for a while, then decided no. There had been too much magic in my life to believe that a presidential election could turn things around.

Only a month after the election, a gas leak at Union Carbide in Bhopal, India, killed ten thousand people almost immediately. Many more were expected to die. Union Carbide was passing the buck, and so was the Indian government. There was no telling if the survivors were ever going to get compensation for their losses. In study group we put the incident into feminist perspective: U.S. corporations like Union Carbide—the supreme symbol of patriarchy's toxicity and irresponsibility—were poisoning the poorest people on the planet, and doing it with impunity. It escaped none of us that analysis by itself was of little help to anyone. But it was all we could think to do.

I missed Grace terribly on that day. Imagined her face going white with outrage. Imagined she might have some insight into how one continues to choose joy in the face of such atrocity. But that was the old Grace, I had to tell myself. The one who no longer was.

19.
Union Street

There have been real betrayals of women by other women—by women who supposedly shared a similar feminist spirit and vision and by women whom one once called friends. Women have also held unrealistic expectations of women friends such that when these were not fulfilled women felt disillusioned and abandoned.

—Janice G. Raymond, *A Passion for Friends: Toward a Philosophy of Female Affection*

BY MIDWINTER, MY HOUSE AND I had settled into a harmonious and sometimes blissful cohabitation. The *Trivia* office took over what had been the dining room downstairs; once I'd lined the walls with bookshelves the room doubled as a library as well, not only for my own books but also for the growing archive of review copies and magazines from all over the world that came in now on an exchange basis. The somewhat dreary front parlour perked up once I removed the vinyl flooring and sanded the floors to expose the wide pine planks underneath. A friend and neighbour helped me paint the walls a light sand colour with rose trim and I had a woodstove installed in the corner. Replacing the canvas shades with wooden shutters was the final touch. The room was luminous, now, and happifying. I felt sure Lillian would approve.

I moved an old desk into the small bedroom room upstairs and escaped as often as I could from *Trivia* work to read and write up there. Glancing from the page to the window, something in me still broke open in wonder at the grove of tall, slim poplar trees out back and the hills beyond, the birds that would swoop and then rise again to perch in the branches. With the arrival of spring a flock of red-winged blackbirds suddenly appeared, and starlings by the hundreds. And every afternoon and sometimes evening too there was the intermittent sound of Poncho's lugubrious wail.

My whole life was now steeped in feminism. It informed the thesis I was writing, on three visionary women writers—Virginia Woolf, Christa Wolf, and Luce Irigaray—all of them fiercely antipatriarchal. It seemed everything else I did fed into either *Trivia* or the Feminist Lecture Series. Study group was still meeting only sporadically, but *Trivia* held us together. The women in the group were my unofficial advisory board, and whenever possible I pressed them into service for bulk mailings—it seemed there was always an issue or a flyer or a letter going out. More and more now I also got help from student interns from the five colleges nearby, or women from the area who'd heard about *Trivia* and wanted to pitch in. And the circle kept fanning out; readers from as far away as Australia sent letters saying how much it meant to them. This was now my community, this international network of women thinkers.

Only sometimes a shadow appeared. A tension. When what I believed and what I saw couldn't easily be reconciled. Given the dense concentration of feminist luminaries in this area, I'd had visions when I first arrived of vibrant dinner parties with ideas volleying back and forth across the table. It wasn't long, though, before I learned the celebrated feminist writers and thinkers of Montague and Leverett had mostly fallen out with each other or drifted apart. When a note from Adrienne and Michelle appeared in the *Trivia* box welcoming a "sister publication" to the scene and suggesting Anne and I come for a visit, those dinner party fantasies sprang back to life. And more: I imagined finally telling Adrienne, as I'd longed to do for some time now, how her words had undergirded our lives on Leverett Road, how her poems had accompanied us in our efforts to love and to create the world anew.

A few days after receiving the invitation, Anne and I crossed the street to join them for tea in the high-ceilinged living room of their colonial home. The talk over our teacups was mostly of the house and its quirks, what grew in their garden, the charms of Montague. I looked in vain for an opening to tell Adrienne how she'd been woven into our lives. The conversation was animated and friendly, but the longer it went on the clearer it became that that it was strictly a conversation between neighbours. There was no mention of our respective magazines, though the fact that we were all feminist editors working out of Montague would have seemed to call for some comment.

When we crossed back to my house an hour later, I confessed my dashed hopes to Anne. She helped me see what I had not wanted to see, what was quite obvious once she spelled it out: whatever differences existed between Adrienne and Michelle and the other feminists in the neighbourhood, the two of us had inherited them. Certainly our first issue, with articles by both Jan and Pat and many allusions to Mary Daly, had done nothing to dispel the notion that Anne and I were in the same camp. "Whatever that means," we both said at once. Neither of us had been especially aware of belonging to any camp at all.

It was becoming abundantly clear now that these camps did exist, and that the ideological differences between them could not be so easily dissolved. In fact, they were becoming more and more pronounced in the movement itself. The writers we published in *Trivia* had always taken a strong stand against pornography and S/M, which they saw as forms of violence against women. I had known there was another side to this issue, that feminists were divided over it, but I had never taken that side seriously. Now, though, those voices were becoming louder and more articulated. There had been a Sexuality Conference at Barnard in 1982 where feminists gave papers defending pornography, bondage, and, yes, S/M, and some of these articles were starting to appear in anthologies—most of them featuring the word "desire" in the title—devoted to women's unfettered exploration of their sexuality.

Andrea Dworkin and Catherine McKinnon had drafted a civil rights ordinance that allowed victims to sue pornographers, and we would be publishing a copy of that ordinance in the seventh issue, along with a stirring article by Dworkin about censorship.

"We," I still said, out of habit and preference, though in practice I was now editing *Trivia* by myself, Anne having bowed out just before the sixth issue, citing overwork.

I was aware there was much opposition to the civil rights ordinance among feminists. Some of them had banded together to form a group called FACT—"Feminists Against Censorship." They had circulated a brief to the feminist press explaining why they felt the ordinance could endanger free speech and possibly result in the banning of feminist literature.

In my editorial in this issue I intended to try and answer the objections put forth in the FACT brief. Most of them would be easy enough to strike down. But some of them, I had to acknowledge, would not. Might the ordinance have a chilling effect on our own creative expression in the area of sexuality? Would it, for example, make it easier to ban a book like Wittig's *The Lesbian Body,* in which lovers perform mutual acts of cannibalism and evisceration? While the ordinance itself did not call for censorship, it seemed important to ask whether in the wrong hands it might serve as a tool to do so. I spent longer on this editorial than on any other I'd written.

ON AN AFTERNOON IN LATE FEBRUARY, as I was still trying to pull my thoughts together, Jan came by collecting signatures for a response she'd written to the FACT brief. She stood over me impatiently, her face flushed, as I read. It was an angry response, accusing the brief signers of betraying feminism. I looked up at her anxiously when I'd finished. I needed time to think about this, I said. Women were already so split on this issue and I was afraid her letter would only serve to polarize us further. Jan just stared at me incredulously. "Whose side are you on anyway?" she said finally and walked out.

The next day I called to tell her I'd decided not to sign. I begged her not to hold it against me as a friend. Jan insisted my personal position on this issue didn't matter to her in the slightest. But my position as editor of *Trivia* did, and since *Trivia's* position was not clear and strong, she could no longer associate herself with it. Consequently, she said, she would withdraw the article we were planning to publish in the forthcoming issue, an excerpt from her book on friendship. Ironically, the title of the article was "Obstacles to Female Friendship."

I was shaken, but there was an issue to put out. I called on my friends. Anne supported me for not signing the letter. The last thing we needed, she said, was accusations and finger pointing.

Soon after, Lena packed a bag with her books and her clothes and came to stay with me in Montague for a few days. During breaks from our work, we talked off and on about the brief, Jan's letter, my response. Lena found some of the arguments in the FACT brief persuasive, as did, she said, quite a few women she knew. She would have refused to sign herself, as there were no easy answers to be had. These words were comforting to me, but even more so was her physical presence in the house.

During those winter days of 1985, as a gentle snow covered the landscape, Lena and I became lovers. The wild hilarity we seemed to always unleash in each other, we admitted, had always had an erotic edge to it and was probably the way we sublimated our sexual feelings. It was such a relief now to express them directly. And it was so good to curl up in bed together and talk when our work was done, or to take walks arm-in-arm around the white meadow.

WHEN SPRING CAME, THERE WAS everything to discover: the swamp cabbage unfurling in the marsh in back, the great forsythia bush in front bursting into flower, the hydrangea just pushing up in the front yard, the lilac bushes by the kitchen porch starting to bud, and the clumps of daffodils in back left over from the garden Lillian must once have had. In mid-April the first tentative piping of the peepers out back gave way to surging screams. In the meadow, bobolinks hovered over their nests and wildflowers began to sprout.

But also in the spring tensions began to surface. Lena had high expectations of love. At the slightest sign of inattentiveness on my part she would explode, announce she was "taking her space." Between the house, *Trivia* business—which now included applying for publishing grants—and the thesis, my life was busy as never before. Instead of hanging out with her after dinner I would return to the office. Some nights I'd stay up typing while she slept. The next day there would be stormy outbursts, or withdrawals, which almost always took me by surprise.

In May Lena began to "need her space" more often and to communicate less. She told me she was going through some deep changes and couldn't take any pressure from me or from anyone. We would make plans to be together and then she'd forget, or change her mind. If I complained her back would go up.

At the end of May I flew to Berkeley to take part in the third national Women in Print conference. Harriet, who'd been to the first WIP conference, said it was a must. There would be booksellers, editors, publishers, and writers from all over the country and Canada, too. I'd network, make invaluable contacts, get a big shot of energy. People Express was cheap. And I told myself it would be good for me, just now, to get a little distance from western Massachusetts, to find out what feminism was to women from other parts of the country. Lena and I had been in a state of barely contained hostility for several weeks now. Maybe the break would be good for us too.

Anne's ex-girlfriend Frieda had offered me her Berkeley apartment, which was vacant for the week. Jeffner, a writer we'd published, camped out at Frieda's with me that night and in the morning we parked on a residential street in the Berkeley hills and set off on foot. The light on my face felt amazingly good. The sky seemed limitless. There were rich fragrances emanating from flowering bushes and trees every step of the way, and occasional views of the bay that made me giddy with pleasure.

It wasn't till I was back at the apartment again at the end of the day, my head crammed full of all the women I'd met and the information I'd absorbed at the workshops, that I read the note Frieda had left out on the kitchen table. At the bottom of the page, after instructions about plants and coffeemaker, there was a request to "CALL HELEN," followed by a number. "You'll like each other," it said. I had heard Helen's name before, from Maxine, who knew her from Berkeley, where she was a graduate student in English literature. "Brilliant," she'd said of her, I remembered now. "Astute." And, one time, "wise." I called the number right away. Helen picked up and knew instantly who I was. We agreed to meet for breakfast the next morning.

Maybe because of her association with Maxine, with her uncouth manner and impish looks, I was not prepared for the person waiting for me at The Brick Hut that morning, in the first booth facing the door. She was blonde—that much she'd said on the phone. She was also delicate, and poised, in an African print top. She had long lashes and a Greek nose. *I didn't know lesbians could look like this.* She was, in short, beautiful, and she was smiling at me—having identified me, I supposed, by my curly hair. I smiled back. She laughed as soon as I sat down. A welcoming laugh, a "so here we are" laugh.

She had just a hint of a Southern accent. Was that what made her so easy to talk to? There was suddenly so much to say. I mentioned I'd first heard of her from Maxine. "Oh yes, Maxine," she said, "and her summer from hell"—laughing softly now again—and then I was hearing the whole story of that summer from Maxine's perspective.

There were few if any points of contact with mine, and from Helen's tone I gathered she was only too aware of the discrepancy. "Somehow I suspected you couldn't have all been evil miscreants," she said when she'd finished. "But I never expected you to look anything like this," she added, a little incongruously. I told her that made two of us.

She was a fan of *Trivia,* she said, had been since the beginning. In her heart and her soul she was a radical lesbian feminist— "though God knows it's been put to the test"—and was endlessly thankful that somewhere in the world there were women keeping this sacred flame alive. A poet herself, she was writing her dissertation on three lesbian poets—Adrienne Rich, Susan Griffin, H.D.—all of them women without whose words she did not think she would have survived. I told her about the three fierce feminist writers at the centre of my dissertation, and we marveled at the coincidence. "Meeting of minds" kept running through my head. We talked about pornography, and the Civil Rights Ordinance. She told me she could see both sides of the issue. She had as much rage against pornographers and the industry as anyone; she had marched with protestors in the Castro district. But on the other hand, well, she said, feminists knew almost nothing about the lives of sex workers. Many of them depended on the very things that feminists wanted to tear down. She hinted that she had firsthand knowledge of this world, which didn't square at all with what I saw before me: this fragile, well-mannered, well-dressed woman who'd been finishing her degree at Berkeley.

More than three hours went by, and before they were over I had told her all about my falling out with Jan. It seemed like the first time I'd taken the measure of it, how it had felt, what it meant. When I finished she put her hand on mine. "It's a trauma you've been through," she said. There was no deeper wound, she said, than a woman's betrayal of another woman, especially when both were feminists. She understood too well how devastating it was. Sometime, she said, I will tell you.

Who is this woman? This blonde angel, so full of light yet on such intimate terms with darkness.

AT THE CONFERENCE THAT DAY I met women whose words I'd been reading for years, as well as women who wanted to thank me for my words and the words of women we'd published. In between the workshops, there was a lot of political talk—about sexuality, racism, ageism, censorship. Though I didn't learn much of anything new in these discussions, it was gratifying to sense that *Trivia* was at the centre of so many of the defining issues of the movement. And I was buoyed by the spirit of solidarity and good will that pervaded these rooms, with women sharing tips of the trade and resources of every kind.

Yet none of these women was anything like Helen, and my thoughts drifted to her throughout the day. I had promised to come see her on Sunday after the conference.

She called the next morning to say she was in bed with a fever and could I bring some cranberry juice? The thought of ministering to her in bed made my heart pound hard all day. I arrived at six, breathless—there were five flights of stairs—bearing the juice and a bottle of wine. She looked pale but was no longer bedridden. After thanking me for the juice and gulping some down she took me on a tour of her apartment. Then she began hopping about the kitchen planning a meal. She was in high spirits, laughing and chattering.

"I thought you were sick!" I said.

"I was," she replied. "It's you. Something about you ... 'Looking at you, I revive with prodigious speed.'"

We both laughed knowingly. How many people, how many lesbians, even, would have gotten the allusion to *The Lesbian Body?* I tried to overlook the fact that Wittig's words were addressed to a lover.

Off the kitchen was a little window-lined alcove with a table and chairs. We ate our dinner there looking out over the hills, talking. A full moon had begun to rise over those hills before we got up from the table. She'd been a hermit for months, Helen told me, rarely seeing people, only emerging to teach her classes and buy groceries. Which made it all the more surprising to her that she had been so looking forward to seeing me. How had Frieda known?

I told her how enchanted I was by the air here, the light, the views. I told her about my friend Lena, who was also a poet. My voice must have given something away.

"Are you and Lena lovers?" she asked me point-blank.

I said yes, and no, and stumbled on about how we'd been friends before and maybe it should have stayed that way. I thought I must be sounding very muddled.

There was a silence. Then she looked me right in the eye and said, in her slow, purposeful drawl, "I'm *very* attracted to you."

A shock went through me. "Oh," I stammered, and complimented her on her candour. "It's mutual," I added, but explained that acting on it was out of the question. Oh, she said, she totally understood. But she hoped I would agree to spend the night—platonically, of course. I said yes.

The walls of her bedroom were pastel blue; a poster of a Greek coastal village hung beside the bed. She lent me a nightshirt and changed into a T-shirt and a pair of black knickers slit up the sides. We talked most of the night, first sitting, then lying side by side on her rose sheets. Not touching. I told her how much I loved the poster on the wall.

"Have you been?" she asked. "No, never," I said.

"Someday I'll take you there. We'll go to the isle of Lesbos. The country of our origins."

"Where'd these come from?" I asked, changing the subject, pointing to her knickers.

"A warehouse in Georgia. My mother likes to buy me smutty clothes." And she began to unreel tales of her Southern family: her manic-depressive mother, her abusive stepfather, her "Gammy" who lived with her aunt. She was a mix of Southern white trash and New England WASP, she told me. Her father came from a very proper Yankee family. Ah, I thought, thus the mix of polite reserve and excess.

I asked why she'd been in hiding all these months.

"You really want to know?"

I nodded vigorously.

"Okay, then. I'm bringing a therapist to court. A woman. A lesbian."

"Oh."

"She seduced me during treatment. I was living here in this apartment with Nan at the time. I left to move in with the shrink. She begged me to. And then, a month later, she kicked me out. Nan and I never recovered." There was more, she said, but that was the gist of it. Her betrayal story.

"I don't know how you managed to survive all that."

"I almost didn't. And believe me, I wouldn't be going to court if I didn't feel my life depended on it.... I don't like using the master's tools," she added, referencing Audre Lorde. But the cause, she insisted, was feminist. Her perpetrator happened to be a woman, but the context for her actions was a system that rewarded domination, punished vulnerability, banished tenderness.

I reached out for her then. Awash in tenderness, I folded her in my arms, like a little bird. She felt so tiny and delicate.

When I woke up after only a few hours, the room was pink and grey. Birds were feeding from a plastic feeder stuck to the windowpane to the right of the bed, and through that window you could see the slumbering shapes of the Berkeley hills. The light was mystical, the very light sent off by the white stucco and sand in the poster on the wall. I gave silent thanks to whatever powers had brought me here before nodding back to sleep.

WE WERE UP AT EIGHT A.M. and dressed quickly, not wanting

to stay in temptation's way. Besides, there was no time to waste. We had the morning and part of the afternoon, that was all. Helen's car, an old, faded blue Ford Fairlane convertible, was parked right across the street. A dog-eared copy of Kingston's *The Woman Warrior* lay beneath the rear window, beside a wide-brimmed straw hat.

"This is exciting," she said as we got into the car.

"What?"

"Driving with you for the first time."

I was in awe of her boldness, the way she gave voice to what was in the air between us. Soon I could glimpse the blue bay in the distance. And today again the air was unbelievably pure, fresh. She stopped at a little square where we had strong coffee and croissants on a weathered wooden deck. I tried to just breathe, as I'd learned to do at the retreat, to take in all the sights and smells through my lungs and my belly. Beginning with this woman beside me in white blouse and straw hat, who with every minute was growing more vast and luminous.

"It's too good to be true," I said finally, looking around. "I didn't realize how much I needed ... all this."

"You're someone who needs a lot of space," she said, as if she already had intimate knowledge of the cloistered valleys of New England, the low ceilings of my house. As if she knew the way I'd been with Kaye, and with Grace. As if she'd known me her whole life. Then: "Why don't you stay?"

It's not as if I hadn't thought of this myself. There'd been plenty of empty seats on the plane coming out here, why not just fly back standby tomorrow? But Lena was expecting me, I couldn't disappoint her. And besides, how were Helen and I to resist each other for another twenty-four hours?

"I'd love to," I said. "But it wouldn't be right."

She did not plead or pressure me. "I'm just grateful for the time we've had," she said. And she reached into her bag, pulled out something wrapped in tissue paper, put it in my hand. Inside the paper was a thick yellow candle.

"Oshun," she said. "The Yoruban goddess of light and air. Whenever you want to return to this feeling of light and space just light the candle." She'd been studying with a Yoruban priestess, she told me, and there were goddesses she prayed to every day. They kept her steady. "Yemaya" was the goddess of the oceans. I told her I felt like saying a prayer to Yemaya this very moment. She said one, silently, for me.

Oh light oh space oh sunlit coast oh Grecian skies. Sprung free I am. From the narrow corridors of New England its quaint little villages town halls and steeples set in troughs between hills. Its cramped bodies, rusted cars.

We drove to Frieda's for my bags. On the way to the airport we stopped at the Berkeley Marina and walked out on a pier. There were strong gusts of sea breeze and gulls wheeling about. She showed me the spot on the rocks where she first came to the decision to take her case to court. I put my arm about her shoulder on the way back to the car, she put hers around my waist, leaned into me. It was uncanny how our bodies fit together. At the airport we had drinks at the bar and stared into each other's eyes till the very last moment.

When the plane put down in Newark at two in the morning Eastern time—People Express was cheap but it was not direct— I called. She was writing me a letter, she said. I was all over her apartment and she had begun to feel a little scared not knowing when we'd see each other. On her altar, beside the cowrie shells and candles, she had set the swizzle sticks from our drinks. She'd returned to the bar and retrieved them after we parted. She was exhilarated, she said.

I knew that wasn't right, I should have given her no cause to feel "exhilarated." But I had to admit I felt that way too.

Back in Montague, my house, which I had had to wrench myself away from less than a week ago, looked tacky and sad. The asbestos tiles were the same indeterminate grey-white as the sky. The air was thick and damp, as if trees and bushes had been sweating moisture. The blooming lilacs were sweet smelling, but somehow lacklustre after the colours and fragrances that had mixed in the air in Berkeley. Inside, the ceilings seemed so low, the rooms so little.

"A LOT'S BEEN HAPPENING," Lena said when I called that afternoon. Since we'd last spoken, something from her past had come back to haunt her. When I asked if I could come over she said no, she needed to be alone.

"But I set aside this time for you," I complained. "We had plans together."

"I'm sorry it's so inconvenient for you," she said, that familiar edge back in her voice.

WE MET TWO DAYS LATER, in a smoky Northampton bar; we'd agreed neutral ground would be best. Heavy metal music blared through the speakers; I got the manager to turn it down. Over cigarettes and whiskey sours, we had it out. Her disappointment in me for not understanding what she was going through. My disappointment in her for shutting me out and canceling plans. Once that was out of the way, she told me a bit about her crisis, the memories from her childhood that were surfacing. I told her about the conference, about meeting Helen. I told her about the light, the smells, the ocean. I said I had wanted to stay, would have done so had we not had plans together.

"Are you sleeping with her?" she shot back.

"It wasn't physical," I parried, aware this was falling back on the literal.

"You know what I'm asking," she said. "Is there something going on between you?"

When I said nothing, she exploded. "A poet! I should have known! You and your thing for poets. A poet who lives in Berkeley, no less."

"Lena! You're getting carried away. I'm not having an affair with her. We never even kissed."

"And you have the nerve to complain about feeling shut out," she persisted, "the nerve to wonder why I can't trust you. Obviously you can't go anywhere without seducing someone!" She was screaming by now. We'd both had two drinks.

"You're blowing this out of proportion. Yes, I'm happy to know her. But my primary commitment is to you. That's why I wanted us to talk. I want to make things right between us."

It wasn't the whole truth but it wasn't a lie either. Lena was screaming at me, which meant I mattered to her after all. I felt as if I'd been snapped out of a fantasy and back into my life here in

Massachusetts, my life with her. But she wasn't buying it.

"A fine way to make things right between us!" she yelled before turning on her heel and walking out of the bar.

BACK HOME IN MONTAGUE, I buried myself in *Trivia* work. Issue #7 was almost ready for the typesetters, but there was some finetuning still to be done. One night I called Andrea Dworkin about a detail in her essay on censorship; she was curt and businesslike. The last time we'd talked on the phone she'd been expansive, had said how important *Trivia* was for writers like her and for the movement in general. I was sure Jan had gotten to her.

In the hopes of making at least one thing right, I decided to write to Jan to let her know we were publishing Andrea's piece, to reaffirm my support for the ordinance, and to ask if she could be possibly be persuaded to reconsider her decision, to let us publish her essay after all. I knew it was a long shot and told myself to expect no response, but when none came I took it hard all the same.

20.
Wild Nights

The seasons. The scent of the trees. And our free existence,
a new joy for each new day.... The citadel did not reach
as far as here.

—Christa Wolf, *Cassandra*

THE LETTERS BEGAN TO ARRIVE NOW, at the rate of two or three a day, in blue ink on pink paper—the colours of her bedroom. When I opened them I'd be in that room all over again, feel the spaciousness, the light. In each of the letters she enclosed a poem by a lesbian writer—H.D., Sara Teasdale, Judy Grahn, May Sarton—invoking the universe she now saw opening up to us both. In one way or another, letters and poems all conveyed the same message: I was what she had been longing for all these years. Her dreams and prayers had brought me to her.

I could not have dreamt Helen into my life. She looked too much like the women I had been in love with in high school, the women I saw in films, the ones who were strictly off limits, so obviously were they for men. I had learned to keep my lust well harnessed in the presence of such women. Was that why I could barely respond to her letters and more and more found myself unable to feel anything when I read them?

More likely, it was Lena. When I called to check up on her she shocked me by saying she'd been offered a generous stipend at Harvard and had decided to take it. I hadn't even known she'd applied. "But ... what about your writing? What about your poems?" I stammered. I knew what grad school was like.

"Just because I'm going to Harvard doesn't mean I won't write poems," she shot back. And then: "You know, some of us need to think about supporting ourselves." It was a well-aimed jab to a tender place.

I was racked with guilt. Harvard was clearly a bid for security; if Lena hadn't felt abandoned by me, she'd be organizing her life around her writing. And if I was ever inclined to forget, if my heart should make even a small move in Helen's direction, it was only a matter of hours before my face was rubbed in it again. Lena had a very large and active support system. Whenever I called Graves Avenue and one of the witches picked up, it was obvious from the sound of her voice that she had taken Lena's side against me. And when I pulled Nina aside after study group to ask why, when I spoke, she either averted her gaze or looked at me skeptically, she said something about my "escapades" out West.

I would often feel something like dread when I saw another fat pink envelope with Helen's blue handwriting and knew that yet again I would be unable to rise to the occasion. I tried to tell her this once on the phone. Don't be silly, she said, you deserve it all, every last word. I realized then that what I had really been asking her to do was to stop sending the letters. I hadn't managed to make that clear.

One day in early June, Harriet called. She'd been living in a cabin in the woods in New Hampshire, a magical studio built by women for women writers. She was going to be away for a week and wondered, would I like to come stay there?

It was a gift from the goddess—maybe one of Helen's Yoruban goddesses. Thanking Harriet, blessing her, calling her my fairy godmother, I took down the directions and began scurrying to finish all pressing *Trivia* business.

THE NEXT AFTERNOON FOUND ME FOLLOWING a long, winding driveway up a hill between tall spruce and maple trees. Inside, the cabin was all birch wood, great windows, and high, vaulted space. After settling in, I walked for a long time up on the hill under the dripping trees—it was a cool and wet afternoon— then came inside and made a fire. And there by the woodstove, surrounded by the wooden walls of a house that had been built entirely by women, in the arms of majestic pines whose branches grazed the windows, I lit the yellow candle and began to reread the letters.

"I want to be outside a book with you—outside rigidities—to escape into life—to breathe—to stare into things—to feel our intimate expanses."

I was back in her element ... the dry air, blue light. It was the element of my poets, I saw now, the ones I had first read at the Centre, whose words had cleared a path for me. "I go where I love and where I am loved / into the snow; I go to the things I love / with no thought of duty or pity." Despite all these years of treading that path, of reading and thinking and loving, I knew I had yet to truly live what these poets wrote. Sitting by the fire, feeling space around me again, a space carved out by women, for female creation, it occurred to me that I had only been in training all this time.

Helen lived the words of the poets. I wanted to escape into life with her, to dwell in her realm of distilled perception and experience, of light and air. Together, I sensed, we would take time for the important things. And we would play....

"Yes," she wrote, "we'll share ideas and work and visions, but let me please be playful with you.... I want to eat cereal with you many times before we save the world...."

Helen wanted freedom, for both of us. And as strongly as she felt about me, she refused to make any assumptions about the form this feeling would take. Above all, she said, we should not try to fit some preexisting mold. She wanted us to explore in our own ways what we were to each other, to make it all up as we went along. It was a task worthy of all our powers of invention, she declared.

She is out on the edge where I most wish to stand. She meets me there and takes me farther....

I spent much of the next two days meditating and walking in the woods. On the second day the sun broke through; the wet pine needles sparkled and the leaves were impossibly green. Helen was with me as I walked. I thought back to that brief walk we took out on the pier, the churning of the bay, the fit of our two bodies. I felt a wildness stirring in me. I began to imagine all the places I might go with her, not all of them on this earth.

At the top of the hill was a plateau where a maze of foot trails cut through moss and juniper bushes. One evening I walked the trails barefoot, paying attention to the contact of my feet with the ground, the way I'd learned to do on the retreat, reveling in the moss and pine needles underfoot. Something was shifting in me, I could feel it. The world felt big and open again, as it hadn't since I first met Grace. And all this walking was helping me to find my footing in a landscape that was now radically altered.

On my last night there I called her. The yellow candle, now a mere stub, was burning beside me. "You are there now, I can hear it," she said.

"Yes, I am." I told her about rereading her letters, how they made me feel, now that I *could* feel.

She was overjoyed. We spoke to one another now, for the first time, as lovers. I answered her fire with mine. She told me she was preparing for the deposition, the first of several. It was hard going. The therapist would be present. She would have to summon all her powers, call on all her goddesses.

BACK IN MONTAGUE THERE WERE NO consoling messages awaiting me at the post office and a thousand little *Trivia* details to attend to. On the phone with Helen that night I complained about having to carry the weight of the journal all by myself. "You don't have to do it alone," she said. "I'll come and help out. As soon as the deposition is over. I'll be free then. It will be good for my soul."

This was not what I'd been angling for, though I could see how she might have thought it was. No, I said, no I wasn't ready for that, to have her on this coast, it was too soon.

On the day of her deposition, I got in my car and drove down to New York. I wasn't sure why except that I had finally dropped all the articles off at the typesetters in Greenfield and there was no reason to stay. My sister was living with her boyfriend now and her place was empty.

It was dark when I arrived. On the Henry Hudson Parkway approaching Kaye's exit (Dykeman, occasion for many bad jokes), I had a sudden stabbing memory of her, of us together. In bed that night, acute physical longing—not for Helen, for Lena.

We had spent a romantic weekend here just four months ago. How did we mess up so bad? I lay awake for a long time awash in sorrow, wondering how many loves and losses one life can hold.

THE DEPOSITION HAD GONE VERY WELL, Helen said when I called to ask her about it. The shrink had been there for the first part. It had been tough. But she had felt my strength supporting her, and it was over now. And oh, she wanted to see me.

Yes, me too, I said. Just not quite yet.

However, two days later I was driving to Newark to meet her plane. She had called the night before to say People Express had a direct flight, it was cheap, and there was space. "If I get there and you decide you're not ready for me to come to Montague, I'll just fly back." She had already picked out a traveling outfit, she told me.

"Give me a little time to think about it," I said. Then sat on my sister's bed and pondered. Something had called me here to New York. What else could it have been? To be honest, what tipped the scales was the thought of her traveling outfit. I called her back and said come.

At Newark the plane was held up on the tarmac for an hour. I paced and paced, smoking one cigarette after another. Finally there she was, stepping out onto the platform—in the red pants and blue-and-white-striped shirt she had described to me over the phone, and a wide-brimmed hat with a red ribbon she had referred to as her "Monique Wittig hat." She was pale, exhausted. I gathered her in my arms; she let herself be gathered. In the car I stole incredulous glances at her profile. We held each other tight that night, then fell asleep side-by-side on my sister's bed.

The next morning we went walking in the park, along the river. It was hot and green and sunny. She was jet-lagged. We were both of us shy and wary. She kept saying how big the trees were, how she'd missed trees like this, with big trunks, lush leaves. Out West the vegetation was so scrubby, the ocean so wild and forbidding. Everything on this coast, she said, was so much gentler. "Yes," she was saying "yes" to everything here. All of it was a way of saying yes to me and I knew it.

The talk turned to feminism, how things seemed to be falling apart between women. I had given her my editorial to read that morning. We talked of the fissures, the rifts, this split over pornography being merely the symptom. She said she thought we had to ride them out. We stopped and sat on a park bench with dull green paint peeling off. I was afraid to sit too close to her. She was wearing a beige camisole with a tulip embossed on it. She said that things had to break down so that something else could break through. That there was something beyond these dualisms, the pro and anti camps, the right and wrong, if we could think with our hearts.

And it's you will help me go there, to that place beyond divisions. We will fight together, and we will heal....

We got up from the bench, walked back along the path with the river on our left. Her bare brown shoulder over that linen top. The way she held her body, as if it were a bouquet she were about to give away. I wanted her. She stopped suddenly on the path. When I wheeled around, she said, "I need you." My groin clenched as if the words had hit me there. Words never spoken to me before. Both dreaded and desired. Terror and thrill.

I put my hand on her bare shoulder I circled her waist— again, that uncanny fit—and we headed back, quickening our pace. Into the elevator and up the twelve stories—to the door to the room to the bed. I flung myself on her, my head in her neck, arms all the way around her, my tongue finding her lips, our kissing wet and savage, slobber everywhere, then both of us undressing her, first the camisole, then the shorts, panties, and *this is now everything, the world down there, to climb down over the ridge and into the wet, yes and inside, the folds unending, that the fingers find and feel, "oh please," she says, finding their way down to the tunnel and then thrusting up into her, "oh God God," as she pulls her whole hips up around them....*

"We'd better hang on to our hats," I said to her afterward. "It's going to be a wild ride." And almost instantly the day began proving me right. We headed out for a walk down Broadway and—purest serendipity—ran smack into the gay and lesbian parade. *Like a giant welcoming committee, this festive train winding through the city, colour and music and wildness out in the streets. And we are part of this massive explosion—of love and lust. It catches up with me now, here, in this dancing crowd. That she is here that she has crossed a broad continent for me. She of the long lashes of the Grecian nose. That she wants me. That there is no obstruction here, none. We are floating in the ether of mutual desire, so strong we have to stop at intervals, run our hands all over each other, kiss, and touch, and gaze.*

We stop at a café in the Village for drinks, neither of us is thinking of food, she takes off her sunglasses—no one who looks like this has ever wanted me back—she says, has anyone ever told you you look like Virginia Woolf? and I laugh—it's both absurd and flattering—and can't think what to say, there's no one to compare with her, she is incomparable.

We sit side by side holding hands on the train heading back uptown, too full to speak, and it is endless, this lust, endless and huge, and it finally spills over when we are back in the bed in the room with its view of the river, and it's wild again, wet and wild … until it's her turn to make love to me … and then it is so feeble, my response, I'm ashamed.

Get ready for a wild ride, I had said, and already then I was aware of some dissonance in the remark, some slippage, as I'd barely come at all. It's all just so new, I told myself, so sudden and new. But now here again, after the march, after the magical day, with all this build-up....

She noticed this time, she asked me why. I began to cry. Her hand on my back as I wept. Not asking for words. "Let go that which aches within you," she said, quoting Susan Griffin, "let go the years within you."

Just let go. *That is all she wants for me.* They were suddenly all there, the millions of reasons, all the bitterness with Lena, my friends turning against me. *Go deeper, she is there for you, let yourself drop down.*

"Please, please come home with me." The words forced their way out when I was done with my weeping. I hadn't meant to say them at all.

She smiled, not surprised, exactly, but relieved, deeply relieved. "You want me to stay, then?"

"I want you to stay."

I left the next morning, having realized I needed a few days by myself first. I had to get ready for her. Clean the house. Call Lena, give her some kind of warning.

Helen was happy to stay in the city, she said. She would go to the Met, do some goddess research in the Greek and Egyptian rooms.

But when I walked in the door of my home—afternoon sun streaming in—nothing was the same. The antique plates in the pantry, the pine table in the kitchen, the roses just starting to open outside the barn. Everything was glowing. *Is this what they mean by seeing with the eyes of love?* I wanted her to be seeing all this with her own eyes. I wanted—I wanted very badly—for my life to be seen by her.

At the post office there were two letters waiting for me. One a typed note signed by Lena, her full name typed underneath, requesting that her name be removed from the *Trivia* title page. So much for that phone call. The other one, almost identical, from Nina.

I called Helen right away. She had just returned from the Met. Her afternoon with the goddesses was okay, she said, but... "The light left with you."

"Then come tomorrow!" I said. It was I needing her now, this was not lost on me.

AT THE BUS STATION IN AMHERST we squeezed each other very tight. She said it was almost too much, to be meeting me in the hometown of Emily Dickinson. All the way up she'd been so aware of approaching us both. "Did you know she was an erotic poet?" she asked as we drove north, our hands clasped. And she began to recite: "Wild nights wild nights were I with thee / wild nights would be our luxury ... Rowing in Eden, ah the sea / could I but moor tonight in thee." As she spoke this last line she unclasped her hand from mine and dug it down between my legs, causing fire to rage. I felt giddy with desire and disbelief: before us lay an endless succession of wild nights.

Helen loved my house, all its nooks and crannies and imperfections. The sloping kitchen floor. The peeling wallpaper in the little bedroom upstairs. It took her back to her Georgia childhood, she said; she felt like a Southern girl here. At the kitchen table I showed her the letters from Nina and Lena. She read them silently, then held me while I cried.

Unlike Grace, Helen enjoyed being the object of my desire, indeed basked in it, and my desire, that week, to the best of my recall, was unflagging—even if, as I was beginning to realize, I would probably never abandon myself in bed as she could, and did, every time. And it was bliss all week, waking up beside her in the morning and coming home to her from the typesetters in the afternoon. One day when I came home she had cleaned the curtains and washed the windows. "To let the light in," she said. "It's nice to know everything isn't falling apart."

No one has ever been this good to me. Something is right, for both of us, as it's never been before.

And then the issue was off to the printer, and we were driving to Maine. We wanted to be on the coast again, and there was nothing to keep us in Montague. In Ogunquit, I found my way by memory to the hotel where Grace and I had met Nicole and Marisa four years ago. It was posher than I'd remembered. Bellhops were hoisting garment bags onto dollies at the entrance. But it was only one night—our splurge night. I handed my battered Ford Fiesta over to the valet and we collected our keys. Our balcony looked out over the ocean; we both stepped out and feasted our eyes on the blue infinity. Before dinner we made our way down to the cove and strolled the tiny path that threaded along the cliffs, ecstatic to be by the ocean.

Down in the bar after dinner the piano man is singing "Night and day, you are the one." And she is singing along, loudly, holding me on the beige velvet couch, looking in my eyes "and this torment won't be through" and there is tingling in every part of my body, I have never been so alive, so in love, and the world has never felt so welcoming; together we are taking it all back, traveling outfits, three-star hotels with plush carpeting, canny love songs in elegant piano bars.

The next morning we headed to Old Orchard, both looking forward to a sandy beach and more affordable quarters. We managed to stumble upon an almost entirely deserted old oceanfront hotel there with a grand old '30s lobby. For thirty dollars a night we had a room with a double bed, a pink chintz spread, floral curtains, a washstand and a dresser, and an armchair by the window overlooking sand and ocean grasses and sea. From our bed we could see the ocean and hear it all day and all night. We settled in here: slept deep and long, walked on the beach, got too much sun, ate too much seafood.

One afternoon we came in from the beach to make love. The surf was loud as our bodies thrashed about on the bed. We lay still in each other's arms afterwards and gazed out at the rolling waves, the beachgrass blowing in the wind. Helen picked up the copy of *Woman and Nature* that lay on the bedside table—she'd insisted we bring it along—and read aloud: "Because we know ourselves to be made from this earth. See this grass. The patches of silver and brown. Worn by the wind." As she read the white lines of foam composed themselves over and over again. After a while, it seemed the waves were breaking in me, then tears began to come down, as if they were breaking right there behind my eyes. *Not since Grace,* I thought, remembering that morning by the tree in Leverett, the earth's plates shifting before me, the earth and her body becoming one. The knowledge I had and then lost. *Helen has given it back to me.*

21.
Ordinary Circumstances

Whoever desires what is not gone? No one. The Greeks
were clear on this. They invented eros to express it.
　　　　　　　　—Anne Carson, *Eros the Bittersweet*

HELEN'S LETTERS FROM BERKELEY had evoked a state of delicious timelessness, where one could abandon oneself to contemplating a beetle she encountered on the path as she walked in the hills, or a book of poetry she had already read several times. "This sinking into air and light I do alone" she had called it. Back in my farmhouse in landlocked western Mass, she continued to dwell in that element—and I, to the best of my ability, kept her company there. On sunny days we took walks through the meadow or bike rides along the rich potato fields that bordered the river. I liked sharing my treasures with her: the hidden trail that wound past deep green fields of rye and dense woods down to the river; the secret waterfall at the end of a boulder-lined path. She delighted like a child in the smallest things: the sight of cedar waxwings dipping suddenly to water or the sound of a lone bullfrog in a pond. It seemed she was inclined by temperament to do what I had managed only fleetingly on that Zen retreat, what I understood Buddhist practice trained you to do: live in the moment. When I mentioned this to her one day she said, "Yes, I've had to learn that these last years. The moment has been all I've had."

Whether it was a matter of temperament or necessity, I envied her for it. As the days went by I found myself slipping out of the moment with increasing frequency. I was behind schedule on my dissertation, there was another NEA grant to write, house repairs, letters to be answered. As soon as we returned from a walk I would shut myself up in the office and stay there for long hours. As I worked, I would be dimly aware of her lounging on the couch in the living room, reading poetry books, and occasionally writing a few lines of poetry herself.

Helen and I both rejected the idea of play as something that had to be "earned" by working at arduous, boring tasks. But it seemed I had internalized this idea in a way she never had. "Pleasure is the highest work," she had written in one of her letters, and I saw now that she lived by that credo. She would rise from the couch and, as if propelled by the words she'd been reading, come to me in the office where I was working and read a passage to me out loud with great feeling. Sometimes she would rise up from lovemaking to write poems. Once she had a memory of the two of us together in ancient Greece, where we were both healers.

My own memories after lovemaking tended to be short-term and to involve appliances that needed turning on or off. Helen's continuous, intense presence served only to throw my distractedness into relief. I would feel like a hopeless drudge as I descended the stairs after lovemaking and resumed work on my thesis.

The few times Helen and I drove to Northampton, to shop or have dinner, I was jumpy and tense; my desertion by Lena and our mutual friends was never far from my mind. But also, Helen assured me, it was all the pressures of work and the thesis. I needed time, that was all. Just a day with no plans or worries or goals.

It was full summer now, and mostly hot. We talked of how good it would be to float together on a body of water. One sizzling afternoon we donned our bathing suits, packed an inflatable raft in the car and drove to Cranberry Pond. We were both cheering at the "Dismantle Patriarchy" sticker we spied on the bumper of an old Chevy parked by the side of the road when I realized I knew that car. It belonged to one of Lena's housemates. Sure enough, gazing out at the lake I saw two of the witches sunning out on the raft. There was no question now of launching ourselves into these waters. We both took a quick dip by the shore then got back in the car and headed for home, where we took long cold showers instead.

On August 6, the fortieth anniversary of Hiroshima, we made love in the afternoon, wanting to insinuate some joy into the heavy air. Helen arced and climaxed and cried out and went far, far away. Once again, my response was tame by comparison, pitifully muted. Why couldn't I bring myself fully to the moment? I told myself it was the images I'd seen in the paper that morning of Japanese bomb victims. But more likely it was the letter I'd written to Lena that had come back to me the day before with "Addressee Unknown" written on it in somebody else's handwriting, and which had called up memories of the poisonous letters from Grace I used to find in my postal box. Why, though, I had to wonder, were thoughts of betrayal and loss so much more present for me than was Helen's unwavering love? Why did I find it so hard to go where I loved and where I was loved?

Helen's birthday was two days later. It began with her sitting cross-legged on the living room floor opening presents, beaming like a little girl. Afterwards she put on the record I'd given her, the latest Kay Gardner album, and began to dance. It was a solo dance, a dance of life and celebration, and she was doing it for me, pirouetting about before me in the living room, a stunned, dizzy look in her eyes. From time to time she glanced my way to gauge the effect.

It was not, I was aware, what she hoped for. My eyes were downcast; I could not meet her rapturous gaze. After several turns about the room her face fell, her body collapsed. She stopped the record. "I'm so sorry," I said, and began to cry.

I wanted her to hold me as she'd done before, to let the tears come and with them the words, the true words that would explain it all and exonerate me. I knew what I would say to her this time, I knew exactly where I'd gone in those moments. I was twelve years old, in my father's living room, *Tristan and Isolde* playing at top volume, his body swaying to the music, wanting my body to sway with his, wanting us to be transported together. I was resisting the pull of the music, resisting him and his need with every cell in my body. It was my father, I wanted to tell her, it wasn't you, not you at all. But this time she did not come to me, and did not want me coming to her. I could see it in her face. She had been up so high and I had brought her down so low. She turned and walked away.

We both recovered from the incident, enough to get in my car that evening and drive, as planned, to a French restaurant in Newfane. On the way there, head bowed, Helen murmured, practically under her breath, "I should probably tell you about Sandy."

"Sandy?" My heart began pounding like a piston. The name had not come up before.

Sandy was someone she had been in love with, she continued, her voice growing dreamy, back before Nan. Sometimes she thought he was her soul mate.

"He?" This was a double whammy.

"It's nothing to worry about," she said, backpedaling, possibly in response to the sight of my hand shaking on the steering wheel. "He's not in my life anymore." And then, "Me and my fantasies. How I carry on sometimes." She apologized and reassured me that if ever two souls on earth were mated they were ours. When I pressed her for more about Sandy at dinner she insisted it was not worth discussing; she'd just been reacting to my coolness in the morning.

After dinner, as planned, we drove across the river to New Hampshire and up the winding road between the tall trees to the studio, where Harriet had invited us to spend the night. She literally jumped for joy to see us, and ushered us right up to the loft, which Helen exclaimed felt just like a tree house. Harriet stayed up there with us for hours, perched on the side of the bed, while she and Helen conversed about spirits and goddesses, chirping like tree frogs. As I watched, and listened, all of the wonder that was Helen began to return to me. Our lovemaking that night was wild enough to make up for the dismal morning, or so I hoped, though I must have been aware of something perverse in this sudden return of my lust.

In the weeks that followed, though, the sense of wonder was increasingly hard to sustain. There was a second deposition in early September, and Helen dreaded going back for it. As her departure date approached, she seemed more and more desperate. The more she needed, the less I felt inclined to give. I felt churlish, stingy, like Lily Briscoe when Mr. Ramsay comes bearing down on her with his demand for sympathy and she does nothing but draw her skirts tighter about her. It was my father, I kept telling myself, not Helen, but knowing this didn't seem to make any difference at all.

ON THE DAY HELEN WAS TO DEPART we were informed at the terminal that her flight was overbooked and she'd have to fly out the next day. I don't think I realized until that moment how much I had begun to crave solitude. When Helen, visibly relieved, decided this was a sign she should extend her stay by a week, I was visibly upset. "You're someone who needs a lot of space," she had said to me in Berkeley. Wherever did that woman go?

"I know you're ready to be rid of me," she said in a self-deprecating tone she'd been adopting a lot lately. "But you'll see. This will turn out to be a blessing."

She was right. After two days back home I had to wonder how I had expected to manage without her. The shipment of *Trivia* 7 arrived, all eighty cartons of it, and we went into gear packaging first for bookstores and foreign subscribers, then for bulk mailing. It took us three days working full time to finish the job.

Three days after that, Helen was truly gone. I could not remember ever having woken up as happily with a lover as I did by myself on the futon in the quiet room that morning. I drank in the adventure, the deep restfulness, of this solitude; there was so much I hoped to realize in it, through it. Among other things, my thoughts turned eagerly to Lena, wondering if classes had begun at Harvard and how she liked it there. With Lena, both my friends and my solitude had remained intact. I missed her.

Soon letters began to arrive again, as passionate and poetic as the ones from before, except they now had a history to anchor them. Helen longed for 11 Union Street, she wrote, longed to perform the most menial duties in my house. It grounded her, she said, to take out the compost, to wash the dishes, to package the journal. Here in Berkeley she felt unmoored.

I told myself the time would come when I could respond to the emotion of these letters as well. On the phone I gushed to her about her poetic powers. "You're a writer, Helen, please tell me you're writing."

"I'm writing letters to you," she would say. "Doesn't that count?"

As I went about my daily tasks, I began to find little love notes, one hidden under the pillow on the double bed, another behind the deodorant in the medicine cabinet. Still another spilled out of the rolodex of *Trivia* subscribers. They made me smile, but they did not make me long for her.

Neediness, Dr. J had observed about me, made me freeze, shut down. A survival instinct, he pointed out, as my father's needs were so overwhelming. That instinct seemed to have kicked in now, full force. I began to worry that fall was too soon for Helen to return. In one of our phone calls, I tried to feel her out about it.

"What are you saying?" she asked nervously. "Are you having second thoughts?"

"Not about you, Helen, not at all. It's me. I just think I might need more time."

She took this badly. The deposition had been moved back, she said, to late September. She was determined to hold on till then, but afterwards she would need to get out of town. "Mine are not ordinary circumstances," she stated.

"I know that, Helen," I said. "But I'm trying to look out for us, to do what's best for us and our future."

"There won't *be* any future if you keep on being this ambivalent," she huffed.

I assured her it was caution, not ambivalence. And only days after that phone call, I noticed aloneness had begun to lose its appeal. Harriet was an hour's drive away; Anne was now living at the boarding school where she taught and had a girlfriend who claimed all her spare time. Her withdrawal had been the deathblow to the study group, which had formally disbanded.

I finally called Lena one evening, having gotten her number from Joanne. She was guarded at first, but warmed up as we talked. Harvard was exciting, she said, and went on to enthuse about the great minds in her department. When she announced she was not ready to see me I thought it just as well; what would we actually have to say to each other?

AT SOME POINT IN SEPTEMBER it began to rain incessantly. By the end of it, there was mold on all the bread crusts, doors were sticking, bugs breeding. And I was strangely depleted, with little enthusiasm for *Trivia* or my thesis. I was out on the kitchen porch painting an old rocking chair Lillian had left in the basement—the sun had peeked out for the first time in days—when it suddenly dawned on me: I missed Helen! It was as simple as that. Did I think I could just shrug off this calling we had one to the other? I'd been killing time here on my own. I wanted to be there with her, in the middle of her life. And after that I wanted her home, here, with me. I called and told her all this. Just tell me when and I'll be there, I said.

"You can't imagine how happy this makes me," was her response; almost instantly, energy began coursing through me again. We would spend ten days together in Berkeley, then fly back East in October. She would buy a one-way ticket this time.

"I'll carry you over the threshold!" I proclaimed, my princely impulses returning.

IN BERKELEY, HELEN WAS THE HELEN I had fallen in love with, the Helen of sunlight and vast expanses. She drove us all over town and into the countryside in her Ford Fairlane. The landscape had transformed since my last visit, the hills were cracked and yellow now, and everywhere there was testimony to what she had hinted throughout the summer: nature here was not friendly as it was in the East. At the lighthouse in Point Reyes, signs warned of violent, deceitful riptides. A year and a half ago, Helen told me, she had decided to come here and let herself be sucked away by these tides. That was before she made up her mind to sue. "And before you sailed into my life," she added.

She took me on a tour of all the women's bookstores in the Bay Area—there were two in Berkeley alone. I was curious to see these places I'd been corresponding with and shipping off big packages to. At A Woman's Place, I remembered Maxine's story about the stickers warning women against *Gyn/Ecology.* There were none now, and the women behind the counter, when told them I was *Trivia's* editor, gave me a hero's welcome. From there we drove to Amelia's, San Francisco's fabled lesbian bar, where I had set up a meeting with an avid reader of *Trivia* from Australia, Barbara Walsh, and her partner, Sharon, with whom she had just arrived in the U.S. for a year-long stay. Barbara hoped to spend the last weeks of that time in Montague with me, working on the journal. Both women were lovely and Helen and I had to admit afterwards that, as much as we shrank from defining ourselves as a couple, it was awfully nice to hang out with two such women who did.

But more than any of our excursions, I enjoyed our talks. How could I have forgotten the pleasure of simply talking with Helen? How she went into the depths. How her insight illuminated my life. Mornings we would lie in bed holding each other and telling each other our dreams; she always saw things in mine that I didn't. There seemed to be no end to what we had to say to each other. We spent hours after dinner at the little table in the alcove. Sometimes we projected ourselves into our future together on Union Street, surrounded by friendly countryside, where we would do work, alone and together, that would benefit all women.

Helen had often talked to me of Sunday services at Mama Bears Bookstore—they'd been her lifeline over the past year. They were centred around weekly talks, or "haggles," given by Native writer Paula Gunn Allen; Judy Grahn, her partner, would often read as well. We attended one of these services the Sunday before I left.

Paula's haggle was about the earth; she talked of the earth moving, bucking, and moaning as if she had a lover, and we all knew she was referring to the recent massive earthquake in Mexico. In the end, she said, the earth would survive, but she might have to throw us all off her back to do so. Afterwards, Judy chimed in with her "She Who" poem—"When She Who moves the earth will turn over"—and I felt myself being lifted with the other women in the room into a community of feeling and knowing, just the way it used to happen at the Centre. Someday, I thought, I would leave my life in Montague and come settle in here with Helen for a spell.

On the last day of my stay I had an appointment with Helen's young male hair stylist, an artist *manqué* who chipped away at my head as if it were a sculpture block. The result was artistic but unflattering. We went dancing at Ollie's that night, after packing most of the day. When we got home, exhausted, there was a message on Helen's machine from a "Brad" saying something about a poem and ending with the words "love you." I was in the bathroom obsessing over the ungainliness of my shorn head. At those words, I blanched. At least "Sandy" was in the past. I had been assuming her traffic with men was inactive.

"I'm really sorry," she said. He was a guy she'd met at a bar on a down night. The whole episode was entirely forgettable. She didn't even know how he'd gotten her number. I felt too guilty about my own lapses of feeling to challenge her about this.

THE NEXT DAY HELEN LOOKED unusually elegant in a new beige traveling outfit, and I was proud to be taking her back East with me. It was our first flight together; we held hands during the ascent. Not long after—Helen had just fallen into conversation with the woman on her left, who was from East Africa—an announcement came over the intercom: there'd been a bomb threat and we'd have to make an emergency landing in Denver.

The descent was extremely rocky. The stewardesses buckled themselves up in their fold-down seats and gripped their armrests along with the passengers. I tried saying something to Helen but had lost command of my jaw. She took my hand again and looked deep into my eyes. Then she extended her other hand to the African woman, who grabbed it thankfully. A model of calm, Helen began to explain to her about her African goddesses. And then, with each of her hands in one of ours, she began to pray fervently to Obatallah. Please, she said, if we have work to do on this earth, let us live to do it.

Ten minutes later we had landed without incident. We were held on the tarmac while emergency stairs were wheeled up and dogs and policemen rushed on board. The plane was soon declared bomb-free, but we were all shaken. And I was reeling with this new information about Helen: her composure in the face of death—or her *sang froid,* I didn't know which.

We both recited prayers of thankfulness to Obatallah that night. We had come through this alive, and vowed to make ourselves ready and available for whatever healing work now lay before us.

22.
Praying to Oya

Still the walls do not fall,
I do not know why;
There is zrr-hiss,
Lightning in a not-known,
Unregistered dimension...

—H.D., "The Walls Do Not Fall"

WE RETURNED TO MONTAGUE to find the great silver maple in the front yard lying on its side. An omen, it's clear to me now, and not a good one. A twister had torn a narrow swath through the town, downing several trees. Mine was the only property on our street to be hit but everyone said I was lucky. The tree had come down between the house and the garage, narrowly missing them both.

Even before we unpacked, Helen set up an altar in the big bedroom upstairs and lit a purple candle. She said it was time to pray to Oya, goddess of creation and destruction.

The first three days back in my house there were violent rainstorms every afternoon. Electrical storms that lit up the darkened skies. As soon as we heard claps of thunder, Helen would come get me, and we'd both sit upstairs by her altar with the purple candle burning and listen to the thunder and the wash of rain and wait for the flashes of light. When Oya spoke, she said, you had to pay attention. Otherwise she'd just keep on being dramatic.

During the days after our return I continued to muse about the contrast between Helen's composure during the emergency landing and my own loss of nerve. It was a blow to my princely stature, already shaky thanks to the new haircut—which, no matter how many times I looked in the mirror and from how many angles, was painful to regard. I began to feel undeserving and anxious. Helen had given up a rich life in Berkeley to come live with me here, and I feared I was not equal to it.

The downed tree lay upended in the yard, its base a fan of gnarled roots. Helen found it beautiful, and would sit for hours drawing sketches of it in her notebook. She mourned when the men I hired came to chop it up and then again when others came to remove the pieces. I tried to cheer her up but was bereft myself; the house felt less private now, less protected from the bus garage next door.

That first Sunday we decided to carry on the Mama Bears tradition and have a service in front of the woodstove. Helen improvised a haggle. She thanked the maple for all it had given us while it stood, and for its beautiful roots, and then had us take several minutes of silence to meditate on the space where it used to be. Space, she pointed out, was the medium of possibility. At times like this it seemed to me that Helen was herself a creation goddess.

MONTAGUE WAS AT ITS BEST IN THE FALL: all lushness and colour. On brilliant October afternoons, Helen and I took long walks or bike rides through the orange, rose, and russet leaves, past verdant fields. We took drives into the countryside to buy fresh produce and apple pie and cider. It felt like our very first days here together in June, discovering the simple pleasures of togetherness, along with the beauty of the countryside. Helen had brought her thesis materials with her this time, and on grey days she holed up in the big room upstairs with a typewriter. She was making slow progress, she said, and between this and weekly phone appointments with her new therapist in California, claimed to be feeling stronger all the time.

We had been back less than two weeks when I got a phone call from a friend in Boston. She'd just been to a talk by Andrea Dworkin in Cambridge where FACT women had leafleted the lecture hall. A passage from my editorial referring to the "intolerance" of ordinance supporters had been quoted in the leaflet to support their position. I knew how sensitive Andrea was, and how often she'd been stabbed in the back by women she'd thought of as allies. I could only pray the leaflet hadn't fallen into her hands.

Maybe Jan was right after all: maybe one couldn't afford to try and be balanced, evenhanded, in this debate. Now I had to do damage control. I sent a letter out to all the feminist newspapers and magazines I could think of, explaining the way my remarks had been twisted out of context and reiterating my dismay at the FACT brief and my support for the ordinance. Even as I did so I sensed I'd been sucked into a useless game of us against them.

I might not have felt so defenceless had I had friends around. I was ever grateful for Helen's companionship, but it did not take the place of study group or the kind of energy—"gynergy," as some of us called it—that more and more I understood had to be kindled by *several* women in concert, or at any rate more than just two.

At the end of October, having decided we needed an injection of wild lesbian energy, Helen and I drove to Boston for a Cris Williamson concert. We wandered around Harvard Square for a few hours beforehand, both of us ill at ease being in Lena's territory. On our way to the concert we hit rush hour traffic and in my haste exiting the car I wrenched my ankle; Helen had to support me all the way to the hall.

When I collapsed into my seat, I looked up to see a big banner over the stage proclaiming "A Harry Lipson Presentation." Gazing around, I saw we were surrounded by straight couples. Harry himself introduced the first act, an earnest woman folksinger.

"Where have all the lesbians gone?" I chanted in Helen's ear as the woman strummed out a series of tepid protest songs. Helen laughed and patted my hand and told me not to worry, Cris would turn things around. But when she took the stage, though her songs were beautiful and soulful, there was none of the magic I had always felt in women's music events, starting with that Holly Near concert in New York, that sense of call and response, of collective dreams surging up from the depths. I sat through the show wincing from the pain in my foot and mourning what felt like the end of an era.

In November the world outdoors began to lose its allure, in part because walking was now a chore for me—it had been a bad sprain. As our walks tapered off, so did our lovemaking. This was ominously reminiscent of that first fall with Grace, and I had to wonder if passion was a seasonal phenomenon for me, if it needed to be fed by light and warmth and vegetation. As I hobbled around the house I seemed chained to that abysmal day in Boston, my limp now a symbol of our faltering movement. Assimilation, retrenchment—we were obviously in the throes of it. We were most of us burnt out from working so hard in the margins, with so little reward, and the Harry Lipsons of this world were just biding their time, ready to pounce.

At least we had *Trivia*, Helen and I. We were editing the eighth issue together and we were both excited about it. Helen had decided the journal needed an infusion of life from nonwhite cultures; she'd gotten Paula to send her some haggles, had solicited a chapter from Luisah Teish's new book, *Jambalaya*, and an article about two Chicana artists in the Bay Area. If there was time, she was hoping she could shape her chapter on H.D., which she said she was very close to finishing, into an article.

As the trial date approached, Helen's team ratcheted up the pressure; she was spending lots of time on the phone with her lawyer. At the end of the month, he called to say the courts were jammed and the trial date had been pushed back to the following year, probably spring. Helen was crushed. Now #8 would be out before the trial was over, which meant her name couldn't appear in it. And she decided it would be too risky for her self-esteem, and for our relationship, to go on working for the journal without acknowledgment.

Though rationally this made sense to me, it was also a great blow. *Trivia* had been our political work, our common cause—our "third thing." If not this, what was the work we were here on this earth to do together? For which we'd been given a second chance at life?

In December the demands of the journal—which I was now, once again, editing alone—were endless and consuming, my thesis committee at Brown was losing patience, and application deadlines were looming for two college teaching jobs. There was less and less time left over for the two of us. Despite all my best efforts, I was often irritable, short-tempered. My half hour of morning meditation, which had been a fixture in my life ever since the Zen retreat, felt more and more like a waste of precious time. Most days I would stop before the time was up or skip it altogether.

For her part, Helen complained about the cold. Being part Southerner, she had little resistance to it, and the woodstove was finicky, the house badly insulated, without even a bathtub to soak in. One evening we drove down to Northampton for a talk by JoAnn Loulan. Neither of us were fans of her bestselling self-help books on lesbian sex. Read a pop psych book about lesbian passion when you could be reading Audre Lorde or Olga Broumas or Monique Wittig? But we were both pretty desperate by now. More and more, when it was time to be alone with her, when it was just her naked body against mine, I would reach inside myself and find nothing there. Sometimes as I lay there glumly Helen would hold me, have me cry and let it out, and my love would start to return. But it didn't seem right for her to be comforting me for not being able to feel anything for her, and lately I thought I sensed resentment building in her not far from the surface.

Loulan talked a lot that night about woman hatred and homophobia. No wonder women have a hard time loving ourselves and each other physically, she said. We live in bodies we're taught to hate, in a culture that hates women. When she asked us to cradle our hated, loveable selves, many women broke down and wept. Helen and I, both allergic to this kind of talk, turned to each other and rolled our eyes. But I had to wonder: was Loulan right? At least about the bodies-we're-taught-to-hate part?

One December afternoon we both finished a good chunk of work and decided to take ourselves to East Heaven Hot Tubs in Northampton to celebrate. The place had been our salvation throughout the fall. With the steam and heat our bodies would start to come alive; before the half hour was up our hands were usually all over each other and we were generating our own heat. But this time I felt nothing, not even a mild stirring. We sat side by side in our white bodies, our backs against the wall of the tub, damp hair plastered to our scalps. Our hated, loveable selves, I thought, trying to summon compassion for myself, for us.

There was shame in not being able to summon desire for the one you loved. There was failure. And by now it was familiar, having happened before with Kaye and again with Grace. That it was happening now again with Helen seemed designed to drive home some lesson—but what? Rejection, it seemed in this moment, would be a welcome relief from this torture.

JUST DAYS LATER, HELEN RECEIVED A CALL from her department chair: could she come teach a modern poetry course spring semester? Deliverance for us both, though it took us a full day of anguished discussion to come around to accepting it as such. Helen arranged for her subletters to leave in January and booked a flight back.

This time she did not seem the least bit sorry to be leaving. I thought it was sort of understandable. It had been bitter cold and the fire in the woodstove kept going out; we had to wear layers and sometimes cover ourselves with blankets. I found no love notes scattered about the house when I returned from the airport. She didn't call on arrival as she'd always done before, and when I called her she sounded distracted.

Two days later I called again, and it began to come out. She no longer had the feelings of a lover for me. In fact, she didn't have sexual feelings for any woman anymore and didn't know how she could go on as a lesbian. It was too difficult, too exhausting. She wanted stability, possibly marriage. I grabbed my cigarettes and lit up with shaking fingers. Why don't you marry me? I said, only half ironically. She laughed bitterly. My stomach began to clench.

I called Harriet. Having been a fool for love herself, she had a deep understanding of its workings. She needs to hear how you feel, said Harriet, I don't think she knows how much you love her.

So I called again, tried to tell her. Her voice was hard. She told me what it was like in the fall living with someone who was always too busy to make love. Did I have any idea how seldom that was? She had kept a record in her journal. Was it in response to her desiring me? No! No! I protested, but I couldn't give her a reason that made sense. Under the circumstances, she said, how could she allow herself to desire me again?

A letter arrived later that week. Telling me not to hope, telling me she had definite ideas of "leaving lesbianism," and I should not plan on coming anytime soon. When I called her, around midnight, she told me: She already did have feelings for someone. A man. She wouldn't say who he was or how she'd met him, but she insisted they had a deep spiritual connection—so deep that gender was irrelevant.

Now the knife went in, deep. I'd run out of cigarettes midway through our conversation and the MiniMart was closed. In what felt like a grotesque twist on my Doris Day dream, I went out to my car and rummaged around in the ashtray for a butt, without success. I didn't sleep at all that night.

23.
Cassandra

O that our human pain could here have ending!
— Virginia Woolf, *Between the Acts*

Like ants we walk into every fire. Every water. Every river of blood. Simply in order not to have to see. To see what, then? Ourselves.

— Christa Wolf, *Cassandra*

TO BE CAST OUT from the tender place of heart-bondedness, to be in freefall, flailing, entrails feeding on something not this, some matter from early childhood that keeps them red and raw and roiling. To be eaten up by it, this all-too-human pain ... even as the other torment—of not feeling—loosens its grip.

In the first months of the new year, in a state of acute longing, I set to work on the last chapter of my dissertation. I spent most of my days in the Amherst College Library deep inside Christa Wolf's *Cassandra* and Virginia Woolf's *Between the Acts*—both novels of unblinkered vision, novels that saw how far Western culture had advanced in its lethal course, how patriarchal thought and behaviour now threatened all sentient life on earth. What slim hope they held out was to be found in bonds—for the most part, nonsexual ones—between women.

I felt no separation from what I was writing. Every word I wrote was real, sometimes terrifyingly real. It was as if I had entered Helen, were experiencing her state of extremity: the stress of the lawsuit, the pain of her mother's depression, the lingering effects of her stepfather's abuse. The desperate need for some grounding somewhere, anywhere. She was Polyxena, Cassandra's beautiful younger sister, who, as the war begins to rage around them, becomes the palace prostitute, offering herself to every man with the gold or the clout to buy her love. I, in contrast, was Cassandra—a Daddy's girl, protected from what Helen came to know in her bones: the terror of being a woman in patriarchy.

IN JANUARY, NO DOUBT HAVING GOTTEN WIND of Helen's departure, Lena announced she was ready to see me. We spent a weekend together in her attic apartment, talking, smoking cigarettes, drinking lots of wine, reveling in each other's company. The old irreverence bubbled up between us again, taking us both by surprise, along with a seemingly imperturbable ease and harmony. Her earlier veneration for her Harvard professors, I was relieved to note, had now been tempered by a healthy dose of skepticism.

Sunday morning we got up late and walked to Inman Square where we took over a booth at the S&S, the *Times* spread out between us. There Lena finally asked me about Helen, and listened gravely as I filled her in on the latest developments. She told me to be careful, to protect myself.

There is this. There is friendship.

Helen's calls became more frequent as the settlement conference approached. The man was never mentioned now, and I wondered if he had withdrawn. Mostly she told me how tired she was. And how stressed. One night she called to say she had come to the realization she had to gather her strength. Every ounce of energy now had to go into herself. Every ounce of care. Please Lise please, she said, just be my friend.

I considered Helen's life, the terror she knew from which I'd been protected, the fragility that had driven her toward that abusive shrink and was now driving her toward men. I considered my own privilege, and the blessings that had come into my life of late. My thesis was finally coming together; I was making exciting discoveries as I neared the end, working in a white heat, turning out several pages a day. Lena was back in my life. And help had arrived for *Trivia*: a young writer and graphic artist who had showed up for a bulk mailing shortly after Helen's departure, brimming with energy and competence. Brett was now in charge of production and was turning out to be a crack editor as well. In light of all this, it should be possible to give Helen what she wanted, to be her friend.

"I'm here," I told her, feeling generous and compassionate, "I'm here."

We began talking on the phone every night, I trying to shore her up as best I could. As the days warmed up, snow melting off, light flooding the sky, we drew close again.

One March evening I began rereading her letters and was suddenly ambushed by fierce longing, lust. She was there again, in all her power and wonder. If only she would let me, I felt, I could love her now as she'd once loved me.

IN APRIL 1986, THE REACTOR MELTED down in Chernobyl, sending a giant radioactive cloud over Europe. The accident made me feel bound to Helen as never before. Life on this planet was now visibly threatened by the exhaust fumes of patriarchy; Bhopal and Three Mile Island had been mere rehearsals. And Helen was my partner in this precious, endangered world.

I said some of this to her on the phone when we talked in the days after the disaster. She said she missed me, did I think I could come see her.

I asked her—it took all my courage—"What if I come and want to make love?"

"That's fine," she said. "As long as you don't expect me not to have other lovers, before or after."

"Oh," I said, the wind rushing out of my sails. "Well in that case I don't think I'll want to make love."

"You certainly are possessive," she said.

There went my generosity. My compassion. My desire to fly across the continent to be with her.

She apologized. She was afraid the shrink had damaged her forever, she said, she just couldn't trust women. "Fucking asshole," she muttered, and we shared a moment of rage at the shrink. At least we were complicit about something.

24.
Nothing Is Foreseen

*Nothing is foreseen, for we do not know what becomes
of the image of the state of the world
when the patience of mouths lays being bare*
  —Nicole Brossard, "*Sous la langue* / Under Tongue"

EVER SINCE JANE AND ZOEY'S VISIT to Leverett five years earlier, when the old farmhouse swelled to bursting with the music of friends reciting poems and weaving strands of thought in passionate conversation, I had dreamt of living in a house filled with women I loved. Each woman would have her own room, where she would spend the day absorbed in her work—creative work, work for women, work that sustained us all.

For a few weeks in late summer of '86 that dream edged close to fulfillment. Teddy, my architect friend, was putting up a deck over the marshy area in the back of the house and had moved into the big bedroom upstairs. In the little room with the futon was Barbara Walsh, the Australian woman Helen and I had met at Amelia's. Barbara had parted from her lover to spend the last month of her American tour in my old farmhouse in Massachusetts—in "radical feminist heaven" as she put it— helping out with *Trivia* #9. And on weekends, Brett drove up from Northampton and took over the third bedroom upstairs.

Talk would begin kindling between me and Brett, stationed at the kitchen table with beer, a bowl of chips and a stack of manuscripts. Talk stoked by the material in that stack, or, just as often, by what was missing from it. It was only a matter of time before Barbara would come downstairs, and soon the three of us would be lighting cigarettes and conversing feverishly around the table. Often Teddy would drop her sawing and hammering to join in.

Each of us brought her own shit-kicking ideas to the table. Barbara, who had five children back in Australia, was hard at work on a radical critique of traditional motherhood. And Teddy had just finished a thesis on Pueblo architecture and Wittig's *The Lesbian Body;* she'd been feeding us little bits on her work breaks. Like indigenous dwellings, went her argument, Wittig's writing inspired us to imagine ourselves outside of the built world with its divisions between inside and outside, private and public, human and nature.

I was full of the possibilities of lesbian writing myself, having just returned from the Second International Feminist Book Fair in Oslo, which ended with an evening of lesbian erotic readings in five different languages. With great relish I recapped the highlights of that evening for my housemates: Daphne Marlatt and Betsy Warland, two tall, radiant Canadian poets taking turns reading poems about their lovemaking on a train moving through the Australian outback, their bodies echoing the wild landscape (Barbara, who knew the outback, was enthralled). Nicole Brossard bringing the house down at the end with her long poem "*Sous la langue* / Under Tongue" in which a lover's mouth approaches the body she desires, launching her into the unknown.

One weekend in August, Brett and I sat across from each other at the kitchen table with the galleys for Sonia Johnson's latest book, *Going out of Our Minds*, between us. I had wrangled them from her at a conference in Amherst where she'd spoken the day before, hoping to find an excerpt for this issue. In it, Johnson argued it was time to rethink our ideas about political action. Our habitual modes of protest weren't working; in fact, if the state of the world was any evidence, they actually served to fortify what we were trying to resist. Like Mary Daly's spider in freefall, she insisted, we needed to launch ourselves into space, trusting our own powers of reinvention. And to do that, we needed to go out of our patriarchal minds.

Brett hadn't looked at the galleys yet, but on the basis of what

I'd told her of the book, she was wary. Was Sonia suggesting we should just leave abusers of power, violators of human rights and freedoms, to their own devices? Allow the powerless, the marginalized, the voiceless, to get mowed under? Barbara and Teddy—who had made excuses to join us at the table and were sneaking peeks at the galleys as we spoke—now looked expectantly my way.

I reminded them that it had been less than four months since the Chernobyl plant had sent a giant nuclear cloud into the atmosphere. In Bavaria, where I'd spent time after the Book Fair, I'd heard grim tales of fruits and vegetables in gardens and fields now unsafe to eat, of women fearing for their unborn children. In the short run, I was sure Sonia would say, yes, we needed to go on resisting oppressive forces as we've always done. But given that the insanity out there was intensifying, was there any doubt that new modes of thought and new forms of action were called for?

"I'm all for going out of our patriarchal minds," Barbara said. "But how do we *do* that?" A Taurus, she always wanted practical explanations.

"We already *are* doing it," said Brett. "Just by living in a lesbian body."

"That is," I said, "if you haven't jumped on the lesbian mother bandwagon."

"Well, but maybe they're doing motherhood differently," Brett argued.

"If they ever read my book they damn sure will!" Barbara said.

"And if they ever read *The Lesbian Body*," Teddy said, "they'll get a taste of what they're missing."

"The fact is," Brett said, "the lesbian body can go places no other body can."

"Well you should know," I said, and Teddy, Barbara, and I all had a good laugh. Brett had something of a reputation with the women.

Brett grinned but brought us back to her point. All four of us, she insisted, were already going out of our patriarchal minds, just by virtue of what we were doing with our lesbian bodies; we were creating new forms, imagining other ways to be in the world.

This felt right to me, and the deck seemed a small but significant case in point: Teddy had built it with boards of uneven length, molding it to the contours of the marsh, with a small set of curving steps that connected it to the sloping ground in back. The effect was not only aesthetically pleasing, it felt as if some rightful order had been restored. For the first time since I'd moved in, the house seemed to be in relationship to its natural surroundings.

THE AFTERNOON TEDDY FINISHED laying out the planks on the deck, a friend arrived at the door with Sonia herself in tow. We had all of us been outside watching Teddy work her magic. Now we moved indoors and hovered around Sonia in the kitchen, sharing with her some of the thoughts that had spun off from her book. Did she agree with us, we wanted to know, about lesbian bodies? And what would it take for us to really go out of our patriarchal minds? Especially when so many forces, some of them coming from lesbians, seemed to be conspiring to keep us locked inside of them? Soon ideas, exclamations, epiphanies were ripping back and forth across the table. Once we'd all quieted down, the deck beckoned. It was a sparkling August day; we all perched in a row on the pale pine planks, our legs dangling over the side. There was nothing between us and the trees, which were resplendent in the late-afternoon sun.

When I look back on this moment, I can see it was historic, rich in symbolism. This new extension of the house thrust us all right to the edge of the marsh—and the great feminist explorer Sonia Johnson was sitting on this edge right alongside us. In many ways, it was a moment such as I could not have dared to dream. It was a moment that should have filled me with resounding joy.

Yet joy was not what I was feeling in that moment, or indeed in any of the moments that led up to it. Excitement, yes, and an awareness that important events were swirling about me. But for the most part, it was all background noise. Helen was in New York, taking acting classes and living with a man; my every other thought was of her. When she called, as she had that morning, everything else dropped away. Sonia came, Sonia went, the conversations around the table resumed, fed by the sensation of her visit, but I was not really there for any of it.

It wasn't so much the man; I knew Helen just needed his support and attention—or, more likely, his apartment, which was in the Village. She had flown east again in July, once the settlement conference was over, and moved in with me for a week. Unexpectedly, there had been balm in our togetherness again, and bliss. I'd hoped she would decide to stay on but it turned out she had other plans. The theatre was calling her, she said, and as it happened she had a place to stay in the city.

Some of the calls were more encouraging than others. As soon as they ended my housemates would surround me, bring me a glass of wine, console me if she'd been discouraging, cheer if she'd given me hope. Sometimes Barbara would rub my tense shoulders. When I decided to drive down to see Helen one sweltering day, not long after Sonia's visit, they stood in the driveway, waving goodbye, wishing me luck. Barbara especially had urged me to go, saying I had to confront her, get to the bottom of things. "Don't forget your reality," were her parting words.

I MET HER AT HIS APARTMENT—he was away. An undistinguished little place, I was relieved to note. Still, it was painful to see her sneakers lined up beside his. We ate at an Italian restaurant on the corner. It was crowded and overpriced and I had no appetite.

Her life was going well, she insisted. She'd had an interview with Uta Hagen, who could tell instantly she was right for her class. "It's about time," I said, trying to be supportive.

My sister's apartment happened to be vacant again, and we moved there that night. Three days later, Helen's case was settled. It was the day of the NEA grant deadline—I'd been at work on the budget all day long—and we'd just returned from the post office when the call came in. From Helen's face, which flushed in a way I'd never seen before, I knew the victory had been a big one. When she got off the phone she fell to her knees and did prostrations to Obatallah, then rose laughing and crying and screaming so loud I worried about the neighbours. The figure was more than they'd asked for, she said once she'd calmed down. I tried to throw my arms around her but she motioned me away.

I took off for a walk along the river and when I came back she apologized. It was overwhelming, she said, but she hoped I knew that she needed me, that she couldn't have done this without me.

We found a good Greek restaurant nearby where we drank lots of retsina and Helen made a long toast, citing everyone who had ever given her support during her ordeal. Over the moussaka, she said it was finally sinking in that she was going to be able to afford to go to Greece now.

"What about 'we'?" I said feebly. "Weren't we going to go together?"

The irritated look returned. "Lise, can't we just celebrate and be light, for once? A night like this comes around only once in a lifetime...."

I turned my attention to the half-eaten spanakopita on my plate, which now I didn't feel like finishing. I was suddenly exhausted from so much excitement and so little sleep. My face must have fallen.

"It was a fantasy," she said then, reaching for my hand under the table. "Don't take me so seriously."

TT HAD NOT BEEN AN ESPECIALLY promising visit; still, at some point that last evening, Helen had hinted that she might want to come visit soon, and I found myself on the drive back calculating how long it would take Teddy to finish with the deck and wondering if Barbara could be persuaded to leave a bit earlier than planned. I wanted the house cleared of my friends so I could be alone with her there. On some level I must have been aware of the irony: a year ago I'd had her all to myself in the house for weeks at a time and then all I could think of was how I longed to fill it up with my friends.

It was good to have Teddy and Margaret to pour my heart out to when I got home. They fussed over me, gave me strict orders to rest and eat square meals. But Barbara also picked up on my need for solitude, and by the end of the week she had packed up and left. Teddy had business in Cambridge and left around the same time.

Our goodbyes were tearful—Barbara would be back home in Australia within the week—but I was glad to have the house to myself again and began to prepare for Helen's visit. I imagined us taking my raft out to Cranberry Pond, or Lake Wyola, where we would float on the water and be in the moment together again at last.

Helen never did make it back to Montague that summer. She was busy with her acting classes in New York. She didn't give me any details, just said she had realized she needed to think of herself as "a hothouse flower," to provide herself with the particular conditions she needed to flourish. "Like a man with an apartment?" it was all I could do not to say.

25.
Being Laid Bare

Let's break the rhythm and forget the rhyme. And calmly consider ourselves. Ourselves.
　　　　　　　　—Virginia Woolf, *Between the Acts*

ON A BLUSTERY DAY IN FEBRUARY OF '87, the thesis was finally done. I drove to Amherst to get it xeroxed and, after mailing the copies off to my committee, took myself to Northampton to celebrate. Wandering about Thorne's Market, checking out music tapes, I expected relief to hit any moment. Instead, scouring the racks in Country Comfort across the street—I needed a shirt for the defence—it was all I could do to hold myself up. Either I was more exhausted than I'd realized or this is what the thesis had been holding at bay. Probably both. One fact proclaimed itself to me, with a kind of dull irrefutability: I was alone. And lonely.

In the fall, Helen had begun making weekend visits to Montague. Theatre was losing its appeal. She missed nature, missed our life together. After some initial wariness I welcomed her back, to my home, to my bed. I knew my friends would not understand—I could barely understand myself—and scolding voices kept cutting in on our togetherness, but they couldn't overpower the balm of walking with her in the woods, of her body beside me in bed, of her telling me this was her home after all, right here with me, and how could she have ever imagined differently. When she began angling to move back in, though, I balked, which enraged her. In the end, she decided to move to Cambridge instead.

Cambridge seemed to me a healthy compromise: it would give us the space we both needed. Boston was close, and rich in feminist culture. I imagined weekends together, her little Cambridge room a launching pad from which we would take off into the city to see films, to attend concerts and talks.

But once Helen settled in—I had driven her there on New Year's Eve, my hatchback stuffed with her belongings—she seemed to have no time for me. There was a sunny, self-sufficient tone in her voice whenever I called. When I remarked on it she said she was finally writing; it was pouring out faster than she could get it down.

Perhaps I should have been clued in by the phone call that came shortly after her move. Did I have any expectations at this point, she wanted to know. No, none, I said—idiotically. "Okay," she said, audibly relieved. "That's clear enough."

I knew from Lena the two of them had become buddies. I knew Helen had time for *her*. I made the mistake of calling Lena (she was my *friend*, wasn't she?) to ask why Helen didn't want to see me. "Maybe you should be asking yourself that question," she said. I hadn't been able to accept Helen's love when it was offered. Why did I want it now, when it wasn't?

I could definitely see her point—but it was like running into cement when I'd expected something more like flesh. Lena had supported me for standing firm about Helen moving in. Now here she was, taking on Helen's perceptions. What sort of complicity had grown up between them? One that ruled me out, evidently.

ON A TUESDAY MORNING IN MARCH, I drive to Providence to defend my dissertation. I've already prepared myself for the fact that my friends won't be there to support me. Anne is off on a wilderness trip and Teddy is redesigning a loft in New York. I planned to invite Lena, but thought better of it after that call.

Surprisingly, there's a small crowd gathered in the Tudor Room when I arrive. In addition to the three members of my committee, there are two or three professors from the Comp Lit Department, and a handful of graduate students.

My readers are all visibly pleased. Their questions are mostly supportive, designed to set me up. The first one—from my director, Naomi Schor—regards the way the distinction between "female," "feminist," and "lesbian" tends to blur throughout the thesis. Can I explain why? I run with this question, which allows me to talk about the lesbian as outsider, generating revolutionary vision. "Lesbian," I say, "is for me as much a moral and political as it is a sexual orientation." There is lots of nodding among my listeners. They feel included now, and continue to nod throughout the session.

Only the last question catches me off guard. It too comes from Naomi. "If you were writing it now," she asks, "would you write it any differently?"

It's probably a standard question to put to someone who's taken five years to finish, but I can't help feeling she's guessed something about my life. Thrown as I am, it doesn't occur to me to be anything but honest.

"As a matter of fact," I say, "when I returned to the first chapter to do the final revision, it seemed to have been written by a different person."

"How different?" she presses.

"More idealistic," I say.

One of the graduate students—she looks like a dyke—wants to know, as if I haven't already exposed myself enough, "In what way?"

I notice a change in the atmosphere: a tightening of focus, a palpable suspense. Academic discourse has been temporarily interrupted by ... reality.

"In terms of what is possible between women," I say finally. "Of what is made possible by love between women." It's more than I ever meant to say in this company. And I can almost hear them all taking in the words on their tongues, savouring them like a tasty *hors d'oeuvre*. I hasten to add that in no way have I rejected radical feminist vision, that my idealism has been tempered, not destroyed. But the words are out.

In my alarm at the realization I've just betrayed my own movement to an Ivy League dissertation committee, I barely hear the closing remarks of my readers, each of whom is paying me a compliment. There is a round of congratulations, after which I'm surrounded. Is it just my imagination or is there, alongside the hearty praise, a barely detectable layer of condolence? No doubt my confession has made me sound mildly defeated.

I tell myself it was only one moment. And before that I did convey the vision, and well. What's more, I'm now, at age thirty-six, the official bearer of a PhD. Yet I feel neither proud nor relieved. *If only I had a friend here,* I can't help thinking. Someone to go back over the whole event with, over drinks or even coffee. Luckily, I've been prescient enough to schedule an afternoon appointment with a psychic who lives in Rockport, just up the coast. She comes highly recommended by friends I trust. And it's become blindingly clear I could use some guidance right now.

I go back over all details of the defence by myself as I drive up the coast. All in all I feel I turned in a good performance, even if I was too confessional at the end. An ex-professor of mine came up to me afterwards to tell me how impressed he was, how "professional" my talk had been. I realize if I'd stayed at Brown I could have been getting this kind of stroking on a regular basis. And, no doubt, would have had a large circle of friends to support me through the event and take me out for drinks when it was over. *It's just possible,* it occurs to me, *that I've made all the wrong choices in my life.*

LOUISA POOLE'S RAMSHACKLE HOUSE sits on a suburban street. She has a gnomish look about her, a deep voice, and a strong Boston accent. She offers me a cup of coffee and lights herself a cigarette. "You don't mind, do you?" she asks once it's already lit. "This is not an easy time for you," she continues. She's already done my numerology chart.

It's all I can do not to start sobbing. She points to the Kleenex box on the shelf behind me. "There's a lot of drama swirling around you right now." She starts drawing tarot cards. "And one person in particular seems to be stirring the pot. Any idea who that might be?"

I nod.

"Good. Now, in relation to this person you're—well, look"— she shows me the card—"you're the hanged man. You're bound and gagged, you can't practice your craft."

I tell her I've hardly been prevented from functioning; I've just got done defending my dissertation.

"Congratulations," she says. "You must feel pretty proud of yourself right now." Smart woman, this Louisa Poole.

"Yes," I say. "But…"

"But?"

"Well, I can't say I'm very happy." In just about every other arena, I admit, I have felt maybe not "bound and gagged" but constrained, blocked, checkmated.

She nods in the direction of the cigarette dispenser on her desk. I've been eying it for a while now. I grab a king-size Salem, mentholated, light it, and drag hard.

"You're suffering a lot now," she says. "But it won't be forever." She tells me I'm someone with lots of dreams—not pie-in-the-sky dreams but practical, realizable dreams. "Someday," she tells me before the session is over, "you'll attract the kind of people that can really help to make your dreams come true."

This should be encouraging but all I can think is if Helen wasn't such a person, then who in the world possibly could be?

AFTER THE READING I DRIVE TO Crane Beach and walk the long shoreline. It's balmy; the big sky is veiled in gauzy clouds. Only a few strollers on the beach, all of them in pairs. The last time I was here I was with Grace and Maxine. What I wouldn't give to have Grace beside me just now, to be listened to with that attentiveness of hers. *Hell, I'd take just about any attentive presence right now.* Or, failing that, just someone to walk beside.

I drive to Woodman's for fried clams—the traditional way to cap an expedition to Crane Beach. Over dinner I consider the fact that Boston is on my way home. Maybe I could call Lena and explain that I'm driving through town, offer to take her out for a celebratory drink. Midway through the meal I get up and call from the phone booth outside.

Lena seems surprised to hear my voice. Says she's in the middle of a paper that's due tomorrow. Doesn't ask what I'm doing by the ocean. I muster a breezy goodbye—there's no way to bring up the defence without sounding pathetic—and return to my fries and clams, half of which I end up bagging.

I drive back home to Montague playing the tape of my session with Louisa. Comforted by the deep, warm voice, the Boston "r's." There is no way to make sense of what's happening around me now, she says. I shouldn't even try. Instead I have to find a way to get some perspective on all this drama, to rise above it. "Are you planning any trips any time soon?" No, I say. "You have the chart of a world traveler. And you're not doing enough of it. You need to go somewhere where there's ancient history. Explore space and time."

I DECIDE TO TAKE A TRIP down to my sister's place in New York. Not the world, but it's a start. I take a stack of *Trivia* manuscripts with me, call friends, spend many hours on the giant bed surfing channels with the remote.

On my last day there, Teddy drops by, takes me to the loft she's been working on only several blocks away. I follow her up a steep red spiral staircase. The space is small but light-filled, with a sweeping view down Broadway. I'm standing at the window taking it in when she mentions offhandedly that she saw Helen in Boston just a week ago. She was "really engaging," she says. They had a great time.

I freeze. If Teddy notices, she doesn't let on. She tells me Helen has been writing her letters, wants to come visit her here. "That's cool with you, isn't it?" she says finally, as I turn to face her. "You and she are history now, right?"

"If that's what she told you then, yes, I guess we are," I say, though my tone is anything but cool. I realize she's testing the waters.

Teddy wants me to stay and tell her more. I make up an excuse and shoot down the steep stairs as fast as I can. Within an hour am in my car driving north, this new information pumping violently through my blood.

I learn something unsettling about myself in the days that follow. Arousal occurs independently of love. Because some days, now, I hate her. She has driven a wedge between me and Lena. She has reeled in Teddy as well. She's been sleazy and selfish and utterly without honour. Yet this does not prevent me from wanting her, and on some days wanting her with even more vehemence than I ever did before. Phrases from her first letters drift back to me and I wonder if I have poisoned that pure stream of passion forever, whether anyone will ever love me with such poetic ferocity again.

IN APRIL, BOTH HELEN AND I HAVE SLOTS to speak in a feminist lecture series in Cambridge. This didn't seem a problem when we both signed on earlier this year. Now I'm having serious doubts.

I'll be talking about the writers in my thesis. "Getting Man off Your Eyeball" is my clever title, lifted from a speech Celie makes to Shug in *The Color Purple*. But "man" is not my problem. I can't even remember a time when he was. Helen is my problem. I know she will come. She will come and she'll stare at me through the whole talk and I'll think of her and Teddy in bed and will lose it in front of everyone.

And Lena is my problem. I call the day before the talk to ask will she be there and can I spend the night afterwards. At first she says yes. Then she calls back a few hours later to say no. She can't get involved, she says.

"Involved?" I say. "I just need a place to crash." (*Not true, I need to know you're still my friend.*)

Obviously she's spoken to Helen between calls. Checkmated. Again.

The afternoon of my talk Anne finds me on my knees on a prayer bench in my little room upstairs. I've lit candles and am praying. "I don't know how I can get through it alone," I say looking up at her, my face wet with tears.

"You don't have to!" she says and takes me in her arms. "I'm coming with you."

We drive to Boston in her car. I tell her Helen will be there and it won't be as a sympathetic listener. Lena has made me sure of that. Anne tells me not to worry. If necessary she'll surround me with a protective shield. Already I feel protected by her.

A BIG CROWD IS MILLING ABOUT INSIDE the hall when we arrive. Right away I see her, sitting stock straight in the front row, a resplendent presence in royal blue. And—this is a shock—she's chopped her hair off. It stands out in spikes around her head. She looks strong. Hard and strong, like the revolutionary guerrilla fighter she always said she wanted to be.

I ask for a glass of water. My jaw has sprung free from its

moorings. They can't find any glasses and give me a can of soda instead. I take the stage trying to look past Helen, but she's hard to ignore. There appear to be doting young women on either side of her. "Victorious"—Louisa Poole's word—attaches itself to her and sticks. As I begin to speak, I manage to reduce her to a tiny blue speck by focusing on Anne's tall figure on the other side of the hall. My mouth is sticky from the soda but I soldier on. At some point I begin to enter the world of my writers, and not long after everyone in the room falls away. Before I know it, it's over and people are applauding.

She's the first one up on the stage, beaming a big, phony smile at me. "That was great," she pronounces, without a trace of sincerity, then walks off. Cementing her victory.

Now Anne is by my side, giving me a hug. Over her shoulder I watch Helen make off with her friends. I want to run after her. I want to stalk her. I want to shake her big, shorn head till her eyes rattle. I actually start off in her direction but Anne reins me in. She gathers me up and herds me into her car and then we're driving back the way we came, heading home.

Once we're on our way I thank her for saving me again— twice in one day. "Did I blow it completely?" I ask. She tells me no, no, I was good, I was fine. I decide to believe her.

IN JUST TWO WEEKS IT'S HELEN'S TURN. "We Bring Violets" is her title—a nod to H.D. and her poem "Sea Anemones." At first I think I won't go, in the name of "taking care of myself." Then I decide I need to go, that whatever actually transpires will be no match for what my imagination is already conjuring up. So I go. I sit by myself in the back. Am pleased to note there is no sign of Lena in the hall.

Her aura is softer today. Her haircut has calmed down a bit and she's wearing muted colours. Her subject is our sadomasochistic culture and how, as lesbians, we can rise above it. Something about meeting violence with violets. I fall into a sort of appalled trance out of which I'm jolted several minutes later by familiar words: she's reciting memories of herself as a healer in Egypt. Memories, she explains, that came to her after lovemaking with "a sacred sister." *How dare she raid our intimacy in this way?*

When she finishes there is loud applause. A throng of admirers presses close. I should just walk out and drive home now, but I don't.

I accompany Helen and her swarm of fans to the Sheraton Commander for drinks. How did she attract such a following in such a short time? I sit across from her and make distracted conversation with the women on either side of me. Afterwards I end up following her home, carrying her tape deck.

On the corner of Brattle and Willard, just a block from her place, I finally unload. "So ... now I'm your 'sacred sister.' Just what is a sacred sister? Someone whose friends you feel entitled to fuck?"

"Don't you dare start judging me. Just because you don't know how to hold on to your friends."

"It's cheap. It's so incredibly cheap." I hand her the tape deck and stomp off to my car.

"Aristocratic bitch," she yells from down the street.

I end up driving a loop that winds back around to her place, parking in front, and knocking on the door. Asking to be let in. "I don't want to leave it that way," I say, pushing my way in.

"Do you see what you're doing? Just assuming you have the right to walk in here like this?"

"Do you really want to talk about who's invading whose territory?"

"Look, if you're coming here to judge me I want you out right now. Do you want to try and have a real conversation? Do you want to try and understand?"

I say yes. She leads me inside, takes my jacket. The apartment is tiny. I grab a chair from the kitchen and set it down beside the twin bed where she's seated. She begins to talk about power. My power, of which I am entirely unconscious. My barging in this way being a good example. Why can't I allow her to have just one whole night to celebrate? To feel good about herself? Her voice starts to break.

It's exactly what I did the night of the settlement, she continues. Brought her down in her moment of triumph. Maybe I just can't stand to see her happy. "You'd rather see me like this," she says, collapsing on her bed, and now the strong revolutionary guerilla fighter is gone and in her place is fragile, tormented Polyxena. "Tonight I felt maybe I'd broken through, I thought for a moment maybe it was all starting to come together. And now look at me, I feel like a piece of shit. Why do you do this to me?" She gives herself over to weeping.

And I ... go over to the bed and put my arms around her. I say I'm sorry. I try and comfort her.

It's the touch that does it, to both of us. It's electrical, alive with possibility—it will take us both to where we want to be. She will feel better about herself, and I ... will be delivered from this hatred, this rage, this fear. The touch will take us there.

We clasp each other on her bed. I begin to stroke her arm.

She says she's afraid. She says she's needed touch so much.

This makes me want to touch her like crazy. And I do. The gateway yawns.

She tells me her body is terrified. "Why terrified?"

"Because of how it responds to you."

Finally, I think, some truth. The truth I've been waiting for.

She can't allow herself to feel that way again, she says. All torn up and needy and begging. "And you hate me when I'm like that, remember?"

I do, yes. Now I do. The gateway shrinks.

"So please, please, don't make me, don't make me give in to that again, I need to feel loved, and safe...."

The effect is almost instantaneous. I'm released. And I release her. The monster I've created stumbles off into the dark. And I see her now as I have not been able to see her in so long: Helen in all her fallibility. Helen who cannot afford to love me, Helen whom I have failed to love. I give her one last strong hug on the bed, then rise, grab my jacket, and walk out. I can feel the fire in my blood dying down as I drive off into the empty predawn Cambridge streets, heading home.

26.
Sparks Street

With love and respect I offer you
The little flower of my heart
Just opened unexpectedly...

—An-Khong, "Unguarded"

We are so much deeper and wider than we can say.
—Maurine Stuart, *Teisho* 1989

THE MEMORY OF THOSE DAYS of sitting and breathing with Maurine at that Zen weekend at Temenos has grown faint and the effects have long since worn off. Though I still force myself to sit every morning, these days my mind starts galloping at breakneck speed the moment my seat hits the cushion and twenty minutes of hard effort do little to quiet it down. The flyers I get from the Cambridge Buddhist Association feel more and more like briefings from a distant, irrelevant world. Yet every so often Maurine's regal figure flashes before me and I think wistfully of her deep, knowing voice and the calm solidity I felt sitting on that cushion in the August heat. That was then, I usually tell myself. Before the thesis madness. Before Helen.

A flyer arrives just before my defence announcing a sesshin with Maurine at the Cambridge Zendo. Five days, all women. This one I keep out on the kitchen counter, glance at from time to time as I make my meals. I like the all-women part. And I tell myself I need to find out if that first weekend of grace and grounding—which has lain indigestibly on the periphery of my consciousness ever since—was a fluke. By the time I decide to register two weeks later, though, all I really want from the retreat is a cessation of pain.

A TUESDAY IN APRIL FINDS ME driving east on Route 2, heading to the city. Not, this time, for a feminist event, not to see Helen, or Lena, but to attend, of all things, a Zen *sesshin*. Sparks Street is tucked away in a quiet part of Cambridge not far from Fresh Pond. I pull up at an old brown Victorian house shaded in front by great pine trees.

After removing my shoes in the cloakroom I am ushered up to a bare room where I will sleep on a futon mat beside five other women. This time I've packed the right clothes: long black harem pants and black T-shirts.

Even before we are officially (nobly) silent, the hush is a force, an element that pervades the entire house, despite the bustle of preparation in the halls, the excited rustle of robes.

We file into the rooms with the cushions. A statue of Kwan Yin occupies the altar in one room, but my seat is in the room with the Buddha. Almost as soon as I kneel on my cushion there is red rawness up and down the front of me, from belly to chest, acute as the pain in my shoulder blades at the first retreat. *Agitated organ syndrome.* I amuse myself for the first minutes of the sitting by coining such phrases for my condition. But by the end of the evening, I notice, there is some easing of this pain. Less rawness. Less agitation.

The first day I have to concentrate hard just to stay with the program. The schedule is tight and you have to keep to it without fail—no escaping to your room to lie down or jot a few lines in your journal. And there are rules for everything. You have to bow when you enter the room—I aim away from the Buddha—bow when you take your seat, bow when you leave or reenter the *kinhin* line, bow when you receive tea, bow when you place your empty cup back on the tray. When you enter the *dokusan* room for your private interview you have to do a very complicated bow in stages that include standing, kneeling, and prostrating.

Maurine's talk is a welcome reprieve from the task of just sitting, which takes up the majority of the morning. This first day it is short: a monk named Obaku asks his teacher a question; the teacher hits him and tells him to go on sitting. I'm not sure I've gotten the point but somehow the talk gets me through the two sitting periods that follow.

When we're finally released from the zendo—there is more chanting after lunch—I am too tired to gallop through the city streets as I've been fantasizing doing all morning. Instead I climb the stairs to my room and collapse onto my pad. I manage to squeeze in a ten-minute walk before we start up again at 2 p.m.

The afternoon is long and I am flooded with relief each time the bell rings to signal the end of a sitting period. The pain up and down my front is gone completely now and my body has adjusted to the sitting position fairly easily. But boredom has seized me like a giant pair of pincers and I've begun to be tormented by questions—above all the question of what on earth I am doing here in the first place. A pile of *Trivia* submissions is awaiting my response back home and the entire house is in dire need of a good vacuuming. Has desperation gotten the better of me? Loneliness? Maybe I needed some time away, but surely I could come up with a less regimented, less bizarre form of escape?

ON THE SECOND DAY I BEGIN to enjoy the rhythm of *kinhin*. We walk in unison, our steps matched to one another, as we circle the Zendo. The old floors creak loudly as one pair of feet after another bears down on the boards in the hallway. The first day it seemed a violation of the noble silence, and I tried gingerly to step around the offending patch. But by now the creaking has been woven into the silence along with the sound of the furnace kicking on and the growling of our stomachs. I try to imitate Maurine's steady forward gaze as we circle, but can't resist glancing out the windows at the new green tips on the bushes and the graceful leaning birches, the just-unfurling petals of the dogwood trees. I think I hear squeals of delight from girls at a garden party next door. *There is more loveliness in the world than I can even begin to comprehend*—I surprise myself with this thought.

By the time I meet Maurine for *dokusan* in the afternoon I've forgotten the bowing instructions and simply lower myself to the floor. My face is red when I rise from my prostration to meet her gaze. She is smiling, brushing it all aside. Do I have any questions she wants to know. I say a bit about my doubts. My impatience. She adjusts my posture. Shows me how to hold my head, relax my shoulders.

ON THE THIRD MORNING, WAKING TO darkness and silence is inexplicably profound. After strong coffee in the cloak room, after tea service, after the first gong, its waves sounding on and on, Maurine leads us in the chant *Na mu dai bo sa*. Her voice rich as black loam, joining, gathering. In the dark, windows shut, all of us sealed in together, chanting, becoming one body. Our voices resonate in the air for a long time afterwards, like the bell.

I begin to taste a state of mind I have never known before, but it's so elusive I doubt it was ever there as soon as it subsides. I oscillate between suspecting this is a) an inanely elaborate waste of time, and b) the most profound and important thing I've ever done in my life. I notice a burgeoning fondness for the women on either side of me with whom I've not exchanged a single word, or even glance. Amazingly, at the end of the afternoon, the dinner bell breaks in on my meditation.

"The noblest man is the man with nothing to do." Maurine quoted this phrase at Temenos. When she repeats it here I have a sudden image of the cheerful, grey-haired woman who often walks by the house in Montague. "Always busy aren't you?" she said one time; I was loading large burlap sacks of bulk mail into my car. I see myself now the way she must see me: racing to and from the post office, a harried look on my face. And then I see my mother. Racing across the apartment trying to get to a spot before it can soak in, to the ashtray under my father's cigarette before the ashes topple. Always rushing, trying to catch up, never catching up....

What do I know? Nothing, really. Only that I'm no longer yanked about. That I feel anchored somehow. Where? Why? Who knows. "Buddha mind," some would say, but they aren't words I would use, I prefer the strange sounds that come up in Maurine's talks—"*mu*" she says, sometimes belting it out, "*muuuu*" or "*muuushin.*" "Simply being," she says once to explain, and I think I understand.

By the end of the third day I've stopped asking why. As in *kinhin,* I simply put one foot in front of the other. Agree to go nowhere with firmness and resolve.

IN THE LAST DAYS, MAURINE SPEAKS to me in my delight. My rapture. A Japanese poem she reads about clouds parting "to let me in / To be with you, my beloved!" brings me to tears. To my great surprise, I realize they have not a thing to do with Helen.

"Buddha Nature pervades the whole universe." One of Maurine's favourite phrases. Her voice so soothing it could be a bedtime story. "Endless dimensions"—another. This is Zen, I think, a window into ... vastness. I sense this vastness in Maurine, these endless dimensions. Sometimes, for brief moments, I get a tiny taste of it in myself.

"Let go of your hankerings. Let it breathe you...." Maurine tells us. This "it" she keeps referring to is more and more a presence I can feel. Sometimes it's a hum. Is this what they mean by "harmony of the spheres"? Maurine, who was once a concert pianist, refers to it as music. "Not music music," she says. "The music that's always there if you know how to listen."

Sometimes it's a place below where everything braids together. A fundament. "Rockshelf further forming under everything that grows" (from Rich's "Transcendental Étude).

"Just this," Maurine keeps on saying. "Just this. Here, now, together, and alone. All in one and one in all. Just what we are doing."

Euphoria springs from this thisness. The sunlight on the polished banister, the cubes of light that play on the golden floors, the graceful white birches in the garden whose boughs blacken on days of rain. The world revealed to me on my midday walks through these quiet streets with large old homes painted in subtle tones of flesh, grey, and green, set off by lacquered black shutters, well-tended gardens with their hyacinths and violets and tulips just opening up. The astonishing dogwood beside a white garage. The forsythia, which I gather on the last day.

When I bow now I am bowing to this "it," to this unnameable yet everpresent thing that it seems I have lived my whole life ignoring. And I am bowing in sheer love and gratitude to all the women sitting with me in this room, who have supported me in coming into the presence of this "it." Why do we in our other lives never get still enough to recognize it?

In my last *dokusan* with Maurine, I manage to get the bowing-kneeling-prostrating just right. When I come up level with her face the air between us is so dense I am dizzy at first, and wordless. When, after sitting for a few moments, words begin to form, it seems they aren't actually coming from me but from the air between us.

"I appreciate..." I say. "Thank you for helping me to appreciate..."

As if to let me know how completely she knows what I mean, Maurine leans forward and kisses me on the forehead. No doubt an unorthodox response, yet it feels like the most natural thing in the world, as if it too has risen up out of the air between us. My whole body is tingling as I prostrate and bow myself up and out of the room.

My life will be different now, I am sure of it. I am so big, I cannot imagine I will ever again be reduced—by a woman—to sniveling, trembling smallness.

WHEN *SESSHIN* GETS OUT ON SUNDAY afternoon, I walk to Harvard Square, where I've agreed to meet Lena for coffee. She's waiting outside *Au Bon Pain* as I approach. We both smile. I bow to her, she bows back, and we take a seat by the window. I hardly speak at first. She tells me how happy I look.

"I am happy." Words feel so strange after five days of silence. "But 'happy' doesn't begin to say it." I start to talk about *sesshin*; the words begin spilling out. When the waitress comes with the coffee I bow to her, and then to my coffee cup. Lena laughs, but bows along with me. She says she's been chanting on her own. She says she wants to sit a *sesshin* with Maurine. She says she thinks zazen is just what she needs. I bow to her. She bows to me. Helen's name never comes up at all.

27.
L'essentielle

she frictional she fluvial she essential / fricatelle ruiselle essentielle

—Nicole Brossard, "*Sous La Langue* / Under Tongue"

O NE MONTH LATER I'M IN MONTREAL for the opening of the feminist bookstore, *l'essentielle*. Harriet, who moved here last fall, is one of the founders. The name is a nod to Brossard's penchant for feminizing masculine nouns, the "*elle*" at the end an added fillip. *L'essentielle* will cater to women writers and lovers of women's literature, both local and visiting. It will also host cultural events, beginning with the launching of a chapbook tonight: Brossard's long poem "*Sous La Langue*," just issued in a bilingual edition from Gynergy Press.

The little storefront bookstore has hot pink shelves lined with literary texts in both French and English, subtle track lighting overhead. On this warm May evening it's crammed with women in dress shirts and bright scarves, hoisting glasses of champagne or white wine. Good thing I'm spiffy tonight in a pair of new white pants. Women in this town dress up for each other. Seem to bask in each other's gaze.

My days since *sesshin* have been suffused with its magic. The euphoria was short-lived, but the feeling of largeness endured: a spaciousness in which need and desire lost all sense of urgency. Here in this city, surrounded by so much colour and female sparkle, I can feel that state begin to dissolve. Did I think I would not be susceptible to the pull of a woman again? Did I imagine that, remembering where it's led me, I would resist that pull?

Nicole, whom I last saw at the Book Fair in Oslo, and who's just been named president of the third Fair, to be held in Montreal next summer, presses her way toward me, looking radiant. We kiss on both cheeks, as is the custom here, she welcoming me to her home turf. "Harriet keeps telling me this is a city in which things are possible," I say. Nicole beams, and so does a woman standing beside her, a tall woman with curly auburn hair in black pants and a white shirt. Nicole introduces us before vanishing back into the crowd.

"Quinn" is a writer. An anglophone. She's older than me— early forties, maybe? Has a roundness about her body and face I like. And a warmth. An immediate sense of complicity, as if she cares about me. She says she knows *Trivia*. She likes it. She was cofounder of a feminist journal herself. Thankless work, but so important.

NICOLE AND HER TRANSLATOR TAKE TURNS reading the poem. *You cannot foresee,* each verse begins, building toward the climax. We all tremble with them on this precipitous bilingual edge. *You cannot foresee so suddenly leaning / towards a face and wanting to lick the soul's / whole body till the gaze sparks with furies and yieldings /... Desire is all you see.*

After the reading there is toasting to the poem, the press, the bookstore. Harriet and her coworkers take the stage, looking both proud and exhausted, and the applause escalates until loud cheering fills the store.

Then dinner at the Symposium, just around the corner on St. Denis. Several tables are put together to form one very long table and soon large plates of toast and Greek spreads and calamari are set out before us. I try to score a seat next to Quinn but another woman beats me to it, and I strain to hear what they're saying throughout the meal. When the woman between us excuses herself to go to the bathroom, I see my chance.

"Did I just hear you complaining about feminism?" I ask, catching her eye.

"Well, yes. It can be awfully moralistic. And narrow.... Don't you find?" Again that bid for complicity. Her empathetic attention reminds me of Grace. The Grace who once was. "I'm coming to see there are things it fails to account for," I say.

She begins to talk about darkness and tragedy, how little room there is for them in the feminist world view. Her brown eyes dance with intelligence. The low collar of her white shirt reveals a lovely breastbone. And her hands. I've never seen such beautiful hands.

Desire, how it blooms. Each time as if the first time, careless of history impervious to warnings reading only the signs it wants to see.

I'm about to move into the seat between us when its occupant returns and Quinn, suddenly nervous, checks her watch. She gets up abruptly, pulls on a worn leather jacket. She scrawls her address on a napkin "in case you have any further thoughts." The way she looks in that jacket, tough and smug, after having been so soft and confiding, makes a fierce heat surge between my legs.

I stay over at Harriet's, on a twin air mattress that deflates in the course of the night. All night I am feverish. Engorged. Blood pounding in my ears. My body's a rocket, it wants to blast off, wants to send me ... and I want to be sent, to be taken, into the wild and the deep, *into a realm unreal.*

Just breathe, Maurine would say, *just breathe.* Everything is right here now.

But I don't want this moment. I want to tear it down to get to the next one, and the next, and the next, to get to the moment when I can see her again.

I want this burning.

28.
Cloistered

The rectangular shape of his book of knowledge, bending. The shape of our silence, the shape of the roofs of our mouths. Darkness.
— Susan Griffin, *Woman and Nature*

"MU SHIN," SHE BELLOWS FROM DEEP in her centre. "NO knowing. NO mind. No teachings. Just this. Just sitting. Here. Now." She hits the floor for emphasis.

How I love being back here with Maurine. Walking in the door of Sparks Street this time was like coming home.

"Why is it so hard for us to let go? To just be? To experience the enlightened mind we were born with?"

Just sitting. Just being. If I'm honest I'll admit I haven't managed to do this for even one second, not on this retreat. I can't let go. Don't want to. I am just back from a tour of sacred sites in Ireland with a group of German and Swiss women. Following Louisa Poole's advice: "Go where there's ancient history. Explore space and time." I am still so much with the caves the mounds the stone circles. The megalithic graves erupting out of the gentle rolling farmland. Isn't this also enlightened mind? The holy shapes of Ireland?

But it isn't just Ireland. I am still so much with Clara. Clara in the dark chamber scaling the stones with her lighter to illuminate the etchings: spirals, waves, diamonds of all sizes. Clara wincing in pain as she keeps the flame going to the end of the wall. Clara emerging from the cave as if reborn—"*voller Kräfte.*" Clara not separable from those holy shapes.

"Singing the song of eternal as-it-isness." The theme of Maurine's talk today. "What holds us back from this? Prevents us from being one with what is? Our cravings."

Clara prancing naked on the beach, her child's belly, round breasts. Clara and her warm hugs, strictly maternal (she's a married woman, a decade older than me). That is until the farmhouse in Ennis, where there aren't enough beds and—all giggles and innocence—she steers us toward the double. Where, after lights out, the two of us lie rigid and silent, side by side. For what seems like hours. And then finally I whisper, "I can't sleep. Can you put your arms around me?" And she does. And she isn't wearing a thing.

Apart from her pearls. Her hands moving up my arms to my hands, covering them. *"So kalt,"* folding them in hers. Her feet wrapping around my cold feet. She turns her back to me, brings both my hands to her chest and holds them there.

"Du bisst so warm!" I say. It doesn't seem the least bit silly, this simple language of hot and cold.

When I'm warm through and through she turns around and lays her arms—gently—on my side. Then she pulls away and abandons me for her own depths.

We mingle with the others the next day, as if the night had never been. But now a dense magnetic field surrounds her and when she pulls too far away I ache. My eyes are always scanning for a sign of her.

I wonder how this is possible so soon after meeting Quinn. But this ache is not like that one: wanting to blast off, be sent. This woman makes me want to go into the earth with her. To kneel by her side.

To kneel down before her? Yes, that too, having seeing Her carved into ancient stones and into the earth itself—so much concrete, irrefutable evidence of this sacred way of life centred around Her.... *To long to be admitted into those secret chambers. To be taught everything by what is found there.*

Catching up with her on the mound, touching my palm to the back of her head. Her head jerking, as if from a shock, the sudden "oh" from deep inside. Relayed instantly to my centre. Uh-oh.

The cigarettes we share, the fork of my fingers meeting the fork of hers for a brief electric moment, then retreating again. Our complicit inhaling.

Finally, in the cave, words of love spoken.

I miss her. I keep thinking I should be home in case she calls. Never mind that I was home every day last week and no call ever came. I want her beside me, red hair red jacket belly breasts pearls. I want her solidness. Her firmness. Her thereness. There are men all around and I want them gone. I want only holy shapes around me, and women, talking, laughing, taking in.

Cravings, yes. I am burning up with them, feverish with wanting. I can't imagine any other way to be. Fire and air—a bellows fanning the flame—isn't this who I am?

"I don't want to get rid of my desires," I say in *dokusan*. "I can't imagine who I'd be without them."

"Desires aren't bad," Maurine says. "It's how you use them. Just keep breathing."

So I do. In-breath, out-breath. Over and over. Minute after minute. Hour after hour. And my ardour cools. I begin to settle. To feel the pleasurable weight of my limbs on the cushion. To notice the greening birch trees during *kinhin*. Fire and air becalmed by earth.

That evening I let go as it seems I have never let go before in this practice. Into just sitting. Just being. Just this moment. The rustle of robes. The scent of sandalwood. The ochre glow from the Japanese lamps. The dependable rhythm of my breath, our breath. "Our"? Yes, I am breathing with everyone else in this room. Men as well as women. Everything just as it is.

All I want now—all I'm aware of wanting—is to dwell in this place of as-it-isness. But it seems I need Maurine, I need *sesshin*, I need these breathing beings all around me to get there and stay there.

29.
Not a Lesbian

*If the lesbian sees the woman, the woman may see
the lesbian seeing her. With this, there is a flowering of
possibilities.*

— Marilyn Frye, "To See and Be Seen"

LESS THAN A YEAR AFTER Clara and I part in Dublin, we meet again in Dubrovnik. I have spent the year in upstate New York as Visiting Assistant Professor of Comparative Literature at Hamilton College. Brett has taken over *Trivia* for the time being, and I've rented my house out to a friend. My first academic job, and while it will probably also be my last—though I love my students, I feel like a misfit in this profession—I have come to appreciate the perks that go with it, among them subsidized travel to anywhere in the world, as long as a conference is being held there and you can write up a clever abstract for a paper.

Which is how I come to be sitting on a twin bed at the Hotel Bellevue in Dubrovnik in late May of '88. The university here is hosting a colloquium on women and words, and writer friends from both Canada and the U.S. will be presenting along with me, among them Nicole from Montreal and Jeffner, my philosopher friend from San Francisco. Soon, if all goes as planned, the empty bed beside me will be occupied by Clara.

I've been doing a countdown for weeks now, but the lower the numbers get the less real it seems. Will we really have eight whole days together? After the conference we plan to rent a car and drive up the coast.

She called just two weeks ago to say she wanted us to share a bed.

"Are you sure?" I asked.

Yes, she said, she was absolutely sure.

I didn't have the courage to say "we would prefer one bed" when the concièrge said they had two for us, so we're stuck with two twin beds, which I've moved together. At least we'll get more sleep this way.

The scenery of our encounter has now been fleshed out. We have a balcony overlooking a tiny rocky inlet with a private beach. The water is deep turquoise. Jasmine bushes waft their intense fragrance into the room.

Clara is a married woman. I know I need to try and have no expectations. That's what we've been saying to each other all along, and so far I've held up my end pretty well. Granted, my life has been full this year. Weeks would go by without a word from her and sometimes I'd be too busy to notice. But when one of her letters arrived, large round script on blue airmail stationery, it was as if there'd been no separation at all. And when we spoke, when she'd call out of the blue, which she did every few weeks, we would chirp together on the phone like the happiest of lovebirds and I would glow for days afterwards.

On a Saturday afternoon in late April, at the end of a week of raw, steady rain in the drab college town I was temporarily calling home, she called from Milan. I'd been feeling pretty low. From Lena, who now sat regularly at Sparks Street, I had heard that Maurine was sitting out *sesshins*. There were rumours she was ill.

As soon as I heard Clara's voice, I perked up. She described the short black skirt she'd just bought for herself. "I look very smart in it," she said. Then she described Milan: the people out on the sidewalks drinking, talking, smoking. Suddenly the world was big and sunny and cosmopolitan.

Here at the Bellevue I check myself out in the bathroom mirror. I look like I haven't slept for five days, which in fact I haven't. Tomorrow I'll lie out in the sun and try and get some colour.

At breakfast I discover that both Jeffner and her friend Namascar are staying in the Bellevue. Later that morning the three of us stroll through the old walled city with its counterpoint of red-tiled roofs and azure blue awnings. We take lunch out on the plaza with their friends Elizabeth and Alice, both lesbian professors from the South. All of us drink to this beautiful city and to the perks of university teaching, which rescue us from the dull far-flung towns our jobs have taken us to. Towards the end of the meal the Clara story comes out and they all listen spellbound.

I'm up at eight the next morning, listening for her footfall.

By breakfast I've given up believing she will ever come and can't stand another moment of peering out for her. I can't even face the door. Jeffner and Namascar offer to keep a lookout and I seat myself across from them. I've just bitten into my toast when I see Jeffner's eyes open very wide. "Lise," she says. I turn around and see her coming through the glass doors. Clara.

I lunge out of my chair, grab her, lift her in the air, twirl her around. She squirms out of my grasp. I stand back, look her over. Her hair is shorter, she's slimmer. Over the short black skirt, which is indeed very smart, she's wearing a checked jacket, with broad shoulders and a gathered waist. She looks every bit the continental traveler.

We move to the steps out of view of the breakfasters. I think she'll give me my real greeting now, but she just hugs me half-heartedly then says she'd like a coffee, she is very tired. Back in the breakfast room, I introduce her to my friends. Jeffner, a believer in true love, has tears in her eyes.

Clara does not seem impressed. Sipping her coffee, she begins to chatter about her morning, about how they weren't going to let her on the plane but she marched her way on, saying, "I did not get up at four-thirty for nothing!" Jeffner and Namascar reward her with rapt attention in which Clara seems to be basking. For someone who's been up since dawn and has just met the woman she's been writing love letters to for a year she seems preternaturally calm.

We take her bags to our room. I'm still hoping for the real hug, or kiss. It was easier to have no expectations when I was across the ocean from her. She takes a seat out on the terrace, where she strips down to a silk slip and lights up a Dunhill. She begins to sun herself, looking out at the ocean.

"Come, sit down, look at me, let me look at you," she says. I can't sit down yet, I'm pacing.

"Why don't you want to look at me? Do I look very different?"

"No—it's that you look the same." It's not entirely true, but what I mean is: she's really here. I'm trying to take this in.

"Take a deep breath," she says.

Why is she so calm? I think this is what's making me so jumpy. That and my fear, which she's just spoken: that I look different. That I don't look as good. Won't bear up under scrutiny. I have on a pale green cotton shirt and my favourite black pants, which just now feel too baggy. The white Reeboks aren't quite fancy enough I know. I try to think: did I dress less casually in Ireland?

"*Never again be reduced to sniveling smallness,*" I imagined on the last day of *sesshin*. How delusional was that?

We change for the beach. I avert my eyes while she dresses, though I watched her parade around naked in Ireland, and look up to see her attired in a bikini and an elegant silk kimono. Down at the beach I'm aware of admiring eyes trained on her. The hotel personnel, suddenly servile, hover about us, asking can they get us something.

We go in the water for short spells. I try to work on my talk while she listens to music on her Walkman. When I realize I'm not getting anywhere I return to our room.

Lesbian writing, I told the students in my "Lesbian Literature" class (only two of whom identified as lesbian), had as much to do with a particular kind of vision as it did with sexual orientation. As some of the most marginal creatures on earth, I explained, we enjoyed an unusual degree of what Woolf called "freedom from unreal loyalties." We were the true outsiders, the ones who could and would remake the world. The students ran with these remarks in their writing, and some of the results were quite stunning. In my talk tomorrow morning I intend to string some of these writings together, along with my own observations about lesbian literature. I'm counting on all of it to gel as I speak.

Clara and I walk the cobbled streets to the university in silence the next morning. I'm the first to present and there's a lot of traffic in and out of the room, but even once it abates I am unable to command everyone's attention. Reading it out loud, the paper feels more ragged than it had before. I gather from the polished, well-turned sentences of the presenters who succeed me that I did not put nearly enough time into preparation. Clara hasn't a word to say about it as we walk back to the hotel. In our room, I notice the twin beds have been moved apart.

THAT EVENING NICOLE, JEFFNER, CLARA, and I meet Alice and Elizabeth for dinner at the Mimosa. Clara has dressed down a bit, is sporting white linen pants and a floral print top. Elizabeth, who's sitting across from her, is carrying on about deconstruction. I worry that Clara will feel bored or left out but at some point she begins to feed Elizabeth questions and takes notes on a napkin. Later I overhear her telling Nicole how much she liked her paper. Afterwards the two of them carry on a long conversation in French—Clara's is flawless. "*Elle est charmante, ton amie,*" Nicole leans over and says to me when Clara gets up to go to the bathroom.

"Do you think they realize I'm not lesbian?" Clara asks as we make our way home along the ocean between rows of palm trees and jasmine bushes.

A shrug is all I can manage.

Back in our room I lie down. She makes for the balcony, sits there smoking for a long time.

"Clara, can we talk?" I say when she comes back in.

"Why didn't you come out on the balcony with me? We could have talked out there. Now I need to sleep."

And sleep she does, snoring loudly, aggressively, all night. It doesn't matter, as I'm not sleeping anyway.

OUR "TALK," WHEN IT FINALLY TAKES PLACE, the following afternoon, on the balcony, lasts only a few minutes. It was a mistake to have come, she tells me, dragging on a Dunhill. She doesn't feel what she felt in Ireland, it's as simple as that, and there's really no point in speculating about why. "It's not very much fun for me, and I know it can't be very pleasant for you." She says all this in English. We haven't spoken a word of German to each other since she arrived. To my disordered mind it seems this is one of the reasons for her change of heart.

She tells me that as soon as she saw me she realized: I'd been a dream.

"But I'm still the same person!"

"It's not you," she says, "it's me."

A few minutes later she admits maybe the context has something to do with it. All these women giving papers, talking, talking, and it doesn't go anywhere. It all feels narrow to her, she says. By "it" I'm afraid she means not the conference, but the lesbians.

DRIVING UP THE COAST WITH THE TOP DOWN in our Citroën convertible, we both grow lighter. In the interest of seeing a bit of the country we've decided to stick to our plan and see how it goes. Do I imagine that, away from the conference and our little room with its reproachful twin beds, we might find our way back? Probably, yes.

In Cavtat we check into a modern hotel right on the water. Our room is large with two double beds. There is sun, salt air, blue bay, a boardwalk along the shore. Yachts anchored in the harbour. Warm thrill in evening air as people sit down to dinner and drinks. And we are among them. White wine and calamari out on the terrace. Dressed up, as we dress up for dinner every night on this trip; I've brought my nicest pants and tops and sandals. Around us swirl conversations in Italian, German, English, Serbian. Nothing narrow about any of this. Clara chatters, pleasantly.

Four days later I watch her enter the body of the giant Swissair jet. She's been cheerful today, and voluble, chirping like a bird. Because she's going home, of course. She has on the black skirt again, with a white lacy top and the tailored Milan jacket. Kisses me goodbye on the cheek. Says we'll meet here again next year. Both of us knowing we won't.

I feel a thud inside as the plane with the red cross on its tail lifts off. There she goes in her smart suit, her smart haircut her red lipstick. Her big round eyes. Eyes that once held deep affection and ancient mysteries, that came to look so cold to me, so inscrutable. Unbearable repetition here.

"Not lesbian." How distasteful it sounded dropped thus from her lips. This word that never came up in Ireland, where we were all women worshipping together, in the caves, in the tombs by the sea. Where she and I lay back to back and then back to front and I held her in my arms. Where I touched the back of her neck and she breathed in, sharply. *The whispering in each other's ear at the farewell dinner. Confessing to each other over the fancy food that we have no appetite. In the midst of the songs and speeches, our getaway up the stairs to her room. Me pulling her to her feet from the windowsill, kissing her, for real. Holding her head in my hands. She kissing back.*

In Ireland those words—"not lesbian"—would have made no sense at all.

Maybe the context, she said. The missing context: stone circles, sacred ruins. The new context assessed in those first moments at the Bellevue: this hotel not the finest, the breakfast room shabby, and these carelessly attired lesbian academics, their unapologetic bulges.... She must have felt then instantly (so I imagine): "I don't belong." She must have felt, "If these are lesbians, then I'm no lesbian."

And it comes back to me now. How I was once no lesbian. How it was women I loved, beautiful women, women in skirts and sweaters, women with gentle waves and slender waists, not those hearty, back-slapping butches not those bulldykes with breasts tucked in their belts. Their unapologetic bulges. If they were lesbians, how could I be one?

How all the chickens come home to roost.

30.
She Who

"when She Who moves
the earth will turn over"

—Judy Grahn, *The She Who Poems*

IT'S A WEEK SINCE WE PARTED. I take myself to see *Wings of Desire*. There's a scene in the bar when they finally find each other: the man-angel and the woman trapeze artist. He offers her his glass of wine. And the camera frames her face, her red lips that begin to speak at last. I notice the perfection of those lips, the smoothness of the skin just above them, beneath her nose. I notice because at the dentist on Monday when the hygienist handed me the mirror to show me a place my toothbrush was missing I saw the hair on my upper lip. It looked shaggy and dark. I told myself it was those dentist lights. But all week I've obsessed over it.

And I notice those lips because of Clara. How perfect hers were. How she kept them rouged and perky. How mine must have looked to her, I think now, with all that hair. Yes, it might have been something that simple that superficial. Maybe she really longed to feel attracted to a woman, to me, and was stopped by something as trite as dark hairs on the upper lip.

And you, L? What was it you felt on those coastal evenings, sitting down to white wine and calamari and cigarettes? Be honest, now, you. Each night dressing up for her—you'd brought your best clothes—a kind of thrill. Each night hoping to see in her eyes that she was happy to see you, that you were beautiful to her. Sexy, even. Especially on the last nights, when you had a nice tan from your hours on the beach. Mornings were difficult, yes, every morning waking up to dull ache. But the evenings ... oh, if it was pain then it was pain mingled with something like ecstasy, to be always on the edge of the unbearable, always on the edge of possibility. The tantalizing possibility that one of *those women* might actually look your way.

Face it, L. There are women—there will probably always be women—who bring you to your knees as surely as any sacred site or Zen temple. And who can draw the line between humble supplicant and groveling fan?

She Who has never been with a woman before, who is not in your world. She Who is perfect in her beauty like the women who came to your father's library. She Who is shy and trembling and wants to be coaxed and brings out your love of coaxing. She Who brings out the Prince Charming the feminist saviour.

She Who has lured you thousands of miles away to a hotel in Yugoslavia. She Who decides very suddenly this has all been a fantasy. She Who moves apart the twin beds you moved together. She Who inspires every one of your old fears about yourself. You don't have the right clothes or makeup maybe there are hairs on your upper lip of which you're not aware. She Who just by the way she dips into her leather suitcase, plunges her hand into the silken mass, the skirts the slips the scarves, tells you she is not your kind and you will forever be subordinated to hers, subject to her whims, at her mercy....

It's occurred to me that what we can least forgive others for is bringing out our worst selves: exposing the gap between who at any given moment we most wish to be and who we most undeniably are. Grace's Southern hospitality, her empathy, her graciousness—how they shriveled up in our last months together, how she turned rigid, hateful, mean-spirited. Helen's expansive vision, her capacious, leonine love replaced by a clinging, desperate, finally vengeful self. And Clara—who had put her hand on my hand in that cave in Ireland, who had thanked the goddess for allowing her to know this love—how she must have hated me for having brought out what she hated most in herself: the cramped, critical, bourgeois snob. Yet apparently I could forgive Clara for reducing me to one who looked doubtfully at her white Reeboks and cheap Timex watch. For seeing me through the harsh glare of dental lights.

It was the ones who loved me I couldn't forgive. The women whom I'd failed in love, for whom my love had failed, which is to say faltered, sputtered, given out—and was there ever a woman who let me in close for whom my love had not faltered? The women who forced me to confront the gap between what I professed with my whole being to want, what my whole life was dedicated to—loving women—and who I was: someone who couldn't. Not, at least, with any singularity of focus. Not with any consistency. Not in such a way as to inspire faith, or trust....

31.
Dumped

The lesbian *is a woman ablaze ... She is an explorer, an anarchist, a feminist who, with her body, invents everything by the force of the attraction she has for other women.*

—Nicole Brossard, "Kind Skin My Mind"

MONTREAL, JUNE 1988: The Third International Feminist Book Fair. Some six thousand women have come here from all over the world. Conversation blooms around the *Trivia* booth, which soon becomes a magnet for women from the Book Fair in Oslo, from the Dubrovnik colloquium, even from the Women in Print Conference in Oakland three years ago. Lena is here, as are Anne and Brett; they take turns spelling me at the table. Del, a writer from *Trivia* #12 I've been corresponding with, shows up fleetingly, but long enough for some spark to pass between us, for me to feel a little tug when she darts away, her red hair flying behind her.

For weeks I've been moping around in Montague, trying to shake off the news that the college won't be renewing my teaching contract. After just one day here though I'm flying, euphoric. What's unfolding around us is essential, historic: the largest gathering ever of Canadian Native women poets; readings by some of the great poets of our time, all of them lesbian—Judy Grahn, Audre Lorde, Olga Broumas, Chrystos, Nicole Brossard; panel discussions about memory, about power, about language and difference. It's never been clearer to me: it is women, and above all lesbians, who are asking the questions, creating the knowledge, that most matter at this time.

On the second day, Quinn comes by. We've been writing back and forth and having long talks on the phone. Yes, there's someone, she's explained; it's off and on, but she isn't really free. We greet each other awkwardly, kissing on both cheeks. She looks tentative, unsure, but—what is it about her? some *knowingness* behind her eyes—instantly I want to ply her with questions, kidnap her to my little dorm room, talk the night away. She can't stay, she says, she has to prepare for a panel tomorrow. She hands me a computer printout, a text she's been working on, her thoughts on the relationship of feminism to tragedy now shaped into an essay. I begin reading as soon as she's gone and then have to stop.

The tempo. The dark humour. The fierce intelligence. The burning is back. I want, I want.

Quinn's panel the next day is on language and the body. She reads from a novel she's working on, and again the words seem to emit heat, reminding me of something I just read about the relationship between "sex" and "text." I shoot up the aisle when the panel ends, intending to say something clever about her language/my body, but when I reach the stage someone is hovering protectively by her side—a tall, gangly woman Quinn introduces to me as "Sonny." Her someone, apparently. I manage a few lame remarks about her novel before backtracking down the aisle.

Later that day, Quinn shows up again at the *Trivia* booth, but Sonny appears moments after and she beats a retreat. I gather the two of them are now more "on" than "off." We'd made tentative plans to meet for dinner at the end of the Fair, but when I call her the next day she says she's so sorry to miss me but she's come down with something.

Having been buoyed for four days by six thousand women, how can I be brought so low by just one? Back in Montague, it's an effort not to allow the residue of those heady days in the *Trivia* booth, the readings, the dinners with friends, to be washed away by my disappointment.

Then Brett calls and almost instantly we're riding that giant wave of feminist energy again, replaying all our favorite moments from the Fair. It was, we agree, a rare celebration of fine writing and cultural difference, with lesbians at the centre of it all, and we want to find a way to commemorate it in *Trivia*. By the end of the call we've decided to devote the next two issues to work that originated at the Fair. The first, *Trivia* #13, will centre on the feminist writers of Quebec, the second on language and difference.

All summer long I assemble writings, most of them versions of talks given at the Fair: an essay on memory and aging by Mary Meigs, an American expatriate in her seventies; Quinn's now-finished essay on feminism and tragedy; a translation of a meditation on memory and desire by Nicole; a translation of Michèle Causse's dense Cartesian text calling for the elaboration of a "gynolect," a language of female subjectivity. Together, I hope these pieces reflect the rich and subversive cultural brew that is Quebec *au féminin*—or at any rate Montreal, where all these writers are based.

By way of context, I'm writing an editorial on the politics of language in Quebec, and Quinn has obliged me with nuanced reflections on the subject, which throughout the summer serve as pretext for long and animated phone conversations. At some point in these conversations, usually just as they're about to spill over into our lives—it's uncanny—Sonny knocks on her door.

IN THE FALL, DEL OFFERS TO COME HELP with paste-up; her day job is in book production. When I protest—it's a five-hour drive—she says all she has to do is jump in her car. Del's writing is deep and raw and droll; I've wanted to get to know her since first reading her, but she's always been elusive, darting off too soon, as she did at the Book Fair. Now she's ready to drive five hours to help out! I accept her offer, gratefully, excitedly—and nervously. This is probably not just an errand of mercy.

She is shy, I decide, when she arrives and we both gravitate instantly to the light table. With her thin frame, black jeans, and long red hair she looks a little like a punk rocker. I *like* her.

Perfect fall days. We go out for walks on our breaks. The meadow, the Book Mill, the wetlands out back—her idea of paradise she says. We laugh a lot; she's sarcastic like me. Poncho the donkey braying for attention reminds us both of our needy fathers. We do Poncho imitations when their names come up.

The second night, after dinner, in the living room, nursing glasses of white wine, we kiss, shyly, on the couch. The rest of the evening kisses mingle with our writing talk and that night we make love sweetly in the little room upstairs.

I drive to see her the following weekend. Am happy in her little place on the lake. Not in love as I've been in love. But she's someone I love and who loves me. It continues that way for several months, driving to see each other, making each other happy.

Until I start to feel it winding down: the being happy to see her, the sweetness of heart. Until it begins: the dreaded tapering off. Same old thing. Afraid to run out of love.

With the dwindling of my interest she begins to dwindle. Grows thin to the point of frail. Is rootless, unmoored. I can feel her waiting on my every word and move. Is this how it was for Bella? Having brought out my ungainly queer girl? Or for Clara in Dubrovnik? *Each night hoping to see in her eyes that she is happy to see you, that you are beautiful to her. Sexy even.*

The phone calls with their long silences. I stand against the wall, the cord curling around my legs, like a stammering teenage boy.

By spring she's gone hard. A mean edge to the humour. Her adolescent sneer when I wax poetic on our walk to the meadow. Like being doused in cold water. Nauseatingly familiar.

Del, *ma semblable, ma soeur.* She who looked slightly nerdish in my dream, lounging around like me in sweatshirt and pants. Sacrificing compassion to humour. "I hope you won't be permanently disabled." More like me than any woman I've been with. My long-lost friend.

We send each other press releases for idiotic books, phrases from politically correct feminist papers—"the words 'art, vision, dance' are in no way meant to imply that these are universally possible." Our acid perceptions sparing no one. "You forgot to underline *potluck dinner.*"

Her self-deprecation, with its tendency to spill out on me. "I think every woman I love is doing just fine. But I think I am wasting my life. Why is this? Don't answer. You're just the one to say, 'Yes—you are.'"

She whom I sat beside in tortured silence above the frozen lake, waiting for a sign to appear. Waiting in my heart, for some pulse of feeling that could be translated by my tongue. *Touch to my tongue*. ("Do you like to have sex with me?" in thin, worried voice.) The words of the lesbian poets who loved so juicily so fervently returning to taunt me reproach me for my stinginess my dried-up heart. Dumped by the wings of desire and left for dead.

She has become one who makes of me someone who when she reaches inside finds nothing there. Who can't feel. Who when she reads a passage from Duras' *The Malady of Death* has to admit she identifies. And in an unfunny funny moment she writes the words on my forehead "dead man." I am what I have always hated. Those men I resented for being so undeserving of what they had been given—her love—for being unable to return it in kind.

I reach in it's not there I reach in again, keep checking, I think sometimes I feel something flickering in there trying to kindle, to rub itself back to life. What I need to do to activate it: be honest. Tell her I don't *feel* anything. I don't feel I don't feel.... But all she has to do is back away, throw me out, throw me over, find someone else ... the feeling will surge back in an instant. Like blood to a wound.

Yet only months ago, November, those moments of frisky, girlish joy. Hilarity. My heart swelling with every phone call. Unreasonably happy despite the world's woes. Watching the returns at her place, George Bush and Dan Quayle, a nightmare descending. The very next day we walk up the gorge together— rotting leaves and branches, sharp white line of froth—then stand in that huge column of space, gaze up at the water drilling down from that high mouth. And skip back down the trail, all gloom dispelled.

It must be the way she's changed, yes, the way she cowers now seems afraid of me the way I feel her pulling at me. Just don't pull at me, okay? I can't feel when you do that, just go on doing your own thing, just leave me alone. But who is this she who cowers and winces? Who is this I who doesn't love? And which is me? The one who flies into the fire until she crashes and burns or the one who stays in, who fends off, who freezes? The one who feels too much or the one who doesn't feel at all? Either way it's She Who decides.

("It's not you, it's me.") She Who always decides.

32.
Bringing Things Up

Same arguments, same quarrels, same scenes. Same attractions and separations. Same difficulties, the impossibility of reaching each other. Same ... same ... always the same.

—Luce Irigaray, "When Our Lips Speak Together"

T: SO DO YOU SEE A PATTERN HERE?

L: Well it's kind of obvious isn't it? The mother thing. Then when they get too close ... the father thing. Isn't that where this is all going eventually? Just trying to save us some steps ...

T: You say you had no expectations of a real relationship with Clara. What was it you wanted?

L: Nothing that we didn't already have, in Ireland, and after. Some delicate, essential part of my soul that bloomed in her presence simply because she was able to be silent, to stand there, not too close and not too far, while this same thing bloomed in her.

T: Tell me about your mother. Did you ever see your mother in her?

L: See what I mean? ... Not in Ireland no never in Ireland ... but then in Dubrovnik ... (considering) ... well okay, my mother used to complain about my fat friends. She said they wrinkled the bedspreads.

T: Ah … (long and meaningful). Tell me more about your mother.

L: We've already gone over this.

T: I don't mind repetition.

L: She had a short attention span. I made a lot of excuses for her when I first became a feminist, she was plunged into this foreign world, there was too much help, my father took over, she was disempowered. But I don't think it's enough to let her off the hook for.…

T: Yes?

L: Well, just not being there for us. Being there and not being there.

T: Being there and not being there. An exact description of Clara during that week in Yugoslavia, wouldn't you say?

L: Well okay, maybe.

T: And you always hoping, hoping. As you must have done as an infant, though later of course you put up armour, your feelings went into hiding, but that little girl must have been … always hoping that this beautiful woman would look your way.

L: (starting to cry, hating herself for it)

T: (hands Kleenex box to L) Anything else about your mother?

L: (wiping her face, getting control of herself) Okay the beauty part … the not measuring up. Not being perfect. Being sent to Elizabeth Arden. I have disappointed you. I am not as beautiful as you'd hoped. The mirrors everywhere confirming it. Okay, yes, I can see how all that played itself out on that trip.…

T: Indeed.

L: But what does any of this have to do with Del? Why do we keep going back to Clara? I need to know why I can't respond, now, with this one woman.

T: Being there and not being there. Would you say that also describes the way you've been with Del?

L: (pondering) Hmmm. I hadn't thought of that ... but how is this supposed to help me? Why do I go so cold and stony? Sometimes I just want her to go away so I can stop hating myself. Why can't I do what everyone around me seems to be able to do without turning themselves inside out? Just love ... the one who loves me?

T: Because it's not something you've had a lot of experience with. One who was supposed to love you didn't. And the one who did....

L: I dreamt about him last night.

T: Well why didn't you say so before? Let's hear it.

L: We're in my green bedroom. He wants in. Into the room, into ... me. My mind, my soul, my heart. Everything he wanted into. And my challenge is to parry—to fend him off. Which I do. He comes back several times, each time with a wounded look, and each time I push him off. He ends up outside the door in the hall, shooting me one last pleading look, and I shut the door, shut him out. As I wake up I'm talking myself into the rightfulness of what I've done: I have a right to my own life, to privacy, my own room, I have a right to say no. He'll survive, he always does.

T: An important dream! So tell me what it says to you about Del, about what you two are going through right now.

L: Well it's obvious, isn't it. I seem to think I need to defend myself from somebody's love.

T: From his, it appears that you did.

L: Okay, so when somebody loves me I'm afraid, of being invaded, of them wanting in, to my deepest soul. Because I always felt that way with him. I'd be playing the piano and I could just feel him behind me, his eyes boring into my back with adoration. Or we'd be watching TV together and I'd sense his eyes were on me instead of the TV, and would look over and see ... it was true.

T: Has Del given you any reason to feel you need to defend yourself against her, other than the fact that she loves you?

L: Oh, no. She's the least invasive person you can imagine. Except that ... she wants something I can't give. The one thing I can't give. Something so deep and central that if they could get a hold of it my guts would come with it.

T: And that is?

L: I don't know.... But I can tell you this. The way I worry about his survival, at the end of the dream ... it's like that with her. I worry about the power I have over her. I worry that if I stand up for myself I will crush her.

T: Crush her how?

L: Just by telling her the truth about my feelings.

T: And what is the truth, L?

L: The truth is ... I just don't love her the way I loved Clara, or feel about Quinn. It's just not the same. It never was.

T: Is it really as simple as all that?

L: I don't know. I don't know.

T: Okay, let me see if I have this right. One woman has the depth of understanding you yearn for, but puts up barriers. Another puts up no barriers at all, wants you to keep on coming, but you won't, or you can't....

L: Well yes, I'm seeing the pattern here.

T: Is it possible that it is the lack of a barrier that scares you—the formlessness of that—and that it's the presence of barriers in the other woman that allows you to imagine ... endlessly ... her depth, her mystery, her ability to love?

L: (pondering) Funny, it sounds a little like Zen ... when I obey all the strict forms, when I really sit ... I imagine a love so boundariless, so fathomless.... "Oceans measureless to man"—that phrase came to me one day during *zazen*, to describe what's possible between two women.

T: But when you're offered this kind of love you run away.

L: But it takes a certain kind of woman. A She Who. A woman who does not lose herself in me, so that there is infinite she to be known.

T: A she who doesn't really want you. Or who wants you but doesn't want you.

L: So what are you saying? What does all this say about me?

T: On the one hand, you want an experience on the soul level, to be shaken to the roots of your being; on the other, you're afraid of being invaded there, of someone wanting into your "deepest soul" (and with good reason, I might add). So you've found a way ... to protect yourself and still have that soul connection you long for.

L: Right. By sacrificing love. Functional relationship.

T: Have we switched roles here?

L: (laughs)

T: (looking at the clock) We have to wrap up now, but let me ask you just one more question. This love you are describing, for this "She Who" you imagine yourself capable of feeling so deeply for: have you ever been able to see yourself as the proper object of such love? Have you ever been able to see yourself as a "She Who?"

L: (looks stricken) Um, I guess I'll take that as a homework assignment ... (beginning to gather her things) Can I ask you something? Do you think there's hope for me? Do you really honestly think this is going to help me? Change me?

T: (reaching for her appointment book) Just let's keep doing this, things will start to move, you'll see.

33.
Starting to Move

Beneath the outrage of betrayal is a very real fear. The enclosure of separatism has failed to protect us. The enemy is within.
　　—Carol LeMasters, "S/M: The Violence of Desire"

*F*ALL 1989. I'M ON MY WAY *to a woman's bookstore bearing a flyer announcing a murder. A gay man was found in a pool of blood with a plastic device beside him. There is blood all over the flyer and blood on my hands.... It seems I did the deed. Me, a feminist, a morally credentialed wholesome white girl.*

In October of '89 I get a letter from two women on the organizing committee for the W.I.T.C.H. (Wild Independent Thinking Crones and Hags) lecture series. They're writing to tell me that my name came up as a candidate for the coming year and was voted down after a heated discussion in which "negative and defamatory remarks" were made about me. Chief among the allegations was that I had outgrown radical feminism and was now a supporter of S/M. The women are writing out of confusion and concern. They are both fans of *Trivia* and can find no evidence of either of these claims in anything I've written.

The rumours are news to me, but not a big surprise. We received several letters of complaint after issue #12, which Brett edited, and which included a review she'd written of Joan Nestle's *A Restricted Country*, a sexually explicit book documenting the butch-femme milieu of the '50s. One of the letters was from Bloodroot, a feminist bookstore and restaurant collective in Connecticut who'd been staunch longtime supporters. The message was clear: in the eyes of some readers, *Trivia* was not toeing the line.

I write back to the women from the committee, thank them for having the decency to write to me directly, and tell them there is no foundation to those rumours. I have never been drawn to S/M myself, and as an editor I can't recall having written anything that could be construed as supporting it. But I can't get up on my high horse and protest righteously as I could have even just a few months ago—since *Trivia* 15, which is now at the printer, includes an article on S/M by a woman who is herself an unapologetic practitioner. (Did those W.I.T.C.H. women somehow get wind of this?)

In any case, just now I have no stomach for controversy. Del has left me. She's taken up with another woman.

She informed me of this on the phone when I called from the production office of *The Voice,* where Brett and I were getting #15 ready to send to the printer.

There'd been a big earthquake in San Francisco, we were following the reports on the radio. I suddenly needed to know Del was okay. To ask when we could get together next.

"Involved with someone" is how she put it.

"Oh you are," I said, trying to match her casualness. As if she were talking about a new car. We'd been lovers for over a year now. Had been in bed together less than a month ago. "That's a pretty quick turnover, isn't it?"

"You have no right to judge. Not after that letter."

So it was a mistake to tell her about Quinn. Possibly a fatal one. There was no time to think about this now, the issue had to be off to the printer tomorrow. I wandered over to Brett at her terminal. "Del chooses this moment to tell me she's involved with someone."

Brett's blank, inscrutable look said she had information she didn't think she should share. She shared it anyway. "Oh, you didn't know."

"No, I didn't know."

I returned to my terminal, then stormed back to Brett's. "How dare she tell you before me? What else do you know that I don't know?"

Brett returned fire. "How can you get all indignant when you were the one who was ambivalent?"

I walked down the hall to the pay phone to call Lena. Needing someone to wail to, someone who'll say don't worry, she'll come around, it's just a childish reaction. Lena was defensive. Unsympathetic. Lena too, it turned out, already knew. Tried explaining Del's position to me. "You weren't in love with her. And you told her you weren't. How can you blame her?"

I was dimly aware of a script repeating.

BACK HOME IN MONTAGUE, bile wakes me up early for days. Boiling blood. Abandoned by lover, betrayed by friends. Now, with *Trivia #15* sent off, I apply my rage to home improvements. Strip the linoleum off the kitchen floors, sand and varnish them. Begin scraping the cabinets, which I'll paint a pale green. My house shaping up, finally resembling the house I envisioned when I first moved in.

Del who railed against feminist orthodoxy, was all for us publishing the S/M piece—we have to start with the truths of our body no matter how heretical—Del who kept begging me to tell her how I feel, then when I do when I finally tell her, in that letter, by way of my dream—*Quinn has come to me, leather jacket, brown ponytail, both of us in a car in the dark side by side*—when I tell her the dream so she'll know how I feel, honesty the only morality I know, she is devastated. The death blow, she says. My final act of cruelty.

So what did you expect, L? If you didn't want her to leave? What on earth were you thinking? Were you even thinking? Okay, I was thinking: the truth will set us free, will help us break out of this cycle. Honestly, L, were you out of your mind?

"S/M: The Violence of Desire" is the title of the article we're publishing in *Trivia #15*. Brett and I both know there will be fallout. *Trivia's* inaugural issue featured an irate response by a well-known feminist to the outbreak of lesbian S/M, a phrase she considered a contradiction in terms. At the time, I shared her outrage. Chains, whips, inflicting pain—wasn't that straight out of the male imaginary? Wasn't our ethic about caring and integrity? And didn't our entire revolution hinge on how different we were?

Maybe some lesbians felt like imitating the worst aspects of male behaviour, but if so they should shut up about it and not ruin it for the rest of us.

Since then my position has mellowed. For most S/M practitioners, I've come to understand—having read testimonies and listened directly to a few—inflicting and receiving pain occurs in a context of mutual trust (something I evidently know little about myself). For some, it can actually serve to build more. Still, I agonized about publishing this article. The explicit parts make me squirm. And I know the decision to publish it will cost us some readers and mortify many others.

I'm counting on my editorial to defuse some of the outrage. In it I point out that the author's purpose was less to defend lesbian S/M than to consider the vehemence of the feminist response to it. Plus, the writing is fine, the thinking rigorous—and the piece is entirely rooted in the writer's own experience. In the name of what definition of feminism, I ask, could we refuse to publish it?

The first response is a call from the author of another article in the issue, on sexual subordination and the state. How could we have published her side by side with a pro-S/M piece? She feels not only offended but betrayed. I refer to my line of argument in the editorial, which she doesn't seem to have read. When we hang up she is not appeased.

Calls and letters begin to come in from subscribers all over the country, most of them complaining: *Trivia* has let them down. They were counting on us to maintain our strong stand against the pro-porn pro-S/M forces. Now we too have caved.

Word comes from Lena that Crone's Harvest in Jamaica Plain is refusing to sell the issue. In its stead on the display shelf is a sign saying: "We do not agree with the direction in which *Trivia* is heading." When I walk into Lunaria in Northampton several weeks later the owner, who usually smiles broadly at me, gives me a dirty look from behind the counter. "That S/M piece was horrifying," her partner pipes up from a corner where she's shelving books. "Starting with the beginning, picking up men in bars." *That* was horrifying? I think to myself on the way home.

I arrive at the bookstore with flyer and bloody hands. The women who work there are all blond, their facial hairs are bleached by the sun. They're planning a raffle, they say, as a fundraiser. They're stacked on top of one another, like pancakes, and speaking from this stack as one voice. There is a gulf between these women and me, I see this now, my bloody secret separates us irremediably, profoundly.

Women's bookstores used to be such inviting places. Beginning with Womanbooks in New York. Later New Words in Cambridge. I'd scan the shelves hungrily alongside women like me, books piling up in my arms, then squirrel my treasures away to a little nook where I'd gorge myself for hours. Women's bookstores in this country were sacred female enclosures housing desperately needed knowledge. Places where women could come and be among women, let their guard down, allow their imaginations to run wild. How did they come to be places I dread entering? Places of constriction instead of expansion? Guardians of feminist morality?

I recall Maxine's tale of the San Francisco bookstore—A Woman's Place, was it?—where a group of women attached stickers saying "don't buy this it's racist" to every copy of *Gyn/Ecology* on the shelf, stickers the staff presumably made no effort to remove. Now it's *Trivia's* turn: banned in a Boston bookstore for breaking with the feminist rank and file.

Of course I can see their point, the Crone's Harvest women. If women's bookstores start selling pro-S/M literature, what's to stop them from stocking the store with lesbian sex magazines, dildos, even whips and chains? And then what will there be to distinguish them from gay bookstores with their window cases of stag magazines featuring well-hung men on the covers? And if what we're about as a movement is trying to bring down a whole structure of power and domination, shouldn't we be wary of an element that wants to introduce that structure into their most intimate exchanges? Isn't it a betrayal to admit it to our ranks?

I know these arguments well since at one time they were mine, and some of them still are. Yet some renegade in me bristles at the repressiveness of the Crone's Harvest response. The righteousness of my "allies," their "with us or against us" attitude—like Jan's bullying that day, marching in with her petition, expecting me to sign—has become more disturbing to me than the reputedly dangerous element that provoked it. Evidently, it's I who have changed.

But of course I have! How is it possible I didn't see this before? I have never been drawn to S/M, but the last woman who lived in my house walked off with two of my friends and called me an aristocratic bitch and I wanted to spit at her. I wanted to rip all the spiky hairs out of her head. I wanted to call her slut and guttertrash. I don't practice S/M but my last lover called me a battering ram, a projectile—then she turned around and rammed it to me herself.

HOUSES HAVE HISTORIES. Memories congeal there, all the sounds of our talking our listening our realizing suspended in the air of the house on Leverett Road, preserved in the walls. *Trivia* was conceived there but it was here she grew up, countless hours of reading and editing bent over galleys, then drafting tables and light tables, waxing, burnishing, stripping in corrections. Fifteen issues delivered by truck unloaded in the garage, our mad scramble to package them for bookstores, stuff them in envelopes, and send them off bulk mail. Six years of bundling and stamping parties, friends lovers students interns friends of friends pitching in. Six years of beer and chips and salsa, excited talk, laughter, friction of minds contagion of ideas live currents in the air.

Six years of electricity. Complicity. Editorials reminding, boosting, binding. Protesting too much? Six years as figurehead. Opinion shaper. Guardian of morality. All those things men do that we would never never never do.

I'm having a claw-foot bathtub installed in my bathroom, to replace the shower stall Lillian made do with her whole life. Cathartic to watch as a two-man demo crew rips out the floor the ceiling the old stall. Three days later I have an airy new bathroom with a cathedral ceiling. Al telling me stories as he bends over the tub: hitchhiking out West with his girlfriend, eating in truck-stop diners. As I scrape rust off the porcelain I steal glances at his naked back. White hairless flanks, thin torso, muscular arms. Sudden nostalgia for my straight days. Pure sex for a change. Friends you can count on. Good times, coasting along on the flow of life.

This house in whose walls are preserved all my hopes and dreams. This house which I now share with two rescued cats, who settled in just as rapturously as I first did, who have staked out their nests on chairs and windowsills, who roam the neighbourhood all day but happily return to sleep at the foot of my bed every night.

This house in whose air is suspended the shutting down the starving out the smoldering the bitter accusations the hateful words. What happens when the truths of our body contradict our visions, our aspirations? *The way we live and love historic, salvific.* Do we ignore them, deny them, bury them in shame?

"The way in which the feminist community chooses to deal with S/M is crucial because it will indicate how it will deal with the unconscious and sexuality itself," LeMasters wrote. What dreams reveal: all the beings who inhabit us, all the creatures large and small. *All the things men do that we would never never never do.*

Every morning first thing I'm out on the deck with my coffee mug, gazing out at the poplar meadow, listening to birdsong, still reveling in my good fortune to have a perch out back among the trees. I'm enamoured as ever of the view from my little bedroom upstairs and this fall as every other fall, when the leaves come down and unveil the meadows beyond where I can sometimes see horses graze, I am struck dumb in wonder and gratitude. Every morning after sitting I walk to the post office trying not to hope and hoping anyway for a letter: of apology of explanation of rapprochement. Every morning I walk back with bills and junk mail.

This house in which I am, except for the cats, finally alone. Alone with my moral outrage. My reading of reality. Look what happens when I tell the truth about my feelings: my lover leaves me, my friends desert me, a whole community rises up in revolt. And I want out. Out of this rigid, oppressive hardware. Out of these walls that once protected me, made me feel I had a home in the world.

This house whose kitchen is now bright and spare and airy, whose bathroom has high ceilings and a tub I can soak in after my day of home improvements. A tub where I can sit for hours and let myself sink deep into sadness that seems to have no end.

34

Last Refuge

Die on the cushion. Give it all up. Die to all the pettiness, all the nastiness, all the self-preoccupation, all the self-pity.... Then see spring come, sparkling and fresh.
—Maurine Stuart, *Subtle Sound*

I'VE MADE EVERY EFFORT not to expect her. They called to say she wasn't well. But when I arrive, a bit late for the evening sit, there she is in the large *zendo*, seated on her cushion behind the bells, just as erect and magisterial as ever, her glorious hair thick and grey and wavy around her head. She glimpses me in the doorway, nods in the direction of the empty cushion in the back; I bow, rush to the cushion, bow again. The bell sounds just as I'm settling in.

When it's time for *kinhin* she leads with her usual zest, toes pointing purposefully in her white Japanese slippers, seeming to thrill when they make contact with the floor. Yes she is smaller than last time, I can see that, but she is elegant in a floor-length black robe I've never seen before and her presence is massive as ever. When she breaks the evening silence—"please, turn round"— there's the same exquisite colouration in her voice. Once we're facing each other she leads us in chanting before sending us all off to bed. Whatever's ailing her has had no effect on her lungs.

Drudgery sets in the next day. Just getting from one bell to the next. Intense boredom and garbage in the brain, like medical waste washing up on the beach. In the *kinhin* line it occurs to me that for someone who hates repetition I spend an awful lot of time in this *zendo* doing the same goddamn thing over and over and over. Maurine would say, has said, there's no such thing as repetition, we're never in the same place twice. Ah, but it takes Zen mind to perceive this. And mine has been churning up the same sludge all morning long. Make that all month. How could they all leave me like this? What did I do?

To feel one's own restlessness—like an incessant rustling in the brain—to feel it to the point of insufferability, even once the breath has slowed down, the entire body, everything but the racing mind, which can't seem to stop wondering whether this really is the right thing for it to be doing.

"Your face looks different," Maurine says to me when I sit across from her in *dokusan*, having fumbled my way through the prostration. The remark catches me off guard, since I'm thinking the same about hers. It's so much thinner.

"How different?"

"More inward." It's as much question as observation.

"I've been disappointed, by my closest friends." An understatement, but I'm sure she'll fill in the blanks.

"Feel it," she counsels. "Feel your disappointment to the dregs."

I nod pensively. Gratefully. So it's possible I've actually been up to something worthwhile these past weeks.

MAURINE'S *TEISHO* THE NEXT MORNING is on what Buddhists call "the fires": desire, anger, grief. These fires I'm so full of. Most of us, she says, either refuse them or are swept away by them. There is another way, she says, a third way: to embrace the fires, in the same way that we embrace this practice. Ride them, but mindfully. Don't reject and don't be swept away. This way shows compassion for the self.

So I try and take it all in, let it all be—my restlessness, my boredom, my disappointment—as I ride my breath in, out, in, all the way to ten and back again. Over and over. And even as I'm thinking, for what must be the hundredth time, this could just be the most monumental waste of time in the whole world, something begins to shift in me. I notice the bare trees out in the garden as we circle the *zendo* during *kinhin*. How much pleasure there is in just looking. The gracefulness of the boughs, the blackness of the bark. The light streaming through the windows even on this grey winter day. Soup smells waft from the kitchen as I pass the door ... and I find myself feeling inordinate love for the cooks.

In the evening, with no warning, joy arrives. My body becomes the opening to a cave. I see and smell damp earth and stone ...

When I kneel across from her the next afternoon I am not the person who sat here the day before.

"Let me see that face." So she knows already.

I break into one of those broad, just-this-side-of-manic *zendo* grins. "You're there again," she says.

"It's amazing. Everything changes."

"But of course it does.... Is there anything else we need to say?"

I planned to say more about all that I've realized: that this state of being, this oneness with the moment, is always there, always available to us. That we can get to it if we persist. That this means everything.

But I don't say more—because she's had a long day and she looks so pale, so tired. Because, though she has risen valiantly to the occasion of *sesshin*, it is impossible to deny anymore ... Maurine is getting sicker.

So I shake my head and we just sit together, face to face, for maybe thirty seconds, until she rings her little bell. I perform the series of bows in reverse order, prostrating, kneeling, bowing, standing, bowing, the way I've learned to do. It's almost effortless by now, but I notice it's not as easy as it was on my way in. There's a tightness in my chest again.

It's Maurine now. I don't want to lose her.

35.
Homeless

To see that we are alone and that every home is a gift, not a normal state of being.

—Christina Thürmer-Rohr, *Vagabonding: Feminist Thinking Cut Loose*

I.

I DRIVE DOWN TO NORTH AMHERST to empty the *Trivia* box. Some fan mail would bolster my spirits. Instead there are more letters from bookstores and subscribers railing about that S/M article in #15. "When we come into ourselves there are no others," Maurine said in one of her *teishos* at the last *sesshin*, and tears sprang to my eyes right away. Thinking of the sex wars. How can we do this to each other? Make each other others, opponents: this camp over here that one over there.

Over here the visionaries the pure of heart and mind, the ones who want a clean slate a fresh start who believe women, especially lesbians, are that fresh start, a way to put all the horrors of patriarchy behind us; over there the sex radicals, who say it is never wrong to want pleasure—especially for women, who've been cut off from our senses, shamed for our desires—who insist on naming and acting on those desires, desires the visionaries claim not to have any interest in, though our dreams tell us otherwise. Me and my Sagittarian arrow always aspiring, always pointing to the loftiest ideals, but then the parts I've repressed show up in my dreams: rapist murderer sexual subordinator.

Sleep is a coy mistress, enticing only to spurn. Moses sleeps curled up by my head, gets under the covers with me when it's cold. I clasp his furry body close to my chest, as I long to have someone do to me. It's the end of the year—1989—the end of a decade, a time for looking back, for taking stock, but that way madness lies. Where did they all go? All the women I loved, around whom my life revolved. Kaye. Bella. Grace. Helen. Lena. Del. Litany of loss, unbearable.

At least there is Brett. We go on talking—over Indian food in New York, over stir-fry in my kitchen in Montague. More and more our conversations are about how women don't seem to be having conversations these days, the communities in which these conversations took place having broken down. As editors, we confess to each other, we're not sure who we're speaking to anymore. Who is our "we"? We've started work on an issue titled "Breaking Forms." We imagine it as our grand finale, we imagine exiting on this dissonant note.

A new intern drives up from Amherst. "I love this room," she says, entering the *Trivia* office, which is lined with books and magazines, and I know it's not the room she means—though it is flooded with afternoon sunlight—it's everything the molecules in this room hold in suspense: meaningful work, shared vision, community. I nod dimly, remembering the innocent me, unaffiliated, not yet entangled with the politics here, who when she first arrived in Leverett kissed the green breast of earth and felt herself to be standing on the brink of a new world. Who saw the women she encountered here as magical creatures, larger than life.

The thought occurs to me: what if I chose feminism—or this particular strain of it—as a way to sustain my own buoyancy? Not to let in the dark? I feel Quinn's presence as I think this, feel her arm about me in friendship and complicity as a phrase from her essay on feminism and tragedy returns to me, something about following Persephone's trail into darkness. I realize I am hard on her heels.

Some nights when I can't sleep I hear the whistling of the Montrealer heading north. I see a large city shrunk to human size, made intimate and warm by the threads spun between women there.

II.

DECEMBER, 1989. FROZEN TWILIGHT SCENE in TV newscast, a crowd shivering behind police tape, stretchers carried out from an institutional building, one after another. Bodies of young women on those stretchers, the reporter says.

City of my dreams. Blue-grey pavestones. Fountains in European plazas. Whenever I come here I drink too much strong coffee, sip wine, and smoke all day. Food eaten mostly after nine p.m., in cafés or bistros. One time in a gourmet vegetarian restaurant, lesbian owned, with ashtrays at every table. My idea of heaven. By the time I leave I'm walking on air.

At the Book Fair. Piling into a car with friends at the end of the day, driving to St. Denis for dinner. Sidewalk café, blue-and-white-checked tablecloth, sultry heat, a round of white wine and then a round of retsina, a waiter who speaks four languages and caters to our every whim. Who apologizes for being "phallocratic" at the end of our meal. Having eavesdropped on our conversation.

Just a block south on St. Denis, *Lilith* and *Labyris,* two lesbian bars side by side. Each of them packed with sexily dancing bodies. We join them, moving back and forth from one to the other.

A city where women dress up, strut their stuff. Where lesbians live out their lives against this backdrop. Where many are themselves such women. And where men seem to know their place.

Now, a year and a half later, fourteen women gunned down by a man who called them feminists, who blamed them for his failed life.

Is it some kind of payback?

My birthday is coming. I decide to take the train up to mark the occasion with my friends: Harriet, and some of the writers I've gotten to know since the Fair. Tall, frail, elegant Mary, with her shock of white hair, her lovely wainscoted Westmount home stuffed with books, paintings, sculptures. Glamorous Michèle, from France, who says she's in Montreal because "here lesbian culture exists."

"My friends," I keep telling myself on the train, though this surging of blood to my heart is not about friends in the plural. I try to stem it. Forbid myself to hope Quinn will have left a message at Harriet's.

She hasn't. Is in no rush to see me when I call.

The city is in the grip of a cold snap. Walking down Mt. Royal, Harriet and I have to duck into a stereo store to warm our feet. The faces all look stricken, I imagine with shock or grief—it's been only a week since the killings—but it could be the cold. No matter, I am thrilled to be here. Even under this shroud of cold and pain the city is alive with pulsation, the drumbeat of possibility.

When we finally meet for dinner she is shorter than I'd remembered. More matronly, somehow. Everyone is numb, she says. The city struck dumb with grief. But of course. Of course. How on earth could I have expected...? At the same time she doesn't look unhappy. She tells me she's been baking Christmas cookies. Says this without flinching.

She notices my thinness she asks about Del she offers sympathy. She thinks it will all blow over, she says, meaning Del's new love. I light a cigarette, gulp down a glass of wine, order another. Watch the strings from which I've been dangling get snapped one by one.

III.

I SPEND MY FIRST DAYS BACK home in the basement trying to wrap the pipes, which froze when I was in Montreal. The papers and TV are full of the faces of people in Dresden, in Romania, all over the Eastern Bloc, crying tears of joy. The Berlin Wall has fallen. They're tasting freedom for the first time. A condition of existence it seems, at this moment, I've frittered away.

I've been translating a book of essays out of German: *Vagabundinnen* by Christina Thürmer-Rohr. Where we are now as a species is more or less her subject. And where we are now, as she points out, in essay after essay, is on the brink of nuclear annihilation and ecological holocaust. It is men who have brought us to this point, she asserts, but women have not been willing or able to stop them, and so women have in our own way been complicit. It's a book intended to kick women out of the cozy nests we've made for ourselves, to block all escape routes into magical thinking. And it fits my present mood like a glove.

Thürmer-Rohr might say I am now tasting freedom for the first time: freedom from false homes, from illusions, from hope. "To live without hope should mean that we concentrate on the life that remains to us, on this present existence..." If she is right, I have a better chance now of concentrating on this present existence. Then how is it that at this moment all I'm aware of is wanting out of it?

At night, the Montrealer's whistle is a cruel taunt: one more siren song I've mistaken for the call of destiny.

IV.

I DRIVE OUT TO ROCKPORT ON A COLD, sunny March day. Have been feeling hope-less and not in a good way. Louisa's gnomish face and figure are immediately comforting.

"Not an easy time you're having," she says right off the bat, her Boston accent stronger, her voice deeper than I remembered. So she's seen it all in my chart. She hands me the Kleenex box; I'm already in tears. "You can't see where you're going. So much is ending and your future hasn't shown itself."

I nod and sob harder.

She assures me in no uncertain terms there is a future—this is, of course, why I've come to see her—and that it's very rich and full. "But you're going to have to move," she says. "If you don't you'll get booted out of where you are."

Yes, I say. No kidding.

The cards are good, she says, when I ask about Montreal. "The woman thing there ... is really something. And it looks like a great place to write, in fact it looks like you'll have just about everything you ever wanted there."

"Including love?" I ask timidly. Why can't I just be happy about the writing part? The "everything you ever wanted"?

There's an ashtray on the table between us, I grab a cigarette.

She lights up too, starts laying cards out on the table.

"Looks like you've got a good one coming, a really nice one ... somebody very beautiful very mysterious ... look, it's the high priestess." She turns the card around for me to see. The figure on it looks very wise, very regal. "You'll have to be a little patient, though, it won't start before August of '91."

"Is it possible it's already started?" I tell her a bit about Quinn, our history.

She fans the cards out again. "Hmm, I don't see lovers here." I must look crestfallen, since she now begins to slap the cards down on the table, one spread after another. "Looks like you two will have a very nice friendship ... but ... I'm sorry, I just don't see lovers here."

"Are you sure?" I feel stupid for insisting but I have to know.

"Well I'm sure as far as the cards are concerned. Of course, the cards could be wrong. Doesn't happen very often, but it does happen...."

After the reading I drive down to the harbour, walk out to the end of the town pier, just the way I did that February—is it two years ago now?—after my defence. How right she was then, Louisa. How right the cards were. And no doubt she's right again this time. I wonder how it is that despite her having snuffed out the one little flame that's kept me going these past months I feel so much better than I did before. Because I'm so much bigger, that's why. Though I thanked Louisa profusely as I walked out the door, as usual I feel there is no way to thank her enough.

Several nights later, when I wake to hear the whistling of the Montrealer heading north, I feel the old thrill. It's calling to me, and I'm going to follow the call. It seems a woman is waiting for me at the end of the line. I strain to supplant Quinn's image with that of the mysterious woman in the cards. She has dark hair, I'm sure of that—and she's French. Maybe she's the city herself, I think. Dark, mysterious, alluring.

PART IV
THE HIGH PRIESTESS

36.
On the Cusp

Where is our home? What does home mean for women?
Can we know our home?
—Christina Thürmer-Rohr, *Vagabonding:*
Feminist Thinking Cut Loose

SEPTEMBER, 1990. HOME IS A NARROW row house in the heart
of the Plateau, around the corner from *l'essentielle*. There's a
patchwork of gardens in back, overrun with cats. Downstairs, a
wood stove. My bedroom upstairs faces the rustic backsides of a
row of cottages. Moni from the bookstore has the room across
the hall.

It's not the house of my dreams. The bathroom has no bath or
washbasin, and pink insulation pokes out from the rafters above
the shower. The kitchen is all modern appliances and fake oak
cupboards. But between the wood stove and a patio door looking
out over the garden, the downstairs has a latent charm which,
after several days of scrubbing, painting, and importing plants
and old furniture, Moni and I succeed in bringing out.

We're nestled in the heart of lesbian culture here. Writers and
editors from the Fair are sprinkled about the Plateau and the
bookstore around the corner is a port of call for writers from out
of town. Harriet is just two metro stops away, Michèle walking
distance. *Labyris* has closed but *Lilith* still stands on St. Denis,
a few blocks away, and just to the north is *l'exit*, a handsome
afternoon bar where you can sit with a book or meet friends
before dinner.

I love walking the streets of the Plateau, love the narrow

bungalows with their wrought-iron balconies and winding staircases, the little *dépanneurs* on almost every corner where you can buy booze, papers, cigarettes till all hours. I love to wander the *ruelles,* peer into backyards still lush with vegetation. Moses and Beauty, as caught up in wanderlust as I am, return from their forays fur tangled with leaves and brambles. Once you know to look for them, cats are everywhere in this *quartier:* taking the sun in those backyards, peeking out from behind fences, occasionally trotting out into the lanes.

In early October I drive back down to Montague to meet with Brett and wrap up the "Breaking Forms" issue. Our new office manager and her partner have taken over the big bedroom upstairs; the small one is still mine. I like having one foot in my old home, especially now, in early fall, when the leaves have begun to turn and the meadows are still deep green. And I love this crooked house, even if I can't live here anymore.

Ever since the issue she edited in my absence, Brett has been working hard to make sure the voices in *Trivia* are not all white, as they mostly were before she arrived, apart from the issue I edited with Helen. For the longest time I did not see the problem. It's not as if we were turning writers of colour away. Did we really have to start actively recruiting? Only now that I'm getting a taste of this mix of voices do I begin to feel what was missing. This issue features an interview with Paula Gunn Allen and articles by Canadian First Nations writer Lee Maracle and Afro-Caribbean writer M. NourbeSe Philip. It is full of hard questioning about language and ethics. Thanks to these writers, thanks to Brett, I'm starting to get it, what the whole identity fracas obscured—that "white" was a part standing in for the whole. And not necessarily the most vital or interesting part.

As pleased as we are by the material we've chosen, Brett and I confess we were both a little discouraged by all the submissions we had to wade through to get to them. Writing in which there was little in the way of experimentation, subversion.

"Didn't we use to be about throwing everything up in the air? Risk taking?" Brett wants to know.

I'm aware there's a subtext here. Lately her lovers—there is always more than one—have been pressuring her, wanting more in the way of structure, commitment.

"What's happened to lesbians anyway?"

"'Safe space?'" I offer.

"You might actually have a point there." Brett, who majored in U.S. history, talks about cycles of revolution, how the sense of frontier and possibility in the U.S. shaped the lesbian/feminist revolution and how, like the first settlers, once we "arrived" we ended up calling all the old structures back into place: monogamy, motherhood, family.

"Yes!" I say. "Exactly." Thinking of Quinn last December and her domestic happiness. Feeling vindicated by this analysis.

Back home, Brett and I resume the conversation at the kitchen table. We take notes as we talk. Something is taking shape, we can both feel it. We scurry off to our rooms and write furiously, return to the kitchen later to read what we've written out loud. Brett's poetic meditation on breaking, juxtaposed with my more discursive speculations on where we are now as a movement. We exclaim, cajole, send each other back to the drawing board. Gradually it all begins to gel, fragments connect, form mirroring content. We write into it our heartbreak and our hope. By the end of the weekend we have the draft of an editorial: a collaborative piece, call, and response, a broken form. We feel great pride and accomplishment when we part on Sunday.

Driving back up to the city, car loaded with clothes and kitchen things, I think back to our conversation and the lament at the centre of it: whatever happened to the dizzying freedom of those first visionary days-months-years? Now, heading north, I wonder. Is that really what I long for—that sense of being on an edge, always?

Breaking forms: is that really my aspiration now? When it comes to love it seems breaking forms is all I know.

It's true I don't want marriage don't want till-death-do-us-part. But I'm about to turn forty and surely I can't go on loving in this helter-skelter, hand-to-mouth way forever? The truth is I'd consider it an accomplishment to maintain any form at all for more than a few months at a time. So who am I to resent Quinn for trying to do just that? For attempting to respect a form? To live inside it?

My second night back in the city I call. I tell her how sad I am not to have spoken to her all these weeks. Yes, she says, it's been strange for her too. Wait while I get a match, she says. I light up too.

37.

Perdu / Trouvé
(of Things Lost and Found)

...but they were all people's tears, weeping for all people
—Virginia Woolf, *Between the Acts*

LATER ON I'LL DECIDE IT HAD TO have happened when Moni opened the door to get some air. The last time I saw Moses it was just before midnight and he was hovering by the front door. Awaiting his chance, it now appears. Moni was entertaining a new friend downstairs, a palpable buzz between them. Both of them no doubt too distracted to notice. In the morning he was gone.

The night was October 25. I remember the date because of how many times I am asked in the weeks that follow: when did you last see him? And I remember because it was a marker, dividing the city into before and after.

Right away I call our lesbian neighbours. No, he's not there. But they'll put out the alert to everyone they know.

I begin to walk the streets, turning into the *ruelle*s. I peer under fences calling his name. A light rain is falling; it's cold and raw. I imagine him huddled under some porch crying. I get on my bike, fan out farther, scan the entire neighbourhood, calling his name loudly when no one seems to be in earshot.

Late afternoon I begin to panic. Call Harriet, who says she'll be right over to help search for him. Call Michèle, who utters a cry of alarm, she has left behind a cat she adores in France. "I will pray for him!" she says. Harriet and I circle the neighbourhood together; her stream of hopeful remarks keeps me from caving in.

Moni, almost as upset as I am, keeps watch with me all evening, ears perked, running to the door at the slightest sound to see if he's there. I spend the night downstairs on the couch, making regular trips to the door. Never dropping down into sleep.

The next day I call Quinn. The thought of her voice at the other end promises some sort of relief.

"I know you're probably working," I say.

"Yes as a matter of fact I am." She wouldn't have picked up except she's waiting for a call from her publisher.

"Moses is gone."

"I'm sorry," uttered tonelessly.

I'm thrown now and have to scramble. "I thought since you had cats before maybe you'd have an idea...."

She tells me to poster. She says many cats are found that way. Just put up signs. On telephone poles, etc.

At least I now have a course of action. I make a sign; Moni helps with the French. Buy tape and staple gun. Bike down St. Denis to the nearest copy shop. Begin to poster the neighbourhood, a rite that I will practice almost every day now for weeks. Getting to know every *dépanneur* lamppost and telephone pole for blocks around, every inch of the *ruelles* between Berri and St. Hubert, between Berri and Rivard, every escape hole and hideaway and *cul-de-sac*.

I call Mary, my writer friend in Westmount. We corresponded regularly when I was in Montague and our cats featured heavily in our letters. Mary gives me the number of Z., her astrologer. Otherwise known as *l'oracle*. "I don't know if she can help find him. But she's always gives the best advice. Very practical."

I call "*l'oracle*," get her machine. Her greeting says she's out of town till the end of November.

REPORTS OF SIGHTINGS BEGIN TO COME IN. Two old sisters with slightly hunched backs who live together in an apartment down the street say in tandem, "*on l'a vu dehors, il vient manger,*" eagerly they usher me down a yellowing hallway, ceiling so low I have to stoop, point to the courtyard. But the cat out there isn't Moses, doesn't look anything like him. A couple on Rivard claim to have seen him, they have three cats in their living room and oil paintings of Spanish cats on their walls, but the cat they've seen isn't long-haired, something it takes us awhile to establish at first since I keep saying *"cheveux"* for fur instead of *"poils."*

A woman on Brébeuf calls to say she's seen my cat, he usually comes by in the morning. I'm out patrolling the street just after dawn. At eight, I see a cat on the fire escape awaiting its breakfast. Grey-brown. Short hair. An old woman emerges with a bowl, sets it down, catches sight of me on the stairs. *"Pas votre chat?"* she says. Almost as crestfallen as I am.

I sleep in fits and starts and wake every morning to pain. Not sharp anymore, not lacerating. Just a dull, continuous ache on the outer edges. Today on my way to the Piscine Levesque for the first time, eyeing the telephone poles along the way, signs and staple gun in my bag along with bathing suit and hairdryer, I thought: I came to the city to write and instead here I am hunting for my cat. I think what Maurine would say: then give yourself over to it! To the hunt. To the grief. Live it out all the way.

I'm in touch with sadness everywhere. Reading about the horses that fell in the Belmont races and had to be put to sleep. The dolphins washing up in the Mediterranean, PCBs in their system. The abandoned cats at the SPCA, the ones with no chance of being adopted. Not to mention the prospect of imminent war in Iraq; the U.S. seems poised to invade.

Almost two weeks have passed when I begin buying the local papers for the lost-and-found columns. I scan them greedily for the words *"gris, blanc, tigré"* feel absurdly hopeful when I occasionally find them in the *"perdu"* section. It's another week before I decide to put in an *annonce* myself. And then have to field the calls. One from a woman who hasn't seen my cat but wants me to not give up hope her cat finally came home. One from a man saying he has my cat then asking if my husband is home. *"J'ai pas de mari,"* I say, so focused on getting the French right that I don't pick up on the obvious till afterwards, when he asks for my address. A message on the machine from a woman saying "we have your cat but we're going on vacation. We'll call when we're back." They never do.

Walking the white streets in biting wind, smell of stale cigarette smoke pumping up from the grates beside the bars on Rachel, aiming for the pet store for lack of a better plan. Hoping for some feline conversation. This move, which had been demonstrating its rightness by way of so many small but persistent signs, now thrown utterly into question. No one is here in this snowy wasteland without a damn good reason and what's yours? I'm aware it might not seem so bleak if Quinn had called to check in on me, to ask: has he turned up yet? And then: oh. I'm so sorry.

"TO WANT, TO WANT, AND NOT TO HAVE." What happens when I stop forbidding myself to want what I know I can't have? When I allow myself to feel it all the way? For her now as well as him. The depth the ache the heft of my longing. When I go on sitting through it, as Maurine would have instructed me to do. Eventually I run up smack against: the exigencies of her life, her own particular history, her life force driving her in a direction other than where I would have her go.

And my little Moses? What happens when I go on sitting, long and hard, with my desire for him? I join a dirge of weeping women: Demeter's tears for her lost daughter. Isis' tears for her slain brother. I merge with the sadness of the world. Sadness for all lost things.

38.
The Oracle

We must radically reject every superficial consolation.
—Christina Thürmer-Rohr, *Vagabonding:*
Feminist Thinking Cut Loose

DECEMBER 20 ARRIVES, THE DAY OF my appointment with "*l'oracle.*" My last hope. I'm feeling the onset of a cold, bundle up in scarf and hat to walk the several blocks north then across the Plateau to St. Joseph. The "*oracle*" is tall, which for some reason takes me by surprise. And very *soignée* in checked blazer and woollen pants. Eyes—large, deep-set blue eyes—heavily made up. Formal, to the point of cold. This impression reinforced by her spare, spacious office with its steel and leather chairs. The green swivel armchair on which she is seated. An architect, one might surmise. A geometric pattern pulsing on the large computer screen beside her desk.

She won't be able to tell me where Moses is. She says this to me right away. Finding lost animals is not part of her repertoire. "You won't see him again, so don't even think about that," she snaps in response to my first spread. "But he's in good hands." Case closed.

There are big changes coming, she says. "You've been very political ... but now ... you'll see, you're going to start paying more attention to the personal. Your own personal needs."

I want to protest, to say "the personal is political." But instead I nod. I can't deny she's onto something. I thought I was coming to Montreal for the writers, for the women, for the politics. And instead all fall I've been walking the streets looking for my cat.

At least if she can't help me find Moses I hope she'll say something about Quinn. Don't astrologers always come around to the subject of love sooner or later? Not this one, not a word. I have to pop the question. "*Et l'amour? Est-ce que tu vois quelque chose?*"

She proceeds to describe the kind of woman I'm attracted to. Very intelligent. But a little removed, she says. A little indifferent. "*Pas tellement disponible.*" Not too available.

I have to laugh. Obviously, she's describing Quinn.

But in the springtime, she says, things will start to warm up. "*Ça va se rechauffer.*"

In the weeks after the reading my thoughts wander to her. *La tireuse des cartes.* Her voice, deep and resonant. Her melodious French, which somehow reconciled me to Québecois. Of course, oracular voices tend to stay with you, as their sage advice resounds in your head. But in this case it's not just the voice. It's her cheekbones. Her penciled eyes. Her very upright spine.

Don't be silly, I say to myself. Why would a woman like that be interested in a woman like you? With your sloppy old parka and your big winter boots? Never mind why I would be interested in someone like her. Who lives on a noisy boulevard. Whose taste in furniture runs to modern and functional.

Even if she isn't straight, which she most probably is. We made a bit of conversation before I left. She'd just returned from Paris. Beautiful, she said, but she could never live there. The men are just too sexist. How else would she know? I saw her going out to fine restaurants with a lineup of suave Parisian men, then dropping them cruelly.

Her serene smile. Her aloof demeanor. Definitely unavailable.

39.
The Red Hook

For love is flesh, it is a flower flooded with blood. Did
you think it was just a little chat across a table
　　　　　　—Marina Tsvetaeva, "Poem of the End #5"

I AM TRYING TO HANG A RED PICTURE on a white wall. I'm
about to do it with a silver hook when Quinn appears. "You
need a red hook for that," she says and produces one from her
bag. I am so impressed: a woman with a red hook in her bag!

Mid-January. Starlings huddling on the rims of stovepipes. Sky
a vaporous white. Cold like no cold I've ever known. A force that
whacks you when you open the front door.

We're tucked away in a dark corner of Jardin de Panos, Quinn
and I, with a bottle of wine between us. Talking about the
impending war. Something still has me by the gills, despite all my
hard-won progress. The irresistible pull of "no." "No" mixed
with an ever-so-subtle "come hither," the ever-so-persistent
vibration of interest of excitement I pick up with my ever-so-
sensitive tuning fork. We've been "meeting for a coffee," as they
say here, whether coffee is actually taken or not. Spurring each
other on to energetic, passionate, sometimes feverish talk, while
respecting the boundaries.

"I almost wish they'd start bombing so I could stop dreading
it," she is saying.

"Don't you hate it? That they can manipulate our attention this
way?"

"I've been rereading *Three Guineas*." A sly smile. She can trust
me to fill in. "It's never been more *à propos*."

The waiter has uncorked our bottle and set down two glasses. I pour us each a glass and raise mine for a toast. "To freedom from unreal loyalties."

"To freedom, period." That smile again.

"I've been thinking about Lesbian Desire," I say, lighting up my first cigarette of the evening. Risky, yes, but it's also one of our pet subjects. "Uppercase 'l' and 'd,'" I add.

"Oh, I like that." She seems to know exactly where I'm heading. She takes a cigarette from my pack, lights up. In our last phone conversation she announced she had stopped smoking. But I shouldn't read into this.

"I used to think it had implications for the whole world. What we desire, as lesbians, being nothing less than total subversion. Now I've begun to wonder if it isn't a tiny bit overblown ..."

"So ... you've begun to come around." It's a game we play: diehard idealist versus hard-nosed realist.

"Maybe a little. Though I'm not sure I can dispense with it completely...."

"Maybe it's the uppercase 'l' that needs dismantling," she suggests. Her fingers curl so delicately about the cigarette. Her exquisite fingers.

"Hmm. Not sure I can entirely let go of that either. Aren't we the sibyls, the bearers of vision?"

"Well, yes, I've been guilty of that belief myself."

The conversation has gotten away from me. There was some depth I'd wanted to plumb with her, some truth I wanted us to confront together. Something about dreams deferred, desire throttled. Something about the abysmal human condition, which makes compromise necessary. All that I've come to understand and accept, thanks to her. Virginia had her Leonard, after all. Jane Bowles needed her Paul. Susan Glaspell dedicated her great feminist writings to her supportive husband.

"So you don't see a problem with uppercase 'd'?" I say, trying to get back on track.

"I'm not sure I believe it exists."

In order to argue with this I'd have to violate my gag order. Upset our delicate balance, our precarious intimacy. Does she understand this is why I fall silent?

As our talk returns to the subject of Bush and Saddam, I touch my leg to hers, surreptitiously, under the table. We did just toast to freedom, didn't we?

Afterwards I walk her home. Up Duluth to St. Laurent. Our puffy parkas. Our squeaking boots. Our breath white against the dark sky. When we get to her gate I grab her. Aim for her lips. She dodges the kiss, sets it right, on the cheek, first one, then the other.

THE NEXT DINNER IS AT MY PLACE. She's had her hair cut short. "I'm trying to be more butch," she says. In an angora sweater that accentuates her curves.

I laugh, shake my head. How fond I am of her. "Tell me you're joking."

I've been helping to form a women's anti-war group: *Femmes pour la paix.* I tell her I'm not happy with the title, would have preferred *Amazons at war with the existing world order.* Not snappy enough, they said.

"I prefer yours," says she.

It's balmy out, February thaw. We walk down St. Denis to *Lilith,* grab ourselves a table. Lesbians are necking all around us. I have my stool right up against hers, am holding on to her leg.

"I've always wanted to taste lipstick on another woman's lips," she says.

"Okay, I'll wear lipstick next time I see you."

"You'd look silly in lipstick."

Walking her home in the rain. Under her small umbrella, which we huddle to fit under. I keep kissing her on the cheek, under the shelter of the umbrella. She keeps telling me to stop. But I think she likes it.

Spring is in the air and things are warming up. Isn't this what the *oracle* predicted?

MONTREAL IN APRIL. Gulls shrieking. Yards wet, slightly smelly. Clothes pinned up on lines. Winds that seem to whip up the fire in my blood. Her voice, the way it dips and crashes. The world inside her, behind her mouth.

Walking the streets and lanes littered with winter's detritus I keep an eye out for Moses; maybe he'll surface again with the warmth. Thought I saw him once at the end of a *ruelle*, fat white chest, thick fur, riveted to the spot as if waiting for me. When I came up close I saw it was a white plastic bag sticking up in a point. Was it a sign? Am I doing the same thing with Quinn? Making it all into what I want it to be?

We're sitting side by side on a train traveling west. Then somehow we're face to face, and our lips come together. I place my tongue lightly against her teeth and she draws it in....

40.
Salon Méchant

A lesbian is a woman who burns with imagination the way one smolders with the desire for beauty, the way women's beauty sweeps through us like wild-fire.
—Nicole Brossard, "Kind Skin My Mind"

ATLANTA. The First National Lesbian Conference. It's a historic event, not to be missed, according to friends, though just now it feels like a not entirely welcome diversion. But when I see "National Lesbian Conference" in lights on the great marquee by the football stadium in the cab coming in, it's impossible not to get in the spirit of it. Almost three thousand dykes have come here from all over the country. We've taken over the Hilton. The carpeted hallways the salons the ballrooms—all there to receive us!

The lobby is cooking with lesbian energy, dykes milling about in every shape size and skin colour, butch, femme, fat, thin, long tresses and short, white heads purple heads heads shaven and bobbed. Wittig's provocative assertion, "Lesbians are not women," has never rung more true. We are women who've thrown off all the shackles of womanhood, the constrictions of gender. We've claimed our own wildest selves.

I make my way up the elevator to my floor. With room doors ajar, the hallway resounds with women's voices, ripples of conversation, barking laughs. It could be camp, or a girls' dorm. We are girls at heart, after all. On this occasion, happy girls. Excited girls.

In my room I take a look at my conference packet, which is

very thick. Fishing around for the schedule, I run across a long section of ground rules designed to familiarize us with the basics of anti-racist anti-ageist anti-ableist anti-sizeist behaviour. The antiableism section, which is larger than all the others put together, has a "dos and don'ts" list. On the don't side: 1) Seeing her as non-sexual. 2) Wearing "ornamental scents." 3) Failing to create a ramp for your home and office. It's hard to believe disabled women themselves had anything to do with these guilt-slinging rules. I think of the ex-friends I'm dying to read them off to: Del, Lena, Grace.

Every day there are caucus sessions where the conference themes—all oppression issues—are aired and debated. The first day I attend one on race, then on anti-Semitism. The girls are not so happy to be together at these sessions. Tempers flare. I'm right back at those anti-racist events in Boston over ten years ago. Remembering what a misfit I felt then. Hell, I'm right back in my queer girlhood: cast out for reasons I don't understand. Unknowingly provoking disgusted looks.

I realize the impulse for all of this anti-oppression work is to make the spaces we share free of the painful treatment we receive in the world at large. Wanting things to be different. But is this the outcome we want? Oppressed groups competing for attention? The rest of us walking on eggshells lest we inadvertently offend?

The next day I blow off the main caucus session to attend a workshop on sex and intimacy. The mood here could not be more different: lots of smiling, knowing laughter. There is exuberant discussion of orgasms, G-spots, sex toys. One woman—she has a great mane of white hair and an aquiline nose—speaks eloquently about women's right to pleasure, a right that, she points out, most of us have a hard time claiming. I recognize her name when she says it. A fellow publisher; we've corresponded but never met.

Afterwards I introduce myself at her booth. She invites me to pull up a chair and we have ourselves a long chat. She tells me she has two other love interests here—one of them walks by as we're talking and waves to her—but she wants to make time to see me. Am I busy tomorrow evening, do I want to come with her to see the lesbian sex cabaret? The *Salon Méchant*. She has a ride, she's sure they can squeeze me in. I say yes.

THE NEXT EVENING WE'RE DRIVEN OUT of the city centre and into a suburban patch of ranch homes laid out in a grid, past a very long row of parked cars. One of them has an open trunk—a woman is selling beer out of it. This could be a high school football game we're approaching, except only women are strolling towards us, many leather clad. All of them looking flushed and relaxed. And music is throbbing from a low concrete building nearby.

Disco music bounces off the walls as we enter. Most women in the audience are in some sort of costume. There are captain's hats, leather caps, cuffs, rings in every possible body part, heads shaved at every angle. And the vibes are ... sexual. Not heavy, not menacing. Just a slow, steady pulse that grows stronger and stronger the longer we're here.

The stage acts begin. My date and I have drifted away from the others in the car and are now stationed close to the stage. A nun in habit enters to Gregorian chant and candles, begins a stately ritualized dance. Church music gives way to rock as she starts peeling off her garments, all the way down to lace bra and panties with webbing in the crotch that she touches periodically, suggestively. Dykes from the audience get up on stage and dance with her. I have an urge to get up there and dance too, but instead I join my date in clapping and shouting and cheering them on. Oh, the girls are happy now. This is fun, uproarious fun!

Why did we ever get so worked up about this kind of thing? It's hard to remember now. Banding together to denounce the sex radicals, the anti-censorship feminists, the ones who wanted to talk about pleasure and danger, who just wanted to have fun. Policing sexual behaviour. What were we afraid of losing? Only everything we believed in, were fighting for. Desire as a force for political change. Desiring out of the wholeness of our being. Did we have any idea how tall that order was?

I realize I'm getting excited, not so much from the stage act as from being in this moist purple underground cave throbbing with erotic energy. I'm acutely aware of my date's sexually evolved body jostling against me in this dense crowd. I want to touch her, and not accidentally. Want my hand on her skin. I'm about to make a move when someone breaks in on us. It's our driver, rounding us up. We exit the cave, our faces glowing now like the ones we saw coming in. Pressed against her in the back seat of the car riding home I long to plant my hand on her thigh, put my lips in her hair—it wouldn't be much of a stretch. I abstain. Then all night am tortured with sexual longing. Her raspy laugh. Her wild hair. Her nose, just this side of hooked. The great dark circles under her eyes.

How is this possible? When I'm so in love with Quinn, have not been aware of wanting anyone but her for so long. The heart not involved in the same way, the heart barely involved at all.

Undeniable, disreputable, lowercase desire. Me moved by my netherparts. Wholeness be damned.

41.
The Cold Shoulder

*After you have practiced for a while, you will realize that
it is not possible to make rapid, extraordinary progress.*
—Shunryu Suzuki, *Zen Mind, Beginner's Mind*

I'VE COME, AGAIN, IN SPITE OF EVERYTHING. *Come again, in
hope. And her brown shoulders compel me, the cradle of her
chest bones. I go to her I try to circle her shoulders and now once
again she is forced to say no. She says it clearly this time, without
emotion. A trace of irritation in her voice, at having to do this yet
again, at my persistence.*

A fiery impulse, followed to its absurd conclusion. Travel to a
distant place where she happens to be. One that promises to be
less obstacle-strewn than the city we both inhabit. Feeling a little
reckless—can ambush be serendipitous?—but mostly expansive.
Glorious. Desire having given me wings.

The landing is hard. The landing is cruel. She is not pleased
to see me. She is not amused. She is not ambivalent. The answer
is no.

Compelled by the cold shoulder—this began at birth. It was
earliest love earliest knowledge. Mother with a short attention
span. Mother whose affections I must try and win, over and over.
In the absence of a cold shoulder I create one, go in search of one.
They are easier to find than you'd think. The warmest shoulder
can become a cold one. It just takes a little distance a little
upending of trust. In this case: A little breaching of boundaries.
Forcing her hand.

What is this awful pull in me toward no?

Must we go back, return, over and over again, to the wound? To the aging star who snubs you by the side of the road? To the one who wants you but doesn't, whose yes is lined with no's, who reels you in only to cast you off. Have I been returning, over and over again, to the wound? And calling it love?

Stay with the sadness stay with the broken heart. That voice again. Till you've felt it all the way: the depth the ache the heft of your longing.

42.
Collaborations; Broken Forms

We made between us an alloy that is at its heart a bond of love, strong and flexible, prodigious and productive. It has not been without difficulties without and within—that's just how it was.... We only know that we are thankful to have been naïve and to have been in love. Now both will always make the possible possible forever.
—Martha Fleming, Lyne Lapointe, *Studiolo*

MONTREAL IN LATE MAY IS WARM and green but grass and city trees are a poor substitute for the peepers and warblers and dense unfurling life in western Massachusetts. I'm spending long hours in immigration offices, each of which seems to have its own set of rules. I need a work permit so I can get a job here. But in order to get a work permit, they tell me, I need a job offer. By now moving here has begun to feel like yet another glorious impulse gone terribly wrong. Is this how my mother felt her first Chicago spring, stuck in a high rise in the big dirty city, the romance having worn off? But by then her belly had already swollen up with me and her fate was sealed.

When I'm not waiting in immigration offices I'm deep inside *Trivia* work. This next issue will be my last. Our office manager, Erin, and her partner, K., are taking over as editors. They were the first to respond to the call Brett and I put out in early spring, and in the end we accepted their offer with enthusiasm, all the more so since it turned out to be the only one that came in. Their lack of experience, we agreed, was easily trumped by their eagerness and indefatigable energy.

"Collaboration" is the theme of this last issue, its centerpiece the collaborative work of Montreal artists Martha Fleming and Lyne Lapointe. I'd been hearing about their large-scale projects ever since I moved to this city, the abandoned buildings they restored and then opened to the public. Then Brett and I literally stumbled onto their most recent site installation as we strolled along the waterfront in Battery Park on my visit to New York last spring. "The Wilds and the Deep" read a sign over the ornate hulk of the Battery Maritime Building. We entered a massive theatre of polished wood floors, painted pillars, and murals evoking the marina's glory days, its former life as a ferry mooring slip.

The installation extended to the roof of a low-lying neighbouring building on which a crowded slave ship had been painted in full view of the traders and stockbrokers on Wall Street. Brett and I wandered about the site, taking in every detail, our mouths hanging wide open. This was at once exquisite art and bold political statement. The whole project seemed a seamless integrity of means and ends, and stirred in me the same sense of transgression and possibility, of official divisions dissolving, as Teddy's pueblo-inspired architectural drawings had years earlier. As Brett and I walked out of the building, we vowed to find a way to get this work into *Trivia*.

In February Brett came up to visit with her main girlfriend, herself a visual artist, and the three of us interviewed Martha and Lyne in their Montreal loft. We sat around an old pine table in their little kitchen area upstairs; below us, a dugout canoe hung suspended between two wooden walls lined with exhibit cases displaying artifacts. Right away Martha and Lyne brought up their erotic bond—it was, they insisted, at the root of all their artistic productions. Theirs was a collaboration born of deep love and intense lust, and intimacy and pleasure had a central place in all of their projects.

The life they were describing was a life I would have wanted for myself, a life I had had briefly with Grace, then with Helen, and imagined having with Quinn. Wasn't it exactly this kind of creative collaboration lesbian bonds were for? At least I had been lucky enough to experience this kind of partnership with friends, first with Anne and now with Brett.

In the afterglow of that interview, which eventually folded all of us into a conversation that spun from insight to revelation, not unlike those heady gatherings in Leverett, Brett and I decided to devote our last issue to the theme of collaboration. It seemed a fitting note to end on, born as *Trivia* was out of the collective imagination of the women in study group. It went to the heart of our mission as we saw it then: love and friendship as the seedbed for all radical thought, vision, creation.

Now, though, I'm not so sure. This issue is on the slim side, our search for active women collaborators not having turned up very many. And in the editorial I'm taking stock of this entire decade of editing, what began as a collaborative undertaking and then somehow devolved into a one-woman operation, at least until Brett came along. I'm having to contemplate, yet again, the way we came together and then came apart. How we did each other in.

But that's not all. Brett and I seem to be coming apart. It's subtle at first. A tension over the phone when we talk about the issue. Just not the same smooth give and take there used to be between us. A curtness on her end, which she denies when I confront her.

I can't believe this is happening. "A good thing we never got involved" we used to say as we watched lovers quarrel, separate, abandon their collaborative projects. We never hid our differences, which were sometimes extreme; the sex wars came home to us and we argued our way through them. We prided ourselves on being able to clash and even duel in the context of friendship. We could always hear each other out, with respect.

In June we meet in Montague. The plan for the weekend is to go over the material for this issue and officially pass the torch to the new editors. Brett and I both arrive late on Friday night and park ourselves at the kitchen table with a six-pack between us. Erin and K. join us and right away want stories from Atlanta. I launch into an account of my flirtation, our evening at the *Salon Méchant*. It's a kind of concession to Brett, who always held up the "pro-sex" side in our sex-war arguments, and she seems grudgingly amused. Erin and K. applaud; being of their generation, they are happy to see me break ranks with what they perceive as anti-sex feminism.

I go on to talk about the caucuses. An orgy of identity politics, I call them. The oppression model gone berserk. Everyone whining, sparring, jockeying for position. Yes, the skier needs to recognize the cripple, I say, invoking Adrienne and her poem. But does she need to cripple herself in the process? This question has been forming in me for a while now, and I've been looking forward to putting it out before Brett, taking it up with her, the way we've always done.

All three of us look Brett's way eagerly, expectantly.

But she is not responding. Brett—she of the sunny, can-do energy, always upping the voltage, making everything seem possible—is quiet, sombre. Closed down.

I cite the conference program, the ground rules for behaviour. I reel off the several ways not to offend a woman in a wheelchair. Guffaws and noises of disbelief from Erin and K. Nothing from Brett. I finally ask her what's up.

"It's not like there's no point to any of these rules, to those caucuses," she says. "Okay, maybe they took it too far. But most feminists still don't get class and race."

Instantly my own guilt kicks in. "You don't get class and race," she might as well have said. Where do I get off making fun, from my position of privilege? When was the last time I did anything about class or race?

"Point taken," I say. "I shouldn't be so derisive." I can feel myself shrinking, just the way I did at the conference in Boston, self-doubt erasing me from the inside. At the same time, even as the old heaviness descends, a small voice protests: "What about you? Doesn't your own experience matter at all?" My question about the skier and the cripple wasn't an idle one. I really need to know, minus the sarcasm, the exasperation: is there a way for a person of privilege like me to make amends without apologizing herself out of existence?

The next morning, Brett and I go over the contents of this issue. Though it's not especially full, I find the issue pretty stunning. If nothing else, it's a testament to the creative brilliance love between women can bring into being.

Brett doesn't seem as thrilled as I am. Okay, most of the writers were selected by me and all of them are white, except for Suniti

Namjoshi, who's an upper-caste Indian. Is that why she's so stony?

We go over the interview. I want to make some changes in the interest of clarity. Brett wants an exact transcription, accuses me of imposing my own voice, my elitist standards. There's an echo here of complaints she's made in the past, except that then she was friendly, conciliatory, and now she is neither. In the end I give in.

We're writing a four-way editorial and each of us has brought a draft to read. We comment on each other's drafts, hole up in our rooms and rewrite, then reemerge for another round of readings. I love this process, my home serving the function I've always wanted it to. If only Brett weren't sniping at me in her editorial, not the least bit covertly now.

Brett and I spend much of the weekend giving advice and support to Erin and K., passing on tips. As long as the focus is on them everything goes well, and we accomplish everything on our list of tasks. But when it's time for her to go on Sunday I'm relieved and the relief is palpable on her end too. It's never been this way before.

A PACKAGE IS WAITING FOR ME when I get back to Montreal: the advance copy of my translation of *Vagabonding*. It's in hardcover with a bright jacket and a jaunty subtitle: "feminist thinking cut loose." Christina Thürmer-Rohr's razor-sharp vision and unflinching truth-telling, now accessible to the English-speaking world thanks to me. I want to show it to someone. Call someone. Brag to someone. Most of all I want to call Quinn. She read the essays avidly as I was translating them, was eager to read more.

The next day I run into her near the mountain. She's on a bike, a girl's bike with a basket, riding right toward me. I wave. She turns her head away. Not believing what I'm seeing, I call her name. She bikes right past me, never looking my way.

Later that week Moni tells me that *l'essentielle* will be closing in September. Not enough business, too deep into debt. Another ending that feels dismally wrong.

In July I drive down to New York to help get #18 ready for the printer. This issue, like the last one, is being produced after-hours on the computers in the *Voice* office, Brett handling visuals and design. She marches me to her screen when I arrive; she's spliced photographs and text of "The Wilds and the Deep" into the interview and draped a photo of the giant archway over the cover so that it now feels like a gateway into the issue. It's a knockout. I rave and rave.

My job is proofreading. I go over the galleys and turn up lots of little errors, put final touches on my editorial. As usual, it takes longer than expected. At eleven on the last evening, Brett's ready to lock up and go home. No, she says when I ask can I stay longer and get the keys to her tomorrow. No, I can't come back tomorrow evening. I plead: It's our last issue. I want to get it right, see things through to the end.

No, I'll have to leave the last details to her. End of discussion. It all ends in this moment.

Between Brett and me there were no haunting echoes of lovers past. There was no cold shoulder, no going cold. We were friends. We always heard each other out. Once that week, when we went out for coffee, I did try and ask: was she getting back at me for something? Would she tell me what I'd done? No, she said. Her face said it was useless. No way was she going to any soft place with me.

I'll never know for sure what did us in. If I had to guess now I'd say: identity politics and its hierarchy of oppressions. According to which I was a poster girl for class and race privilege. At the time all I knew was I'd provoked yet another definitive "no."

I considered the irony as I left the *Voice* office that night, on my way to crash at a friend's. Coming apart over an issue on collaboration. Splitting up over an issue on coming together. Last issue's theme would have been more appropriate: Breaking Forms. But this was not a form I would have wanted to see broken. Not when it had brought so much possible into being.

As for that other one—the one with Quinn. The one that was already broken. I thought for sure it could be mended. And even if it couldn't be mended, I thought we could find a way to go on. Find a new form.

The end of us, that's hard enough. Even harder: the end of all the possible we could have brought into being.

43.
Girl Music

SEPTEMBER 1991

THREE OF US IN THE TENT. Telling stories at night instead of sleeping. Forgetting to whisper. Giggling. Snorting. Losing it when the others tell us to hush up. Waking up giggling. Giggling as we decamp. The murmur of the brook, all night, a gurgle like our gurgling. The music of girls.

A women's hiking trip in Maine. Outside together day and night rain and shine for a week.

On the first night I speculate. Of the twelve of us on this trip maybe half are lesbian. Of the three of us in this tent, maybe two. By the third day I've stopped counting. It's a meaningless calculus.

"Thermarests should have Velcro bottoms so they don't slide around."

"Why not slide around, don't we know each other well enough by now?"

"Yeah, let's be palsy-walsy."

A women's hiking trip, but we're not women, we're girls, we're three girls in a tent we're twelve girls around the campfire and when we dip into the cold water no one is not shrieking, when we lift off from laughter or singing....

I know this I know this it's my heart's fondest place.

"Look what I found!" Kneeling side by side. "A fossil. A fairy toadstool. A Petoskey stone...." Arm slung cowboy-like around her on the long bus ride home.

Would do anything for you, stay by your side forever.

Pals for life.

301

44.
The Company of Strangers

...Everything, everything is living and dying, moment after moment

—Maurine Stuart, *Subtle Sound*

IT'S EARLY OCTOBER AND I've been stretching out my stay in Montague, basking in New England fall. A launch party for Mary's latest book, *In the Company of Strangers*, is my incentive to return to the city. I arrive early at the Double Hook Bookstore, bringing roses for Mary and a big balloon for Marie-Claire, her longtime companion, whose birthday happens to be today. Mary is sitting at the end of a table signing books, already surrounded. I station myself at the other end, hidden from her by an enormous flower arrangement. When there's a brief lull in the parade of admirers, I rise from my seat and make a dash for her.

"Leeza!" she says, setting down the roses, gripping me forcefully by the shoulders then planting a firm kiss on my lips. I've come to know and love the several contrasts in Mary: on the one hand, the stiffness and formality, vestiges of her patrician origins; on the other, the sudden explosions of affection and confessional outbursts, the fondness for gossip. We often send each other into gales of laughter.

Mary's face brightens suddenly and I wheel around to see Marie-Claire behind me. She spends winters in the U.S. now but she and Mary share a summer house in the country and I drove out there for a visit in June. Marie-Claire was all sweetness and solicitude, hovering about like a little bird as Mary cooked, pouring me one glass of wine after another. Not quite what

I'd expected from one of Quebec's most celebrated writers. The two of us stayed up talking that night long after Mary turned in. Before I went up to bed she insisted on turning the sheets down for me.

"Marie-Claire!" I exclaim, kissing her on both cheeks and handing her the balloon as I wish her happy birthday. She thanks me but declines the balloon. I'm considering how to divest myself of it when she grabs my wrist, pointing to the entrance of the store.

"*Regarde! C'est Z.!*"

And indeed there she is, *l'oracle* herself, sailing in like a tall ship, in an elegant green ensemble. Z. is an old friend of Marie-Claire's and, for some reason I couldn't fathom at the time, was the main focus of our conversation that night at the summer house. After raving about the drawings she always scrawled in the margins of her letters and declaring her a fine artist, Marie-Claire somewhat dramatically announced: "*Elle a renoncé à l'amour.*" Her heart had been badly broken, she went on to say, almost ten years ago. Not by a man.

And now here she is, making a beeline for Marie-Claire. I'm feeling way too casual in my T-shirt and vest. And I'm holding a blue balloon. Every bone in my body wants to run in the other direction. But Marie-Claire is anchoring me to the spot as she and Z. plant kisses on each other's cheeks. Afterwards she stands back, as if urging the two of us upon one another.

"*Est-ce que tu te souviens de moi?*" I ask, feeling stupid as I say it. You don't forget someone you spoke to for over an hour, even if it was almost a year ago.

But it seems she has. Her expression is blank. It now occurs to me she has intense conversations with people several times a day five days a week.

"*Oui, on s'est vu,*" she says finally.

"Leeza," I say, helping her along.

"*Oh, oui, c'est ça, Leeza,*" she says. She seems relieved when I excuse myself to run off to the bathroom. There in the mirror I spy a great mass of yellow powder on the shoulder of my white shirt—pollen from the flower arrangement, which I attempt unsuccessfully to brush off.

Marie-Claire is waiting for me when I emerge. "*Elle est timide!*" she insists. "*Elle m'a parlé de toi, je te le jure.*"

Z. speaking of me to her? This seems improbable. Marie-Claire says they're all going out for drinks, why don't I join them. Maybe in a bit, I say.

Back at the autograph table Mary has been collared by a long-winded, white-haired Westmount denizen. No sooner do I sidle up next to them than Martha and Lyne appear. It's unexpectedly good to see them; we haven't seen much of each other since that interview. We exclaim and fling our arms around each other.

Over Lyne's shoulder, I see Quinn trailing just behind them.

Hair pulled back. Thinner. We step discreetly away from one another as Martha and Lyne take turns embracing Mary, who has liberated herself from the tenacious fan. Quinn is not glowering at me. She seems to be smiling, ever so faintly. Of course, we're surrounded by mutual friends. And, I remind myself, I do have a big blue balloon attached to my hand. And yellow spots on my shirt....

"*On part, Leeza!*" Marie-Claire calls to me. Her friends are filing out of the store, Z. among them. The café is right after the bank, she says, they'll save a place for me. Okay thanks, I say. Without conviction. Why go off with strangers when I have friends right here? Friends who speak my language.

Martha, Lyne, and Quinn are huddled around Mary, who's signing someone's book. I stand by, waiting to see how the situation will sort itself out. Maybe we'll get caught up in a wave of conversation that will carry us somewhere together. Maybe that faint smile was an opening....

Mary hands the book back to Quinn.

"We need to toddle on," Martha says as the three of them inch apologetically backwards, toward the door. So, they're a "we" now. A "we" with somewhere to be—a show to see, an appointment to keep. I should have known from the noncommittal way they were all standing there.

"Leeza," Mary says when they've gone. "Your timing is uncanny."

"No kidding." I tie the blue balloon to her chair—it looks incongruous but Mary seems amused. "Marie-Claire invited me to join her and her gang for drinks down the street."

"What a wonderful idea!" says dear Mary, who can no doubt see how I'm suffering. "You better be off then." I give her another firm kiss on the lips then bolt out the door and down the street.

Less than a block away, just after the bank, Marie-Claire hails me from a table on the sidewalk. A seat has been saved for me right beside Z. At least now I can light up a cigarette, which I do immediately.

It's somehow momentous to be sitting right next to her. Oddly, given that they came here for drinks, she's nursing an herbal tea. As she brings the cup to her lips I notice her eyebrows, perfect semi-circles way up high above those hooded eyes. Aloof like the rest of her.

I order a beer. Then think to ask does she mind my smoking.

"*Oh, non,*" she says, "I smoked almost all my life. And drank wine."

"Then you stopped?"

"I stopped everything."

I laugh uncomfortably, recalling the information I have from Marie-Claire. Z. is very thin, and pale for October. There's a mild purplish tint to her complexion and lips that matches her cool demeanour. I think of her office with the traffic roaring by, the fancy computer on rollers with the blue screen. Has she stopped going out in the sun, too?

"*Puis,*" she says suddenly, "*t'as jamais trouvé ton chat?*"

Our conversation, it seems, has begun to come back to her.

"Non."

"*Mais ça va?*"

Right at this moment I can't answer in the affirmative. I wonder if she remembers her prediction: "*Ça va se rechauffer.*" Not terribly accurate—at least not for more than a few giddy moments. I shrug.

She says Sagittarians are hard to satisfy. So she remembers my sign, too.

Then she gets swept into conversation with the others, who, from the way they laugh and carry on with each other, I gather have been hanging out together for years. Z. loosens up in their company. There is much joking and kidding, most of which I can't follow, and even when I get the meaning I don't get the humour. It's not the kind of dry, subtle humour I like. Is it even possible to be dry and subtle in Québecois?

I miss Mary. I miss Quinn. I miss all the subtle, dry ways we know to convey feeling to one another.

Someone hoists a glass to Marie-Claire, and now everyone is toasting her birthday, me with my beer glass, Z. with her teacup, which elicits laughs from all around. Marie-Claire, deflecting the attention, as usual, says we should all be toasting Z., who'll be turning forty in just two weeks. So she too is a Libra. Une balance. Together with *les filles*, I lift my glass to Z.

Before the party breaks up, Z. says something about meeting me "for a coffee," but I recognize this for the formality it is. I don't really expect anything will come of it and I can't honestly see why anything should. It's not as if we have that much in common.

And it's just what I need. Another cold shoulder. Another red hook.

45.
Anything But This

M Y FATHER'S IN THE HOSPITAL, as he has been on and off all winter. I've flown here to spell my mother at his side. The doctors say it's serious this time, but they can't say exactly what "it" is.

"Overwhelming metabolic insult," I hear one of them saying.

"His brain is pickled," is the family doctor's diagnosis, delivered less sympathetically than you'd expect. He ordered him to stop drinking years ago.

"What am I supposed to order at the bar, Shirley Temple cocktails?" my father whined. Though afterwards he did make an effort to substitute wine for Scotch and sodas.

"He was fine when he went into the hospital," my mother keeps insisting.

"He would be dead if he hadn't come to the hospital," the doctor replies, the one who heads the team, when she directs this complaint at him.

"Well maybe that would be better."

He drifts in and out of consciousness. When he comes to he begs for his pants and his shirt, he asks for cigarettes and a drink. I swab his mouth, he sucks on the swab. I play along, pretend to light the other end. He grabs the swab, holds it between his third and fourth fingers the way he always held his cigarettes, sucks hard. It seems to placate him.

He the king of witty repartee. Necessary always to have a thought at the ready. Books spilling out from the shelves, piling up on the coffee table. What is man if not the sum of his learning? Always clothed in Brooks Brothers suit, Phi Beta Kappa chain strung from the breast pocket. On black tie occasions, his medals.

My father. My mentor in loving women. He who initiated me into the greatness of She Who.

How often did I catch him gazing into the mirror in the front hall before a party, composing his face? Pressing his lips together, jutting out his chin to make the folds beneath it disappear? Every day trying to adjust his face into something he could make peace with. Just not this. Anything but this. The little Jewboy, bad at sports.

For hours on end now he will lie here in a hospital gown shorn of his props, his accoutrements. His intellect. Nothing now between him and it, the Jew-hating world.

The whole pageant of his life, the feast of it the festival. The musical score that orchestrated it. The strains of *Pal Joey*, the straining out of history into ... a European idyll with stunning Scandinavian wife, set on mid-American soil. Foreign guests entertained on Louis XV furniture. Aperitif, drinks with dinner, literate conversation. Cognac after. Then up and down Michigan Avenue from one world-class bar to another.

But now the reel has run out. He is lying in the hospital with tubes up his nose. A body in spite of himself.

When I called from Montreal just a week ago he enthused over the phone. The concièrge was so kindly. The decor was soothing. He enjoyed the sound of the fountains outside.

"He thinks he's in Vienna," Mother interjected.

"So how's Vienna?" I asked on my end of the phone.

"*Oh Wien Wien du bist so schön*," he chanted. "I just wish somebody would get me my pants."

"He wants to tip the chambermaids," Mother explained. "He keeps trying to fish in his pockets."

By the time I arrive he's mostly not there. Can't get words out and for the most part doesn't seem to want to. Around him nurses and visitors scurry and fuss and worry.

I sit beside him in the hospital room. Day after day. I realize we have never simply sat side by side before. There's no pressure now. No push no pull.

Beautiful May days, a veil of green just beginning to adorn the city. The lake shimmering as I walk beside it to and from the hospital. The same route I used to walk to school.

I come every day to sit beside you.

"Are you feeling okay, Daddy?"

"Yel, I'm okay."

"Can I get you anything?"

"No. I'm okay."

Such exchanges as we've never had before.

His hand goes up, sideways, thumb out, he wants something. "What do you want, Daddy?"

"My glass."

I get him his glass. He sips, makes a sour face.

"Sorry about that. Do you want me to read you the paper?"

"Yel."

I read him stock reports, it's what he asks for. He nods, he nods off. Noises issue from his mouth, somewhere between a baby's soft cries and the snores that used to ripple from his library in the evening.

Only one moment of sheer lucidity: his left eyelid hoisted open with enormous effort, closing, then hoisted again, like a curtain, and then he's suddenly wide awake, blinking hard. For the first time, he is there, in his brown eyes, seeing me, and I'm looking back. A light is on and I need to pay attention.

He speaks, enunciating very clearly. The words are not idle or playful. "I want my grey hat."

Sorry, Daddy, I don't know where it is.

"My cane."

Sorry, I can't find the cane either.

Then it starts: "Please. Get me out of here. I want to go home."

You want to go home, Daddy?

"Yes, I want to go home."

"Do you know you're sick?" ("Ask him," the doctors said, "if he's ever conscious, if there's a window of opportunity, ask him.")

"Yes, I know."

Do you know if you go home you'll die?

"I don't care. I want to go home."

"You want to go home?"

"Yel … yeah."

There we had it, an answer. From his wide-awake self. Not a life without cigarettes, without drinks, without Brooks Brothers suits.

The doctors have him scheduled to be pegged tomorrow. After that he's to go to a nursing home.

I confer with my sisters, with Mother. We all agree. He should have it his way.

"We don't want the peg in," I say to the doctor who heads his team.

"You want to let him die? You want to kill him?"

If that's the way you insist on seeing it. Yes.

The nurses are on our side. We win the sympathy of another doctor and finally get our way. They move him to hospice.

The very next day he begins thrashing and moaning. The moans sound exactly like Poncho the donkey. I have an impulse to dial Del's number and put the phone up beside him so she can hear. The nurse says it won't be too long now, the dying process has begun.

I have to leave before it's over. My sisters have come to relieve me at his side. It feels like I'm leaving him in his last throes, fighting for his life.

I tell myself where he's concerned I was always leaving too soon. I tell myself he's had me for ten days now, all to himself—he finally managed to win the war for my attention! But when I bend down to kiss him goodbye—on the forehead, where he's always kissed me, where he's always kissed his three girls—all the blood drains out of me, and my legs buckle on the way to the elevator.

I have to tell myself he'll spring back to life, he always did before.

46.
Girl Music #2

Your first love has no beginning and will have no end. It is still alive, in the stream of your being.
—Thich Nhat Hanh, *Cultivating the Mind of Love*

A CONVERTED FARM ON A HILLTOP In the South of France, with sprawling plum orchards, sloping meadows, walking meditation trails that wind through the woods. "Plum Village," the home and main retreat centre of Vietnamese monk Thich Nhat Hanh. I'm one of a motley group of Westerners who've been carted here from a tiny French railroad station, dazed and jet-lagged, in an old flatbed truck piled high with our belongings. "You have arrived," says a large painted sign in the main office where the truck deposits us.

It's not my first retreat with Thay, as he's called by his students. Around the time things were deteriorating between Del and me, Anne showed me his book *Peace is Every Step*. The cover impressed me: an Asian man with a shaven head stepping peacefully on the earth. Walking his talk. His message of peace, I learned from the book, had been forged in the fire of his people's suffering during and after the Vietnam War. When I heard he was leading a five-day retreat at Omega not long after, I signed up.

After the austerity of retreats with Maurine, Omega felt like summer camp. There were only two sitting periods a day; the rest of the time was taken up with sing-alongs and community meetings. It was hard sometimes not to laugh. Nor could I wholeheartedly join in as the others chanted "present moment wonderful moment" or "peace calm joy ease." Songs about the simple joys of eating a cookie, or an orange, brought out a jaundiced, disaffected Thürmer-Rohr voice in me. Escapist impulses are born of dire times, it said.

But there was something about Thay. His gentle presence was powerful and seemed to touch everyone in the hall. When you walked out you felt as if you could radiate goodness and kindness to everyone you met. And by the last day, when I joined the throng braiding gently behind him as we all walked slowly, mindfully down to the little lake, the snide, disgruntled voiceover had fallen silent. The mindfulness bell rang from time to time, bringing the procession to a halt, and each time I could feel myself filling up with something. "Peace calm joy ease"—yes. Those words they'd been chanting all week.

I called Del as soon as I was home. She responded to my enthusiasm about the retreat with her usual sarcasm but when I told her what I'd come to understand there about her, and me, and us together, she was silent, she was *listening*, and it seemed in fact we were listening to each other as we never had before. ("Love is understanding," Thay said in one of his talks, and that felt instantly right.) It was only a temporary reprieve—the bickering started up again a few weeks later—but for those weeks we were simply two hearts, open and full. *This works!* I kept thinking. *This Thay guy really knows his stuff.* But the idea of flying across the ocean to spend three whole weeks meditating and singing along with the monks and nuns in his order would not have entered my mind.

Yet here I am, and the first days it feels like a big mistake. It rains and rains and it's cold. Thay's talks go on way too long and in my jet-lagged state I am mostly on the verge of nodding off. During meditation I think obsessively about the thick sweaters I left in my closet at home. And there is way too much smiling and talking all around.

At Omega, each time someone spoke of having been to Plum Village for a long retreat, I would peg them as either ultradevoted or desperate. By the end of this past winter I fell into the second category. My father was going downhill fast. My new housemate, a young, self-absorbed poet who left large clumps of long red hair in the stall every time she showered, was a constant reminder of the loss of Moni, who moved in with her lover over the summer.

In December there'd been an unpleasant run-in with Quinn. And the breezy little birthday card I'd sent to *l'oracle* after our exchange in the café had gone unanswered. In the vacuum left by Maurine, my thoughts turned to Thay; I imagined myself walking wooded trails in France, filling up with "peace calm joy ease."

My bed is a narrow mattress in a small dormitory loft. Every time I lay my head down, I am overwhelmed by images of Daddy; it's been just a month since he died. I see his bald head in the hospital bed, smell his pampered, powdered, tucked-in baby smell. One night I dream he shows up suddenly on a city street in a grey suit, dapper and elegant. I'm with a group of friends and we're on our way to a ceremony, to celebrate his passing. "Perfect timing!" I say to him. "We're just on our way to your funeral!" His absence from this earth feels a little vertiginous sometimes. Like leaning back in a chair only to discover it has no back.

Luckily there's a small *zendo* right next to my dorm. I retreat there often to sit by myself. Almost always the same girl is sitting in there when I enter. *Girl,* I think, though she's probably around my age. She has long blonde hair and wears the same pale green sweater every day. Her appetite for sitting seems endless; I always leave the *zendo* before she does. Often a man comes in and sits near her. He, too, is usually still there when I leave.

When I see her outside on the meadow she tends to be surrounded by men. She is very thin with long arms, and when it's cold she wraps herself in a beige shawl. The earth spirit, I dub her, because of the way she blends into the trees. And I don't exactly know why but she reminds me so much of Del of everything I loved best about Del that every time I see her my heart wants to break.

The first tea ceremony is held in the big tent in the Upper Hamlet. An old Swiss man with a distinguished goatee sings a Swiss mountaineering song and the earth spirit chimes in. I notice she has something like a bird's nest on her head. A young Vietnamese monk in robes tells of entering Thay's room when he was urinating and deciding instead of retreating to just listen. It was the most beautiful sound he'd ever heard. "Even urine can be a source of the *dharma*," he says, which prompts the dark flute player to tell the story of how she once overheard a famous lady musician pissing and it was a loud healthy sound and after that she learned to control her piss, to get it to come out slow and steady, and soon she was learning to do the same thing with her flute. "That's how I became a musician," she says. By now I notice my face has broken into an ear-to-ear smile.

Just before the ceremony ends, the earth spirit takes the crown of branches from her head and sets it down on the cloth in the centre of the room. "A poem without words," she says. Even her voice—high, lilting, fairy-like—is not quite human.

TWO DAYS LATER THE SWISS MAN AND I are having a smoke outside when the earth spirit emerges from the *zendo*, gives him a peck on the cheek, and then turns to me with a mischievous look.

"All these people, all this smiling," she says. "It's a bit hard to take." Then she whispers in my ear "please keep that for yourself" and gives me a little hug.

So she's irreverent too. Like Del.

The next time I see her I plaster a fake smile on my face.

She laughs.

Thay's talks aren't getting any shorter but they are getting more interesting. In installments, he is telling us the story of his first love, a young nun he met in a monastery when he was a monk in training. The nun embodied all the qualities he cherished: she was calm, compassionate, beautiful. After a very short time in her presence, he understood: he loved her. He only wanted to be with her. There is now no temptation to nod off.

Most evenings everyone convenes again in the large meditation hall in the lower hamlet for a concert or a lecture. Often the girl and I—Catharina is her name, and she's Swiss—walk down together. One evening she collects stones on the way, hands me one as we enter the hall. "If we don't like the lecture tonight let's click them," she whispers.

A folksinger is opening for tonight's speaker, and just as I'm thinking I wish she'd hurry up and finish it comes: a gentle tap on my stone. The laughter seems to start from way down near my sacrum. I writhe in anguish trying to contain it—we're seated right in the middle of the hall—and rush out as soon as the singer's finished.

She catches up with me in the bathroom later. "Beat me up," she says. "Come on."

"Would that make you feel better?"

She says she had no idea it would crack me up that way, it was inconsiderate of her. I can see she's suffering, and though I sort of enjoy having her at my mercy I'm aware it's extremely unfair. The writhing notwithstanding, that stone-clicking moment was for me the best moment of the retreat so far.

"You know, I would have probably done it to you before the act was over," I say, grinning, letting her off the hook.

"FIRST LOVE? CAN THERE BE SUCH A THING?" Thay asks us all to meditate on this question. How could his love for this nun have come into being without everything that he had loved in his life before her? "My first love has always been there. She has no beginning." I think back to Miss Reynolds. Was it already there in me, just lying in wait? How else to explain how big my love for her was? As big as any has been since.

One afternoon Catharina shows up by my side in the upper hamlet and offers me peaches and cherries—she's been shopping in Lourbès-Bernac. We kneel down together on the grass eating cherries and she says, "You must come visit me at my home in the forest." I follow her along the path. Her tent, which is long and low and green, sits amidst a cluster of tall trees. In the crotch of the closest tree she's created an altar: a stick adorned with a necklace, and a painted stone. She hands me the stone.

"I painted it for you." There are little footprints painted all over it. From all the people passing by doing walking meditation, she explains.

"I love it!" I say. "I *knew* you were some sort of artist."

"Well not the usual kind. I used to write poetry and make things. But now my artwork is mostly ... my life."

Normally such a statement would call forth the snarky Del in me. Instead I want to kneel down before her. I want to squirrel this new information away with my stone and contemplate it in the privacy of my little loft bed. I thank her and walk back to my dorm. In his very first talk Thay spoke of desire, deep desire. He talked of how to reach the seeds of deep desire that lie in our store consciousness. Could he be talking about Pure Lust, I wondered?

When I think of the earth spirit I think I know what he means by deep desire. Not that I feel anything like desire for her. But if I did it would be that kind.

Later that night I take a long walk in the moonlight. The cows are grazing, the frogs are loud, and there is birdsong too, multiplying like stars. I wish she were stopping with me to hear the frogs and the birds to see the cows.

ONE MAN IN PARTICULAR SEEMS TO GRAVITATE to her, the one who sits with us in the *zendo*. He's handsome and greying and it seems every time we sit down to talk he approaches and asks does she want to go walking with him. Usually she says yes. Today I caught myself glaring at him, willing him to leave us alone. After supper I grab her and ask her to walk with me. We stop at her tent for her shawl and then set off down the path.

Words form as we walk. "What I came for, why I'm here … I've noticed you're starting to get in the way of it," is what finally comes out. "And I don't want that." Something leaps out of the underbrush to our left just as I finish. We both turn around to look—it's a huge toad, bigger than any toad I've ever seen. It exactly matches my self-image in this moment.

We continue walking till we get to the main path, which is bright and white. When we round the bend, there is the moon, pink and yellow and full.

"You know it's the same for me," she says after what feels like minutes. "I don't know why I came up to you that day, as if I knew you, and talked to you like that and gave you a hug. I don't know why I clicked those stones."

"That," I say, "was very endearing." I could cry with relief.

She says she doesn't think any of these feelings are a problem, what she doesn't want is desire or clinging. She's mostly alone and she likes it that way. Not that it isn't hard sometimes. But she loves the trees the birds the rocks the air. And she needs her freedom. "I like to be in my shoes," she says.

Oh, I think. *Could it be the main difference between the two of us is she knows herself and I don't?* Those agonizing weeks with Helen: desire snuffed out by relentless expectation. Desire sputtering, the shame of that, with Grace, and again with Del. But ... to choose to live without it?

We decide to return to the *zendo* to sit before bed. Before entering I give her a big strong hug. She hugs me back, just as hard. Then we sit together, just the two of us, facing the white stone walls.

"YOUR FIRST LOVE IS ALWAYS HERE, continuing to shape your life," Thay declares during his talk this morning. So it is for him with this nun, even if he has not set eyes on her now for forty years. Again I think of Miss Reynolds. Whose eyebrows would arc in a peak of compassion, whom I loved with all my heart. And who left to marry a man in Washington without any protest from me. There was no reason on earth to assume it should interfere with our love. Not in any deep way.

That night in her tent Catharina lights incense and we sit together in silence in her temple of tall trees with its dome of leaves and sky. It feels so full, this silence, and I find myself thinking of Kaye, wondering if this is how it felt to her. Remembering how little tolerance I had for it then. How hard I would try to get her to talk.

The next night I come to her tent bearing fruit and cookies and a bowl of water to wash the fruit in. My offering. It's cold and I've come wrapped in my sleeping bag. She lights candles, arranges the fruit and cookies on the canvas floor, and we help ourselves.

Then I begin to talk about Maurine. Her name has come up several times—"my teacher," I call her. I try and evoke her—the fierceness, the kindness, the powerful voice. Her love of Bach, of the sound of rain, of good food, of any kind of pleasure, really. Catharina drinks this in. I tell her about the last *sesshin* at Sparks Street. Late February, a gentle but persistent snow falling outside. Maurine in the hospital dying, all of us sitting without her for the first time. How I sat with more concentration than ever before, how her presence was stronger than it had ever been, as everywhere as the snow. Then on the last day, suddenly, the tidal wave of pain. Bowing to her *rakusu,* which hung on the mantle. The flourish of emptiness behind that *rakusu.* No body behind it, not now not ever. Breaking down in sobs. So what if her great spirit was everywhere now, her teachings absorbed. I wanted *Maurine*.

Catharina is nodding, I can see she is moved. She talks a bit about her teacher in India, her endless gratitude to him. She says she goes off for long retreats by herself, sometimes for weeks at a time.

"I hope you don't mind my asking," I say, "but what do you *think* about all that time?" I'm aware you're not supposed to be thinking when you meditate, but I just have to ask.

And she has an answer at the ready. "This is it," she says she repeats to herself as she sits hour after hour. "This is it."

The last candle goes out, she asks should she light the torch, I say no. Swaddled in my sleeping bag, her shawl over my legs, I descend into myself. Then words start to force their way out. "I think you're amazing," I say. Minutes pass. I can't see her face in the dark. That toad on the path reappears. "What's hard..." I haven't rehearsed this, and the words surprise me as they come out. "What's hard is having so many feelings and not being able to touch you."

Silence again. I feel like a leper, pressed up against the wall of her tent.

I say it's late, I should leave, she says you're not keeping me up. I take her hand to my face, I press her hand against my cheek, then my heart. *This is it.* I take her by the shoulders and put my head against hers. And then we hold each other, we take turns holding each other, for what seems like a long time.

She walks me back to my loft, her long arms slung around me. On the way we pass Thay's hut. His light is on, the only other soul awake on this night.

NOW WE WALK TOGETHER EVERY DAY, sit side by side at meals. We're not too shy to fling an arm around the other's waist or shoulder from time to time. I love the way she encircles me, like a tall tree with long branches.

My hours away from her are full of realization. These years and years of failure. Beginning with that meeting on the ferry from Staten Island sixteen years ago, embarking on what I was so sure was a journey to wholeness—mind-body-soul finally in accord—a journey that would allow me, finally, to actualize my love....

Grace and I, how determined we were to "love with all our intelligence." Helen and I too, in our own way. Wanting to make it all up as we went along, to apply to this task all our powers of invention. All our noble ideas about love, all our lofty hopes ... undone by dailiness. By who, in our dailiness, we turned out to be.

I think of Del, who has been so much with me these weeks, of all the love lost between Del and me. How the question of desire, of sex, upstaged everything else we shared: the riotous friendship, the delight in each other's company.

Driven by desire, driven by "oh, you attract me" and "do I attract you?" driven to feel the flames to fan them to achieve a state of heightened intensity *à deux*. The lengths I will go to make sure I feel it, and she does; the force of my panic the depth of my despair when it's gone missing. Always testing has it stood the test: am I still attracted? Am I in love/is she? (In weak voice, "Do you still want to have sex with me?")

How I wanted to be wanted, how I wanted to want ... how, being wanted, I would stop wanting, start looking for a way out....

The tyranny of desire. What a wild card it was, wayward and unpredictable. It reared its head when I was feeling wary, estranged—abused, even. It flagged when I was fondest and most trusting. It trumped love, over and over again.

I COME TO HER TENT ON THE LAST NIGHT. "I don't know how to thank you for all the things you've given to me," I say: "the stone, the picture, the poem. And all I can think to give you is food." To which she says, "You don't know how much you give me just by recognizing me. That is rare. And precious."

"Yeah?" I say. "Really?" "You sound surprised."

"I've botched things so badly," I say. "I've caused so much hurt."

"What about yourself?" she says. "You must have been hurt too."

"Oh," I say. "Yeah, I guess so. I guess I have."

I put my head down in her neck, her hair is all around me my arms around her, I'm beginning to get the smell of her skin.... I say, "I'd better leave before we get into trouble," and Catharina says, simply, yes.

When we part. She takes my hands in hers. Her long fingers. She strokes my hand with those long fingers. The greying man is hovering nearby and I suspect as soon as I'm gone he'll close in and she will let him, maybe not as close as me, but she will let him in. It causes a twinge but it doesn't interfere, not in any deep way. Stroking my hands with her long fingers she says, "Protect the space in you. Protect your inner freedom."

47.
A Lesbian Going Extinct

A lesbian who does not reinvent the world is a lesbian going extinct
> —Nicole Brossard, "Kind Skin My Mind"

I AM JUST BACK FROM MONTAGUE and am upstairs on the phone with Harriet, absently rifling through a mound of little scraps of paper with scribbles on the hall table, when I see a tiny white slip with the words "Z. August 9" and a phone number.

I excuse myself from the phone and knock on my new house mate's door.

Yes, she says, she called.

"Did she say why?"

"No. She just asked for you. I said you were away."

I call the number the next evening. She picks up.

"*T'es revenue*," is all she says. As if it were natural for her to be noting my comings and goings. "I wanted to thank you for the birthday card."

"Oh. That was quite a while ago."

"I'm a little slow sometimes." Then she starts to talk. Just talk. She the unapproachable. The unreachable. Unavailable. She tells me she's bought a bike, has been biking around the city. To the river, in the parks. Really? That pale Morticia in the café?

It starts like that. We talk on the phone. I call her after teaching my first class, a night class on women and literature at McGill, the work permit having finally come through. I tell her about the students. She listens. She wants to hear.

"You can speak English you know," she says, in English, after

I've stumbled along for several minutes in French.

"Really! Well it would have been nice to know that before the reading."

She laughs. An open laugh. I laugh too. We're laughing together.

We agree to go for a bike ride. I pick her up outside her apartment on a Sunday afternoon. She is indeed less pale than at our last meeting. Though every bit as *soignée* in a fitted brown blazer. Gives the same impression of *hauteur*. Astride her bike, she seems to tower over me.

We decide to bike up the mountain—she's never been up to the top. She'd be content to turn back at the plaza by the chalet, where tourists are snapping each other's pictures, but I make her follow me all the way to the summit, where I find us a patch of grass in the sun. You can glimpse part of the city and the river through the trees here, especially now that the foliage has thinned out. We park our bikes, seat ourselves on the grass. I take out an apple I've packed in my sack. She's says she's glad I made her come this far. After that we don't know quite what to say to each other. It was easier talking on the phone. I bite into my apple.

"Do you ever dress down?" I say finally. Pointing to her jacket. Her polished black leather shoes. I've been feeling self-conscious in my hiking boots and windbreaker. Wanting to get this out in the open.

"*J'ai toujours eu … mon style*," she says. She doesn't follow trends, she tells me. Hates political correctness.

I wonder is this a swipe at me. "I hope you don't hate political people."

"*Ça dépend*," she says.

Whatever was Marie-Claire thinking.

She explains she was part of the movement here at the beginning. Then there was a split. The radicals went to demos; the party girls dressed up, wore makeup, went out to bars. She went with the party girls. Refused to be guilt-tripped by the radicals.

On our way back down the path we discover a great marble disk embedded in the hillside with words engraved around the edge. They're simple words—something about the happiness of perching here with a book, looking out at the view. We set our bikes down and trace the words with our feet.

It's the beginning of something, we both know it. Later she will tell me she first knew when she saw our bicycles propped up against each other that day. *Collés.* She "had a flash." By this time I will have learned to pay attention to her flashes.

After our ride down the mountain we're both chilled. She invites me up to her place to warm up. Her living room—only glimpsed from her office two years ago—is vast and white, with high ceilings. Spare. A large, expensive-looking stereo system against the wall. She offers me sherry, steering me to her black leather couch.

"So," I say as she pours two glasses. "You're drinking again!"

Yes, she says, smiling. Herbal tea was beginning to get very boring. She tells me of her epiphany, around the time of her birth day: life is too short to forego pleasure. She took up drinking wine again, bought the bike. Began enjoying herself more. "*Au plaisir,*" she says, raising her glass.

A deep female voice issuing from her speakers—Juliette Greco. Late-afternoon light glancing off the amber glasses in this vaulted space, the crystalline notes of the song. Some meaning relayed from my senses that my mind can't quite absorb. The accordion swirling about the voice, that peculiar French brand of devil-may-care *joie de vivre.* I'm entering a foreign story. A new script.

I COME TO SEE HER A FEW NIGHTS LATER. She plays me more music: Mahler, "*Das Lied von der Erde,*" sung by Kathleen Ferrier, a contralto with a mystical voice. Sends me home with her Walkman and a tape of *Kindertotenlieder,* sung by Christa Ludwig. Again some meaning here I can't decode. The cavernous depths in these songs rending the plates of my chest all the way home.

What does she want from me? Why is she there, intensely, the moment I wake from sleep? I decide she has to be that high priestess Louisa went on about, it's some kind of spell she's put me under.

Her palm, the shock of it, the first time she shows me, criss-crossed all over like the sole of a new shoe scored with scissors.

"*La décadence totale,*" she says. Though later in the kitchen she puts carrots and broccoli in a juicer just to show me she has a wholesome side too.

I ask her about those years she spent in the bars. Or at *l'Express*. With her friends. *Les filles.* Having made a quick calculation: those were the years I was busy planning lecture series, coordi nating mailings, editing feminist essays. Falling in and out of love with my collaborators. "What did you do there? What did you talk about?"

"*On ne discutait pas. C'était une question de vie, de chaleur. On buvait, on s'amusait.*" (We didn't have discussions. It was about life, warmth. We drank, had fun.)

Not a good fit.

TWO WEEKS AFTER OUR BIKE RIDE I fly to Chicago. My sisters and I have planned a memorial service for my father. The morning of the service, in his library, under his bookcases, I'm fishing out his old LPs. *Parapluies de Cherbourg*, the musical romance he loved, used to conduct in the living room, stopping every so often to draw our attention to tasteful nuances. It was a little sappy, had to be defended. Unlike Strauss or Mahler. "It's just this side of sentimentality, yes, but it's so lovely, so irresistibly lovely," he used to say. I put it on now, and it is ... lovely, even if the record is scratched in several critical places. Achingly lovely, in fact. "*Nous aurons des enfants, j'appelerai ma fille Françoise,*" "*et si c'est un garçon,*" "*ça sera une fille, il y a toujours des filles dans notre famille....*"

Suddenly it's unbearable. To be enveloped in this world of his books, his music, even as I'm poised to bid farewell to it. If it weren't for my sisters just a few feet away I would cave in under the weight of it. And unaccountably—I've only known her two weeks—she is there in this tumultuous emotion, inextricably part of the sadness, this music, this moment. *It's just because it's French*, I tell myself. *French romantic schlock*. But it doesn't let up all weekend.

I call her when I'm back: can I come? Ride over in pouring rain bearing the record in my knapsack, wanting to play it for her. The shock on her face when she sees the cover. She dashes to her bedroom, emerging with the CD: "It just came out. I bought it on Friday." She's been listening to it all weekend. She puts it on, the song booms out of her big speakers. "*Nous aurons des enfants, j'appelerai ma fille Françoise...*" How to take this in? We are both reeling.

There's a moment that night I'll look back on as the point of no return. We are singing along with the CD, we both know the words but she's faster: they're reciting their dreams, they'll marry, he'll open a gas station, "I'll smell of gas all day long," "*Quel bonheur,*" he adds—and she sings along, with vehemence, my pale decadent misanthropic friend—"*Quel bonheur!*"—her chest expelling air, music, rhapsody with abandon.

It's not the way love used to happen. Coming home to Grace, my entire being saying "yes"—not just to her but to the world we were creating together, what our love was helping to build. This one is not a co-conspirator. Not a collaborator. She's not interested in any other world. Seems to feel perfectly at home in this one.

"A lesbian who does not reinvent the world is a lesbian in danger of extinction." She would laugh at these words.

She says sexual difference is irrelevant in art. Wears a thin string of white pearls below the collar of her sweater, grey flannel pants in September. She leaves me sitting on her leather chair listening to opera while she goes to the cleaners. Arrives a bit later, toting blazer on hanger. I watch in awe as she slips it on, elegant grey/green Merino. Formidable, the way she swings into a jacket, steps into a look.

My troubled history with things *French*, stirred up by her. My father's cousins, the dark, glamorous beauties in whose eyes I needed rescuing, the ones with the French names who made me over to look more like them, their prototype mysterious, irresistible Anouk Aimée in *Un Homme et Une Femme*, raven-black hair, eyes lined with kohl. My French "sister," Françoise, whose family I lived with when I was sixteen, who tried on my dresses and looked so much better in them I wanted to leave them all with her.

Coming home? More like being swept up by a funnel cloud and flung far away.

I can't get her to read any of the books I love. She starts them then puts them down. She rarely asks to see anything I write, not even when I shove it in front of her. I try not to be insulted. Doesn't she want to know what I *think*?

I write to Catharina. To say: I've met someone. Was not expecting to meet someone, so soon after meeting her. I tell her how confusing it is, how it makes no sense, none at all.

"Let yourself be surprised," Catharina writes back.

48.
La Petite Mort

Aimer c'est mourir.

—Antoine de Saint-Exupéry, *Le Petit Prince*

THERE IS NO TOUCHING. She makes that clear. She keeps a distance. When I sit down beside her I can feel her flinching. When I try to hug her in her doorway she pulls back. French people don't do hugs. She kisses me on both cheeks instead.

I know I must keep the lid on, haunted as I am by my history. Not wanting to be driven by desire. Not wanting to be snubbed.

One day it erupts, like shot from a cannon. "When I wake up in the morning, you're right there and it's all I can think of." (I do not say: It's rare for me to wake up in the morning, I'm awake most of the night thinking of you.)

She does not throw me out. There is that to hold on to. But neither does she seem pleased. She says she's been alone for seven years and it will take her a long time. She says she's slow. "*Je dégèle.*" She repeats this phrase several times over the next weeks.

Mid-October and we're sitting up on my bed side by side looking out the patio door at the yellowing trees in my yard and the burnished wooden porch with its French windows across the way. It's her first visit to my place. She's come, on her bike, by way of the garden, entering through the kitchen. "*Il a du charme,*" she said, gazing around, only half ironic, and I wondered why I'd been so worried about the ceiling cracks in the kitchen, the insulation poking through in the bathroom. Now I imagine she is seeing the magic, why I've stayed here two years even though all my belongings are crammed into this little room and there's no tub or sink in the bathroom and the downstairs is dark and gloomy. It's all for what you see from this window, this magic garden, this little patch of verdure, all hushed and wild, in the heart of the city.

She sits ramrod straight, in jeans and a black turtleneck, facing the window, as if appreciating the view. We've never sat together on a bed before and we're both very focused on the window.

"It's a little cramped," I say, apologetically.

"You know, when I first came to Montreal I lived in a little place by the bridge, with rats in the walls."

"Really? I can't imagine it." "No, well, I changed."

"*Evidemment!*" We both laugh but I'm busy trying to assimilate this new information, which makes the thickness in my chest grow painfully big.

Through the trees, in the distance, I see a pencil-thin V, a flock of wild geese; by the time I point them out to her they're already gone.

"Shall we go for a walk?" I say, since it seems we've come to the end of sitting here and I'm not ready for her to go.

"Oh yes, that's a good idea!" More and more it is this way; we reach an impasse and she's helpless and then it's up to me to find the way out. But each time her "yes" is right there at the ready.

We put on our fall jackets, her leather jacket with the fur collar (fake, I hope but don't ask), my grey punk jacket, and walk down Duluth to the park. Bright red leaves on the surface of the pond. We walk close so our jackets touch, there's enough padding between us so it feels safe. We circle the pond twice, neither of us wanting to stop.

All night I dream of us walking by the pond, our jackets touching. How long is it going to go on like this?

SHE TELLS ME SHE DREAMT OF ME, I was two cards in the deck: first *le monde*, the world, then in the next moment, I was *le fou*, the fool, and I was leaving.

Why would she dream that when it's she who keeps me at a distance? On the other hand, she *has* read my chart. Knows of my distance-loving Aquarius moon. My predilections in love. "A little removed.... A little indifferent.... *Pas tellement disponible.*"

Then one night. At my place. She's just hooked up my VCR, she's handy that way. Now she sits down in the chair across from me and starts shooting me questions. Questions that seem to have no other purpose than to fill the space between us.

I can't answer them. Can't form sentences. I try, but the words won't fall into line. "Can't you come and sit here?" I ask, patting the space on the couch beside me.

"No, no," she says. Peremptory. Dismissing the idea with her hand.

My whole body wants to fold up, there on the couch. Finally she rises, brings her long, awkward body to my side, lowers it. Maybe she's realized, too, that this phase has run its course.

We take each other's hands. I put my arms around her. "Is that better?" she asks. As if this were all for me.

"A million trillion zillion times better."

"Yes, for me too," she admits. I've taken her out of her misery, I can feel it.

We decide to go to her place and make dinner but when we get there we don't make dinner. We sit down on her black leather couch. And it begins. Both of us tentative at first. Shaking. Not daring. Until we do. Lips meeting lips. The deep groan from inside. The falling away of everything. The I knowing you. The you knowing me. The bottomless. You could plummet forever and ever. "The deep end," they used to warn you. "The drop-off." That kind of scary. Her hooded eyes, so deep so dark—though blue—so compelling. How did any of her lovers ever get over her, why aren't there a million women in love with her. Maybe there are.

"*J'adore le temps perdu,*" she said to me once. So is it her world I'm lost to already? Lost, lost. "*Mon inertie.*" When we get up from the couch hours have passed. Or seconds. Or years.

So the beginning has ended. The ending—of what I don't know yet but I know something has ended—has begun.

49.

Impossible Fit

...the longing
is to be pure. What you get is to be changed.
—Jorie Graham, "Prayer"

WALKING THE DIAGONAL TO HER PLACE. Up Gilford, right on Hôtel de Ville. Ringing her buzzer. This door, so recently the door of a stranger. How foreign it was the first time, the boulevard, the traffic. The blue graph and spinning galaxies on the computer screen. The vaulted whiteness, the spareness. How impossible to be with a woman who lived this way. Who was so poised, so elegant. So remote. Yet why did this thought occur to me at all. Because already I was doing just that—imagining it. Now the distance has been breached. But the strangeness persists. Through cooking together, eating together, lovemaking, waking up to each other ... no getting used to it.

She the unapproachable. Unreachable. Unassimilable.

We like to eat out together. After two years of gazing into restaurants envying the people inside drinking smoking eating talking, now to be among the ones inside. To be seated across from my dinner companion, she with her wine, I with my beer, lighting up before dinner.

But not tonight. The new Thai restaurant on Laurier in Outremont. Her idea. All plate-glass windows, upscale, ascending tiers. Tables jammed, mostly with young couples. Professionals— it's Friday night. How well she fits in. Sitting back with her wine. What kind of life is she sucking me into? I won't sit back. Can't return her gaze. Won't help out with conversation. Keep silent as we walk back to her place in raw drizzle. Slightly ahead of her the whole way. A bourgeois individualist, that's what she is.

Bad fit. Impossible fit.

SHE COMES TO SEE ME ON HER BREAK. She only has an hour. It starts slowly, with protests and feigning of surprise. Then it goes very fast. Off with her grey flannel pants, her black shirt. My sweater, my jeans, our bras, etc. The pile on the floor by my bed. Afterwards she pats herself down, checks herself out in the full-length mirror downstairs. I point to her face—telltale flush. She says she'll put on some powder at home. I watch her being carried off in the cab. In a daze, in my robe and slippers at two in the afternoon. Whatever's come over us?

Looking into her eyes again across the table at la Cucina, enjoying this again, being among the anointed ones, drinking and talking, feeling that unearthly shock at her beauty, that dark secret passionate self so unmanifest in any of her daytime personae. When it comes back it does so rushingly it seeps in through all the cracks, and the doubts I had just hours before ... evaporate.

Stop, go. Open, closed. Fits, starts. Distance between our two homes—a sixteen-minute walk—yesterday a blessing, today a torment.

The films we go see together: *l'Amante, Damage, Un Amour de Swann, la Femme d'a Coté*. Always her choice, always a romance. Stormy. Dangerous. Bourgeois. Heterosexual. "Timeless," she says. "Love doesn't change."

I rent *A Question of Silence* from La Boîte Noire. I've talked about this film in class. A retelling of "Jury of Her Peers," I say, maybe the most powerful feminist film ever made. I've seen it three times. We play it after dinner. She falls asleep halfway through.

Why? Why? What is the place where we meet? What is our third thing?

Next morning she's on her stationary bike. Reading an English exercise book. Hard white face, thin mouth betraying nothing (to think she's accused me of being rigid). Did she even notice the distance I kept all night? Bodies never touching. Feeling of doom so familiar. No way out without great devastation on both sides.

I'm coming down with a cold. She will never care about the things I care about. When I try to talk to her about this she looks stricken. She starts to sniffle too. We are making each other sick. Time to admit I've made another mistake, and cut our losses.

I dream of women who speak my language. I dream of earth and big trees and birdsong in Maine and Vermont. Thinking she'll never understand this part of my life, thinking I've got to be with someone who understands what I mean when I say feminism. Lesbian vision. Refusing the givens. Beginning with O. The epiphanies. The fervour. Splitting the world open, creating it anew. Thinking I'll die if I can't talk about these things.

Reading about Christa Wolf in exile in Santa Monica. Wanting to explain to her, that's what this city is for me: a place to survive, to keep on. After the fall.

"You just want to be free ... politics is just an excuse. An escape!" Her stony, white, impassive face. Furrow between her eyes so deep.

I put my hand on her forehead and she sighs, then tears come down, then sobs. She can't stop. Says she doesn't know why. Then she rubs my back and neck and I cry too.

We go to bed and there it is all over again. The fit of her limbs of her chest of her lips. The sweetness suffusing, enveloping. And I think she may have a point about my politics. Because when she opens she is so open, and I'm so tight, so tense. She too beautiful, I ... not beautiful enough.

Coming in from the cold, *"un frisson dans le dos,"* she wants me to warm her and I do, we throw ourselves on the futon and I hold her and rub her and nuzzle in her neck. And am so happy. We make dinner and eat in front of TV, not really watching it.

Standing in her hallway putting on my boots. Late-morning light. She on the threshold of her office, face pale, worried but rallying her arguments. Why she loves Proust, or any writer who tells it like it is, in all its complexity. Why she hates political art, art that tells you how to think. Finds it so narrow, reductive.

"But what if all we're left with are the old ways of knowing? Of loving?" (Marcel and his obsessive fantasies.) Anticipating her answer. Love is love. You could do with a little more of those old ways of loving. "Don't you ever feel like shaking up the old order? Are you really satisfied with the way things are?"

"Of course not. But women are no better than men, look how they act when they're given a little power. Lesbians aren't anything special; we're just a sexual minority. Why can't you accept that?"

Wanting to cry violently, to get up and leave. Impossible to love someone who thinks like this. One last thrust and boots are on. Wanting only to have my body all over hers to be all pressed up against her.

"This is no way to love," she says.

I leave to get the Sunday papers. Out in the wind on the way to Le Lux. Am I just desperate? All we have in common is sex. Music sometimes. We could disappear from each other's lives without a ripple, the ties that bind are so frail so few.

Lesbians, she is saying—I'm back in her hallway, taking off my boots. All your ideas about lesbians. But she's opening her arms to me as she says this. She's asking for forgiveness. Admitting she was *bad*. She was infantile, reactionary. All the things I wanted to say and didn't. It was because she felt abandoned. She wanted to get back at me.

It begins to surface. The dark side, the hidden. Soft, vulnerable beneath the carapace. She the fourth of six children, too many for her mother to cope with, she used to pray to God every day before they came home from school to help her put up with them. A teacher once wrote on her report card, "*Elle manque d'affection.*" Easily feels abandoned.

"You've got to learn to be patient," she says. "This is just the beginning."

I say I'll try and believe her.

50.
The Father's Return

And Mr. Ramsay? She wanted him.
> —Virginia Woolf, *To the Lighthouse*

HE APPEARS TO ME NOW, again, night after night, in the first months with Z., just as he did right after his death. Leaning forward in his green leather armchair, engaged in animated conversation with a guest. Standing before the mirror in the marbled entrance hallway, adjusting his cuff links, preparing to go out.

Dapper, energetic, pleased with himself.

Or: I'm walking with friends on a city sidewalk, by a large hotel where we used to stay, and his deep bass voice pipes up from behind us, elaborating on the historical importance of this hotel in my life. His timing impeccable.

At the end of *To the Lighthouse*, Lily's longing, which has fastened on Mrs. Ramsay in one way or another throughout the novel, suddenly shifts. While Mr. Ramsay takes off with his youngest children on the long-promised trip to the lighthouse, Lily, standing on the shore by her easel, attempts to complete her painting. She muses about Mrs. Ramsay, who has died, whom she misses terribly. Finally that formidable woman appears, flicking her needles, casting her shadow on the step. And moments later Lily's gaze moves out to sea: "Where was that boat now?" she asks. "And Mr. Ramsay? She wanted him."

How to explain this sudden reversal? Mr. Ramsay, the man who bore down on her at the beginning of this section demanding sympathy, Mr. Ramsay, the famished wolfhound whose bottomless need she wanted to escape at all costs—now Lily Briscoe wants him. In fact needs him in order to complete her painting. Has distance given Lily the space to feel what she could not feel when he was breathing down her neck?

He's coming towards me on the sidewalk in the sunshine, dressed in tweeds and sunglasses. Foreign journals tucked under his arm. Then I'm adjusting his collar, yanking at the two stiff white triangles so they stand up alongside his neck. I do this with great tenderness and love.

How to explain my father's metamorphosis in my dreamlife into a man who is always dapper and charming, with no trace of the neediness the heaviness that marked our relations to the end? And mine into a daughter who delights at his opportune appearance, longs to adjust his collar, mourns the fact that she could never attend to him with such simple gestures of affection when he was alive? It would seem that death, the ultimate distancer, released us both from the roles in which we'd been frozen.

And allowed me, finally, to complete the picture. To fill it in. Now that it's over his lifeline comes forward, the long span of it that converged with mine; now that he's gone he returns to me, the father I loved. Is it she who helps me remember this? A time when it was not his wanting I felt, but his love.

The clanking in the elevator hall, the door opening, his call—"Children?"—the rush to the door, "Daddy!" my heart pumping hard, he's back from New York, exciting in his fedora, his greatcoat, dark hair, and moustache, smell of scotch and cigarettes. He fiddles with the clasp of his brown leather grip, it springs open, and out they all spill, our presents: gyroscopes, magic tricks, salted licorice, even, one time, soon after he'd taken us to see "Peter Pan," stardust. All the romance of New York distilled into that little suitcase.

The living room our theatre, where we three had starring roles. "*Sank Heaven,*" he would sing along with Maurice Chevalier, adopting his thick accent, "*for leetle guhls ... for leetle guhls get beeger every day,*" our cue to launch ourselves from behind the couch, to pirouette across the thick carpet, twirl and leap across the room. "*Sank heaven, for leetle guhls, zey grow up in ze most delightful way*": conducting us, along with the music, his delight in his three little girls written over every inch of his body.

Following him down the thickly carpeted hallway of a hotel in Paris smoke from his cigarette trailing behind him. The little jig he'd do, tripping down the hotel corridor, or down a Paris street. His Paris jig. Always happy in Paris. Trading quips with cabdrivers, shopkeepers, waiters. Making conversation with barmen, all of whom knew him by name. Basking at the head of a great round table, white linen, wine uncorked, he's invited friends, he tastes, nods, indulges, urges on us all a delicacy we've never tried, at the end of the meal a dessert we have no room for.

We are here to enjoy. Civilized pleasures are at the root of this joy, and France is the seat of all civilized pleasures. Beliefs we imbibed from the time we were old enough to sit at the dinner table, with the bottle of Pommard, the jar of Dijon. It seems to me now that all these years I've repressed the great allure of France, the irresistible magic of it, just as thoroughly as I've done the great allure of my father himself.

"*On ne discutait pas. C'etait une question de vie, de chaleur. On buvait, on s'amusait.*" When is it this occurs to me. He's returned to me through her. Francophile that he was. Enjoying nothing so much as an afternoon whiled away at the counter of an elegant upholstered bar. That uniquely refined blend of warmth and life.

This script I've entered not so new after all.

"It was your father who brought us together," she says one day in April, after one of our reconciliations. By this time it does not seem all that odd. "He was looking out for you after his death."

"Looking out for me! More like finding another way to get to me." This my first, impulsive response.

Much later I think, no, she was right. He was looking out for me.

Either way, his aim was true.

51.
Les Mouvements du Désir

---

*So much depends, she thought, upon distance: whether
people are near us or far from us.*
—Virginia Woolf, *To the Lighthouse*

STRANGENESS HAS MELTED AWAY. In its place now, a complicity
that I love that I treasure. Except when it seems a trade-off for
an element I miss. What, exactly? The strangeness, alas. I've been
restless, distracted—e.g., by sun emerging from the clouds as we
make love on her bed, I hurry things along so I can dash outside.

It's not as if she hasn't noticed. "*Tu n'es pas assez amoureuse,*"
she's complained shyly, in a moment of discouragement. What
she wants from me and doesn't get: *des après-midis blancs,* time
talking about us, rehearsing all the pivotal moments, when we
first met, when we first knew.

She's just not in love anymore, she says one night. We're not
compatible, things shouldn't be so difficult.

"Not in love anymore?"

No, and doesn't think she'll feel that way again.

"Never?" Me pleading now.

No, she doesn't think so.

Okay then, I say. Okay. And retreat down her stairs shaking,
shaking. How can this be? The whole way down expecting her to
call to me, don't go just yet, I didn't mean for you to go.

Weeks go by and it no longer feels like a separation, it's a
rupture, a *rupture violente.* Irreparable damage. *Damages.* I
should have known.

Everything I see and hear and read refers back to this pain.

Even the suffering in Sarajevo after the siege. Sarajevo, where just now horror reigns. Yet on the radio a boy who lived through it all, lost parents and a limb, says to the interviewer what he is feeling for a fourteen-year-old girl is causing him more suffering than any of that.

"Love?" asks the interviewer.

He nods. "Yes, love."

So it's not just spoiled Westerners like me.

Nights I go out, seeking life, warmth, diversion. Léa Pool's *Mouvements du désir*, a Via Rail train bound for Vancouver hurtling through snowy plains mountain gorges, in the dining car the strangers meet, both are journeying to unknown destinies, in the smoking car they talk, come to feel they have known each other all their lives. In the sleeping car they make love. I imagine her in the seat behind me, this her kind of film, I imagine her spying me when the film ends, taking my hand as we walk out together. Having realized, thanks to the film, that our train is still moving, that neither of us has gotten off.

But she is not in the theatre and I walk home alone in the dense spring air. Past restaurants we've eaten in. Mazurka, where we had to escape to the ladies' room to make out. Ouzeri, where we argued and couldn't finish our meal. The city imprinted with our erotic life.

Then I come home to the unblinking red light of the answering machine.

Her coldness. Her cockiness.

Those times when I would come to her pleading. Wanting to find a way. She looked on, indifferent. The night she pointed to my corduroys, which I'd altered in the seam with a safety pin. "*Franchement*," she said. Lip curling in distaste. A sign of my ineptness, my sloppiness. Of how I just couldn't keep things together.

I dream she has pincers for arms—all sharp and steely. She's the Bad Mother. Good riddance to the Bad Mother, the hard bitch.

I pray for clarity. There are mornings when I do nothing but this: I sit on my cushion, I breathe, I cool the fever. I try to see. The moments come rarely but when they do a calm descends. And I see: it is not Z. I am desiring in this fever. It is the Z. who left me, far away and foreign and indifferent, like the very first version of her in her high-ceilinged office with her high arching eyebrows. Z. rejecting. Which is not, I have come to know, the truth about Z.

IT'S BEEN A MONTH NOW. I leave a note in her door. Then wait. Agonizing. She calls the next day. Agrees to come over.

We start up again. Slowly. Weekend expeditions. To the market at Jean Talon to buy flowers. To the mountain for a walk around the summit. Edging closer. Warily. *Tranquillement.*

There is the night I sit beside her on her couch (her two-thousand-dollar couch, but I'm no longer thinking this), tears coming down because I can see by her eyes—she is open to me, open as I thought she'd never be again.

"*C'est parce que j'étais venue de si loin,*" she says, to explain the coldness, the bitchiness. Meaning: she was that much in love.

A bolt of fire to my centre. And then we're on her bed. She's on top of me twisting and turning like a snake, her body has never felt so sexy so infinitely wonderful. Her beautiful, long, abandoned body.

At the Brazilian restaurant, after, hanging on her every word. Intensely, giddily, ecstatically in the moment. Holy oneness. All made possible by grievous, excruciating separation. (So is it all then this theatre of desire, fire and ice, my history and hers, reversing them in our common bed as lust washes over us, healing the wounds of years?)

"To the new *nous*," I quip, full of hope, and we both hoist our glasses.

52.
In Defence of Desire

Pure Lust ... is in its essence astral. It is pure Passion: unadulterated, absolute, simple sheer striving for abundance of be-ing.
—Mary Daly, *Pure Lust: Elemental Feminist Philosophy*

BACK IN LEVERETT, WE USED TO TALK of desire as the original, if not the ultimate, creative force. From our desire for women all other desires flowed: above all, the desire for a world in which women would be not marginal but central, in which all life on earth would be honoured, protected. From Lesbian Desire flowed not only the desire for such a world but the energy to bring it into being.

That flame in our centre, the blazing thing that moves us out beyond where we would have thought possible. For days on end for weeks even we can do without food or sleep our energy is boundless. We climb the twisting path through the woods, spy the giant moon through the trees, oh light of revelation! How wondrous we are amidst the infinite shapes and sounds of creation. How moonlight becomes us ...

Integrity. The word that's made flesh that night. Simply, simply to allow a life to spring from this moment, to allow *life* to spring from it, as already it has been, all spring, unbelievable the green wet pulsing never-endingness of living life. To protect, above all, to live in such a way as to protect not just her and this love but these trees and all this green growth this *real world* we are knowing now, loving now as if for the first time.

We used to talk of desire, our desire for women, as the most powerful force in the universe, our particular gift to the world ...

Yet desire flags when we are fondest, most trusting. Rears its head when we're estranged.

Serves as conduit for childhood wounds (this awful pull in me toward "no").

Gets mistaken for love, though so often at odds with it.

Sitting *zazen*, hour after hour, day after day, you watch it burn off like fog. One moment it's the element you live and breathe, *desire is all you see.* You stand poised, quivering, at the lip of possibility. Then the pulse slows, fever breaks. Vision clears. You see her now, absent the fog, as the mere mortal she is. As she *is*, not as you have wanted her to be—some would say this is the beginning of love.

But wait ... the She Who I apprehend through the eyes of desire ... shot through with moonlight, gateway to infinity ... is that not also what *is*? Is she not also goddess? Even if it can't be sustained. Even if I play a role in its demise. Bella's bigness, her visionary power. Grace in all her graciousness, her ethical fervour. Helen's poetic intensity, her pagan wildness ...

I am, after all, a *Lesbian.* I dwell in possibility. I don't want to give up on Pure Lust, *that unadulterated, absolute, simple sheer striving for abundance of be-ing,* any more than I want to give up on my desire for a world wholly other than the insanely life-denying, patriarchal world we all inhabit now.

And why should I? Why not see women in ways that accord with the highest intuitions we have about ourselves? Why not fall in love with our most evolved, most powerful selves?

Simply this: we fall from grace. Often spectacularly. *She is not who I thought she was,* wails the lover betrayed. (Though in this she is not entirely right.) And in a matter of months if not weeks either she or her lover has bailed.

The dream unravels. Stars come unaligned. *A life of integrity?* How easy it was to imagine back then, before I came to know us as the slagheap of conflicting impulses, needs, desires we are. Myself above all. Before the years of feuding, accusing, undermining, attacking.

Integrity. The word sounds quaint now, abstract, refuses to flesh out. We're left with jagged pieces that won't mesh.

Perhaps this is the fate of us uppercase Lesbians. As beings who, it seems, were put on earth to practice astral striving, to soar on the wings of desire, perhaps we are doomed to fall, and to fall hard. Doomed to get caught over and over in the gap between who we (mostly) are and who we want to be, between the world as it (mostly) is and as we ache for it to be. (No wonder we ripped each other to shreds at those conferences, no wonder our collaborations fell violently apart. We wanted things to be different! Wanted it so desperately we rode roughshod over each other to get there.)

How easy it is now to look back at us, we desiring Lesbians of the seventies and eighties, and see only the quarrels, the betrayals, the fallings-out. For those of us on the inside, who expected nothing less than the world from each other, how difficult not to get stuck there. I am speaking of myself here, of course. Myself and this book you hold in your hands, this tale of broken forms, so awash in loss.

How easy to forget, especially now that it's all but vanished, that we *did* create a world together. A culture of resistance. Those of us who weren't writing poems or essays or fiction, making films, art, videos, music, were founding journals, coffeehouses, bookstores, art galleries, theater companies, hosting book fairs and conferences and festivals. Together, we managed to give a shape to our needs, our values, our longings. To give weight and heft to our dreams.

How can I not marvel at all the possible we brought into being?

Especially today, when our cultural networks, our meeting places, our bookstores, book fairs, music festivals, magazines, newspapers, have almost all disappeared. When hardly any presses exist anymore to publish our work. (Even as the forces against which we struggled then despoil more and more of what we held precious, even as the poisons extend their reach.)

How can I not love us for our wanting, our desiring, our aspiring? And in honoring the glorious soaring, how can I not forgive the ignominious crashing? My own included.

Desire is not a practice. It does not teach patience or sustainability. It does not teach kindness or understanding. (Whence comes kindness? And whence understanding? "From pain." My instinctual answer. The pain of losing what is most precious.) And yet Desire, deep desire, is the motor of transformation: what makes the possible possible.

53.
Abiding. *Je me souviens*

...And the ecstasy burst in her eyes and waves of pure delight raced over the floor of her mind and she felt, "It is enough! It is enough!"
— Virginia Woolf, *To the Lighthouse*

...as all lovers leave all lovers much too soon to get the real loving done.
— Judy Grahn, "A Woman is Talking to Death"

SHE'S HAD HER HAIR CUT, a duck bob, two frisky waves meeting at the nape of her neck; from the back she looks like a handsome boy, an elegant boy, in her jeans and navy V-neck cashmere sweater. These days she just wants to bury that head in my neck, she says it's *une maladie,* she's afraid of crushing me; I keep telling her don't worry, I love it. Though admittedly sometimes I worry. Still.

We've settled into rhythms. Dinner out once a week, then back to her place. A night out to see a film. Meeting midway in the metro. Waking up happy to muffins from the Commensal. Telling our dreams. Sometimes making love after breakfast.

In the winter, we go skiing in the park. She wears parkas now. Has bought ski pants and hiking boots. *Une sportive,* thanks to me. We've bled into each other, our differences attenuated, she's taught me to enjoy a glass of wine with lunch. To colour my hair. To indulge in the pleasures of the city. Spinach salmon mousse from the Atwater Market on Russian bread. Paper-thin pizza with goat cheese and vegetables. Sometimes, even, shopping for clothes: a woolen vest, a dressy scarf. Especially in January, when there are sales.

To want, to want, and finally *have*.

What happens to desire when the unattainable the mysterious one becomes sister, mother, best friend. *Familiar.* When the cold shoulder becomes the warmest shoulder ever. Something falls away—even as love grows, even as you *cleave* to her, can no longer imagine life without her—only to be reawakened, with a needle-sharp pain, when she pulls away.

Repetitions. Over and over I walk up St. Joseph to her place over and over we cook dinner or eat out over and over we climb into bed together. Lie side-by-side *collées*, clasp each other when we wake up. Nights when I can't sleep—there are many—she takes me in her arms. She presses on my wrists, then my palms, then my wrists, till I feel my heart slowing down. They're acupressure points, she says, I can treat myself, but when I try it on my own there's no effect.

In repetition there is dullness. Sitting on the same cushion in the same spot with the same people on either side of you minute after minute hour after hour. It's nausea-inducing, at first, to know that each time, after *kinhin*, you must return to the same stale thoughts, the predictable drivel—you, who fancy yourself a writer!—the endless cycling of old memories worries fears obsessions. Or to be cleaning and recleaning the same goddamn bathroom that was never dirty to begin with. In repetition there is anguish. No way out of this joint now. Just go through the motions, along with everyone else. As the whole body burns with the longing to be anywhere but here, to jump out of its own skin.

Usually it takes three days. Sometimes four. Though already on the second day you might notice that returning to your cushion does not feel like torture. By the third day you've slowed way down and have begun to notice ... how much there is to notice. Even on the same twenty square feet of floor all the changes, not only what you see but how you feel, limbs heavier when you sit and when you rise lighter, or the whoosh, whoosh of air as you all walk so briskly through it. And that pinch in your shoulder blade, how it's gone now, completely. Not to mention that phone call you were obsessing about the first days.

In repetition, over time, there is ... revelation. A moment, maybe it's the last day, when you notice you are walking to your cushion with great alacrity. You long to settle there, this oh-so-random point where your body meets the ground, where every day now, hour after hour, you have been showing up for this appointment with ... yourself. This place where there is nothing to do.

My mother never understood people who just accepted things the way they were; you didn't suffer things in silence, you vented your grievances, took action to make them better. There was no end to her refusing, her *oofing* her *ishing*. Trying to make things unhappen. Why *did* she have to spill right on the beige carpet? Why *did* the sun have to disappear the moment she stepped out the door? No wonder she was moving all the time, there was so much she couldn't abide. Beginning with this city— how in God's name did she end up here?—all the noise and soot and grime. The first time her brothers came to visit her here she managed to get the city to clean out the underpass to the beach so it wouldn't reek of urine.

Let's face it, I'm my mother's daughter. For better and for worse. All my marching demonstrating protesting advocating, trying to make the world the way I want it to be. In my case, a just world. A woman-centred, nature-centred world.

Trying to make *her* the way I want her to be. More pagan, more political, more intellectual. Why? Why? Why this person?

The difference between my mother and me is: I stopped. I knelt down. I staked out a spot on the floor and returned to it, hour after hour and day after day.

What if you stay with it? The there's-no-point-to-this-none-at-all. The oh-no-this-was-all-a-big-mistake-and-I've-dug-myself-in-too-deep-to-exit-now. What if, instead of railing against God, you open to it all: the boredom, the disappointment, the pain. The wine stains, the grey skies. The lost things.

What if, after falling into the hole, you stay in it for awhile, take a look around.

Agony, at first. Agony maybe for some time. But then. Gradually. Undeniably. Amazingly. It lets up. Tapers off. Melts away. The rage. The pinch. The itch. The ache. And you find you have settled. Like a giant bird folding its wings. Brooding over the world. You've put down.

And it begins then. The wonder. The music. The mystery.

The realm where she feels at home. Reading cards. Palms. Charts.

"I couldn't get any work done at all today, things kept breaking down and all I could do was fix them."

"The Sun's in Capricorn in the twelfth house, your house. Tomorrow it moves into Aquarius, it'll be better, you'll see."

Things that can't be explained, only known.

Her spare apartment, the white walls, the vaulted space. Her "convent," she calls it. Brought to her knees by the same thing I was. Those long hours in the bars, *perdant le temps*. Always, never far from the surface, her hopeless love for Y., who kept drifting toward men. There were several loves after that, each imperfect, each crushing in its own way.

She spent seven years alone here. Not drinking. Not smoking.

Hardly ever going out.

"What were you doing all that time?" "Developing a relationship to myself."

"O Solitude," she plays for me, Purcell aria, sung by a male contralto.

"Protect the space in you. Protect your inner freedom." How good she is at this.

She tells me about what it was like to eat an apple after she stopped smoking. To be really eating an apple.

Most days we keep to ourselves. Have different beats. "Go to your lectures, go march in your marches," she says. She prefers to stay home and paint.

Her *no's* always forceful, unmixed with come-hither with equivocation. What they call forth in me, once my protesting subsides: *Je me souviens*.

IT'S TRUE WHAT THEY SAY. Patterns persist. Grievances pile up in their insistent way. Our needs don't get met. So much we fail to be for each other.

Failures we acknowledge, we accept. (Sitting on the bed smiling my guilty smile. "I know. I've been caught up in my things all day. Ignoring you.") ("Go out and talk to your intellectual friends." Teasingly. "Your feminist comrades.") Except when we rail, when we balk. Over and over again still on both sides the righteousness the rearing back the shutting out. My fits of recoil. Her answering archness.

But then too ... on the other side of those failures ... such exquisite surprises.

A beautiful wristwatch on the table with scenes from all over the world, including the Arctic. It's a present from Z. Attached to it a note saying, "*toi et le monde.*" In a dream, but still.

Her watercolours, bursts of yellow and orange. "*La joie!*" she says. "*C'est comment je me sens ces jours-ci.*"

Skating at the Bonsecours rink in the February sun, the frozen river, the yellow stone walls of the old city, the silver dome.

What is our "third thing?" Do we have a third thing? If we do it's this city. Make that, this world.

HER BIRTHDAY—IT'S BEEN A YEAR AND A HALF since our last separation—we decide to drive to the mountain, climb up the path. Like a dog I run circles around her, then come to heel. I put my arm through the big leather sleeve of her jacket as we walk to the chalet. There we look out over the city. Both of us thinking of the first time, then finally saying it to each other. How it was all contained in that moment, a seed tightly wrapped. Our bikes leaning tenderly against each other.

Back home I pinch my finger in the garage door. Cry out in shock, then pain, and can't stop crying, am racked with sobs. Inside she takes me in her arms, it's not just my finger anymore and both of us know it, it's everything I feel and never say ... she is there for me, *you've got somebody who loves you.* Even after a bad haircut. Days I can't stand to look at myself in the mirror. Even after I've withdrawn, stayed away, been bad.

Dinner at the Tibetan restaurant on Ontario after a film at ONF. We're happy tonight and in love. In the metro a woman approaches us, her name is Rose-Aimée, would we like her to write some poems for us? Yes, we nod, I hand her two dollars, she takes just a few minutes with pen and paper, then reads us what she's written. Z. is "*la plus belle madame du monde,*" and I am "*la lumière de l'aube.*" "*Je vous souhaite de l'amour,*" says

Rose-Aimée, handing us the two slips of paper. We walk off hand in hand, Z. feeling very beautiful, I feeling full of dawn light.

"BUT, BUT." ME SPUTTERING STILL SOMETIMES. "Don't you want to know what I *think*?"

She holds me and looks in my eyes. They look worried, she says. "It's your lunar return." And she takes me in her arms. She tells me I have a hand language in addition to an eye language. Making little fists all the time. She pries the fingers open, pulling on them, making them relax.

IN THE SPRING WE GO WEST TO THE OCEAN. All the "whys" have quieted down now. Fighting has subsided. We walk the high trail with the great infinite blue down below. Who she is not: one who walks out to that edge with me and sees what I see, sacred sister in this perilous time, who knows herself to be part of the ocean's wildness, feels our interconnected tides. No poems are recited, no prayers to Yemaya. No common destiny unites us. Our work is not one. She walks beside me and I have no idea what she sees or what she thinks. All I know is what I feel: her joy at this cerulean blue this dry air this sun. Just this. Her joy, and mine.

A resting place. A folding of wings. A settling. Not settling down. Not moving in together. Not nesting. Just stopping, at last.

Time stand still here.

My head against her chest, my hand on her palm, open, fleshy. This perfect fit.

CODA.
Side-by-Side Love

And the world discovers as my book ends
How to make two lovers a friend.
　　　　　　　—Rogers and Hammerstein, *Pal Joey*

And there is a dignity in people, a solitude; even between
husband and wife a gulf, and that one must respect....
　　　　　　　—Virginia Woolf, *Mrs. Dalloway*

THE KISS; THE LOVERS' KISS. Which as the camera withdraws
I see—oh horror—is being performed as well by the lovers'
feet, two bodies fusing to form a wheel, a snake swallowing its
tail. Is this why I tend to fall in love with one whose body leans
away from mine? So as to feel myself intact? Feet on the ground.
To remain free to respond to what moves me ...

In our wish to explain we resort to psychology: the mother
wound, the father wound. The fear of being smothered, the
history of being snubbed.

But beyond mother, beyond father, there is also this: what we
came into the world with, bequeathed by the stars.

She Who needs space around Her, more than She's ever known.

Sho Who is all fire and air and needs to burn.

She Who is in love with the world and longs to feel it in their
embrace.

She Who wishes Z. could share Her ardour. How would it be if
Z. too wanted to see the gospel choir, despite her fatigue, despite
their troubles, they might go and be uplifted—together!—or if Z.
wanted to hear the intelligent lesbian dialogue on television so

badly she couldn't stay put over the frying pan and the sauce got a little burnt. Or if Z. too had a passion to be outdoors kicking through the leaves when the light was yellow. So it wasn't always Her leaving, being distracted, diverted, tempted away by Her lateral vision....

All our *ideas* about love. What it looks like, feels like. After a lifetime of doubt to discover: there are infinite versions.

To make peace with my own.

My girlfriends and I. Singing our lungs out on those long bus rides home. Arms slung cowboy-like around each other. Would do anything for you, stay by your side forever. Pals for life.

In Ireland, belly-down over the cliffs of Moher, gazing out at the green, roiling waters down below. Feeling her beside me, looking out.

Sparks Street. Side by side on the cushion hour after hour day after day with women—and men. No words, no direct gazes. Bowing to one another as we seat ourselves. Bowing to one another as we rise.

Sitting beside him in the hospital room. Day after day. As I realize we have never simply sat before.

Side by side on her couch. The couch where our bodies went down together for the first time, those deep hooded eyes with their dark lashes, unable to imagine those eyes would ever not compel me to follow them down to her deepest places. The couch where we kissed for the first time and fell into timelessness and the great unknown. Side by side now on this couch watching TV on her large screen. Our bodies close but not entwined. Sometimes touching sometimes not. Sometimes she'll take my hand in hers and keep it there. Sometimes I'll lay my head against her chest. Mostly we just watch the screen.

We're not lovers now, strictly speaking. No push, no pull. When we travel together we lie side by side on the motel bed, sometimes touching mostly not. But if lover means one who loves who is there to listen to comfort to protect. If lover means one who holds you in her accurate perception of you—who you are, what you need—whose life is sane and serene enough to act on that perception....

Coucou, sweetie! Here are your flower remedies: *Star tulip:*

enables inner peace, meditation and prayer. Opens and softens the emotions. Indian pink: to remain centred amid activity.... J'espère que tu vas mieux aujourd'hui.

I can't say I don't miss the rapture. The breathlessness. The fire. Those days when the mere sight of her—*oh la voici la voici la voilà!*—made my heart rate soar. When flinging her down was the thought called up by the sight of a motel bed, when sitting across the table from her at a restaurant soaking in her beauty, I longed to kiss those eyes and touch those elegant bones with my fingers, when all the way home from the restaurant we would hold each other and kiss and kiss again. But if lover is one who is for you without qualification without hesitation, if lover is one whom you trust who trusts you—

We walk arm-in-arm along the coastal trail the great blue ocean far below soaking up the California sun after the long winter back East, and there is nowhere else I want to be no one else I want to walk beside. No push, no pull.

Dream: *We're riding on a train side by side, the train splits in two, each of us is carried off in another direction but the farther we travel away from each other the closer we are.*

Pals for life.

Acknowledgements

Thanks to the editors in whose journals earlier versions of chapters from this book have appeared: *Trivia: Voices of Feminism* #3 and #16, *Carte Blanche* #12 and *Women's Studies Quarterly* # 43. And thanks to Inanna Publications for the care they have brought to the production of this book.

"It is the person who remembers—not memory," wrote Christa Wolf in *A Model Childhood* (*Kindheitsmuster*), her novel about growing up in Nazi Germany. Though most of it was supplied by memory assisted by detailed journals, my account of events and conversation in this memoir has no objective status, all the more so since I relied on imagination to fill in when memory came up short. With this in mind, I have changed most of the names—except in the case of public figures, and/or when I had permission.

This book was long in the making and I received much help along the way. As a U.S. citizen who moved to Montreal in 1990, I have been amazed and graced by this country's—and especially this province's—embrace of and support for its artists. Generous grants from both the Quebec and the Canada Council on the Arts arrived exactly when I most needed them and were an incalculable support to the work. The book began as a series of meditations on lesbian desire which first began to coalesce into memoir in Anne Charney's 2003 workshop in creative nonfiction, sponsored by the Quebec Writers Federation. The mentorship I was awarded by the QWF soon after with Elaine Kalman Naves was the most precious gift an emerging writer could receive. Elaine's generous support and expert guidance inspired boundless energy and confidence; I wrote furiously during those months.

A residency at Hedgebrook not long after that mentorship provided sustenance, beauty, and intimacy a writer can only dream of (and ocean! eagles! sand dollars!). Writing has never been as euphoric as it was in those three weeks. Subsequent residencies at VCCA and Ragdale supplied not only invaluable time away in lovely, meditative surroundings but also, as at Hedgebrook, the gift of writing community. Donna Johnson, Martha Dudman, Jennifer Dickinson, I'm thinking especially of you. I bow down to all those who keep these priceless refuges for writers going. My friend Ann Stokes (1931-2016) created such a refuge for women writers and artists in the woods of New Hampshire. I owe much of my writing life to those luxurious studios, where I've been a regular since the mid-'80s—and which make a brief appearance in this memoir: http://welcomehillstudios.org/. I am grateful also to Deena Metzger's Pine Mountain Writing Intensive, where a small but critical portion of the book came together.

This memoir would have been much longer, less coherent, and much less readable were it not for the attention and advice of a series of readers and editors. A manuscript consult with Betsy Warland in the early stages of the writing was generative and encouraging. A manuscript exchange with Renate Stendhal once I'd finished a first draft was grossly uneven; I had almost no criticism of her novel whereas her copious and illuminating edits and comments kept me busy for years. Jill Dearman's eagle editor's eye was critical in helping me trim down and give shape to what was at the time a sprawling unwieldy mass and she also helped me see my way clear around some sensitive political issues. Verena Stefan was a generous reader who had valuable input, especially in the style arena. I also received excellent feedback in Paul Lisicky's nonfiction workshop at the Juniper Summer Institute. Jennifer Lawler was an extremely helpful, knowledgeable interface with the world of agents and publishers.

Kim Chernin jumped in as editor at a moment of doubt and discouragement. Without her enthusiastic coaching this book might not have seen the light of day. Her deep understanding and brilliant prompts made this a richer, more full-bodied text.

When I first fell in love with women I was lucky enough to be also stepping into a movement that supported this love, that celebrated it and provided countless venues for me to act on it. I want to thank all the feminists and especially the lesbians who created the culture that's at the heart of this book—bookstores, presses, magazines, newspapers, performance spaces, radio shows, music festivals, book fairs, camps, conferences—which in my snarkiness and my naïveté (I thought they'd be around forever) I'm afraid I did not always appreciate sufficiently. Now that almost all of these venues have disappeared I see what we had, and I bow down to those of you who envisioned and brought them into being—and especially to those who did and do the often thankless work of keeping them going.

Finally, deep and endless gratitude to Zonzon, for oracular vision and "deep recognition" every step of the way.

Lise Weil founded *Trivia: A Journal of Ideas*, an award-winning radical feminist literary and political magazine, in 1982; she edited it for nine years. She was also editor of its online relaunch, *Trivia: Voices of Feminism*, from 2004 to 2011. She founded the online journal *Dark Matter: Women Witnessing* in 2014. *Dark Matter* publishes writing and artwork created in response to an age of massive species loss and ecological collapse. Weil's short fiction, essays, reviews, literary nonfiction, and translations have been published widely in journals in both Canada and the U.S. Her collection of Mary Meigs's writings on aging, *Beyond Recall* (2005), was a finalist for a Lambda Literary Award in biography in 2006. Weil teaches in the Individualized Master's program in Goddard College's Graduate Institute. She lives in Montreal and spends summers in a cabin in the woods north of the city, where she hosts annual retreats for women writers centred around dreamwork.

Many back issues of *Trivia: A Journal of Ideas* are sitting in the author's garage and can be had for the price of postage and handling. Rarer ones at a cost. To order: lweil22@gmail.com.